NEW LATIN COMPOSITION

by
CHARLES E. BENNETT

Bolchazy-Carducci Publishers, Inc.
Wauconda, Illinois

ation:
e, Mary Johnston,
Published by Scott, Foresman and Company, 1957, p. 316

Cover design:
Bensen Studios

Printed in the United States of America

2000

Bolchazy-Carducci Publishers, Inc.
1000 Brown Street
Wauconda, Illinois 60084

ISBN 0-86516-345-6

Reprint of the 1912 Allyn and Bacon edition

Library of Congress Cataloging-in-Publication Data

Bennett, Charles E. (Charles Edwin), 1858-1921.
   A new Latin composition / by Charles E. Bennett.
      p.   cm.
   Originally published: Boston : Allyn and Bacon, 1912.
   ISBN 0-86516-345-6 (alk. paper)
   1. Latin language - - Composition and exercises. 2. Latin language -
- Grammar. I. Title.
PA2087.B56 1996
808'.0471 - - dc20

                                                        96-27400
                                                            CIP

PREFACE.

PART I of the present work is based exclusively on Caesar. The illustrative examples are drawn directly from Caesar's own writings, either unchanged or with unessential alterations designed to adapt the passage for practical use. The sentences of the Exercises bring into use only Caesar's vocabulary — chiefly the common words — and Caesar's constructions. The passages of continued discourse in Part I are devoted partly to a summary of the familiar episodes of the early books of the Gallic War, but deal mainly with the stirring events of the year 54 B.C. as narrated in Book V.

Part II is based on Cicero, and follows in detail the plan of Part I. The passages of continuous discourse interspersed among the Exercises deal with Cicero's life up to his consulship. The remainder give a somewhat detailed account of the career of Verres.

Part III is intended for the last year of the high school or academy, and consists of some thirty passages of continuous discourse, dealing with the subject-matter of the Fourteen Philippic Orations of Cicero.

In compliance with the request of a large number of teachers, I have included material for oral exercises in connection with Parts I and II of this book.

CHARLES E. BENNETT.

ITHACA, May, 1919.

TABLE OF CONTENTS.

PART I.

PART III.

SENIOR REVIEW.

PART IV.

ORAL COMPOSITION.

NEW LATIN COMPOSITION.

PART ONE.

BASED ON CAESAR.

LIST OF ABBREVIATIONS.

Grammatical references not preceded by any initial are to the Revised Edition of
the author's *Latin Grammar*.

A. & G.	Allen & Greenough's New Latin Grammar
abl.	ablative.
acc.	accusative.
adv.	adverb.
c.	common (gender).
cf.	compare.
conj.	conjunction.
dat.	dative.
dep.	deponent.
e.g.	for example.
f.	feminine.
gen.	genitive.
H.	Harkness's Complete Latin Grammar.
i.e.	that is.
impers.	impersonal.
indecl.	indeclinable.
intrans. or intr.	intransitive.
lit.	literally.
m.	masculine.
n.	neuter.
obj.	object.
pl.	plural.
pred.	predicate.
prep.	preposition.
semi-dep.	semi-deponent.
subj.	subject.
trans. or tr.	transitive.

LESSON I.

GRAMMATICAL REFERENCES.

1. Subject Nominative. 166, 166. 2; A. & G. 339; H. 387
and 1.

2. Predicate Nouns. 167, 168. 2; A. & G. 283, 284; H. 393
and 8.

3. Appositives. 169. 1, 2, 5; A. & G. 282; H. 393 and 4.

4. The Vocative. 171; A. & G. 340; H. 402.

EXAMPLES.

The heavy-face figures in parenthesis following the examples
correspond to the heavy-face numerals under the Grammatical
References. Thus (**1**) indicates that the Example illustrates the
Subject Nominative; (**2**) Predicate Nouns; *etc.* The other numerals refer to the Notes on the Examples.

1. **Mosa ex monte Vosegō prōfluit,**[1] *the Meuse flows forth from
the Vosges Mountains.* (**1**)

2. **Germānī impetūs gladiōrum excēpērunt,**[1] *the Germans met
the attack of the swords.* (**1**)

3. **Usipetēs et Tencterī flūmen Rhēnum trānsiērunt,**[1] *the Usipetes and Tencteri crossed the River Rhine.* (**1**)

4. **apertō lītore nāvēs cōnstituit,**[1] *he stationed the ships on an
open beach.* (**1**)

5. **is**[2] **lēgātiōnem ad cīvitātēs suscēpit,**[1] *he undertook the embassy
to the states.* (**1**)

6. **ejus bellī haec fuit**[1] **causa,** *this was the cause of that war.* (1)

7. **extrēmum oppidum Allobrogum est**[1] **Genava,** *the outermost
town of the Allobroges is Geneva.* (**2**)

8. in vīcō quī appellātur [1] Octodūrus, *in the village which is called Octodurus.* (**2**)

9. vir fortissimus, Pīsō Aquītānus, *a very gallant man, Piso, an Aquitanian.* (**3**)

10. duae fuērunt Ariovistī uxōrēs, ūna [3] Suēba, altera [3] Nōrica *there were two wives of Ariovistus, the one a Suebian woman, the other Noric.* (**3**)

11. dēsilīte, commīlitōnēs! [4] *jump down, comrades!* (**4**)

Notes on the Examples.

1. The verb in the Latin sentence *regularly* stands last (348 ; A. & G. 596 and *a* ; H. 664), but it often precedes a predicate noun or adjective.

2. The subject is here emphatic ; hence the pronoun is expressed.

3. ūna and altera are in partitive apposition with the subject, uxōrēs.

4. The Vocative regularly follows one or more words of the sentence.

VOCABULARY.

alarm, commoveō, ēre, mōvī, mōtus.*

barbarians, barbarī, ōrum, *m.*

brother, frāter, tris, *m.*

build, faciō, ere, fēcī, factus.

camp, castra, ōrum, *n.*

centurion, centuriō, ōnis, *m.*

come, veniō, īre, vēnī, ventum.

direction, quarter, pars, partis, *f.*

draw up, īnstruō, ere, ūxī, ūctus.

foot-soldier, pedes, itis, *m.*

friendship, amīcitia, ae, *f.*

horseman, eques, itis, *m.*

lead across, trādūcō, ere, dūxī, ductus.

leader, dux, ducis, *m.*

lead forth, ēdūcō, ere, dūxī, ductus.

messenger, nūntius, i, *m.*

tribe, gēns, gentis, *f.*

troops, cōpiae, ārum, *f.*

winter quarters, hīberna, ōrum *n.*

woman, mulier, eris, *f.*

---

* In giving the principal parts of verbs, the perfect passive participle is given instead of the supine; if the verb is transitive, the participle is given in the masculine form, otherwise in the neuter. Where the perfect passive participle is not in use, the future active participle is given, if it occurs.

EXERCISE.

1. You, Titus,[1] were the leader of these horsemen.
2. The Ubii, a German tribe, had made friendship with the Romans and had already given many hostages.
3. Children and women were seen on the wall. 4. We shall lead forth all the foot-soldiers and draw (them)[2] up before the camp. 5. The barbarians were alarmed and sent messengers in[3] all directions. 6. Quintus, brother of Marcus, was a lieutenant of Caesar. 7. Narbo and Tolosa, most flourishing cities, were in the Roman Province. 8. In this great forest were many strange animals. 9. The Germans slew Sextus Baculus, a centurion and brother of Publius Baculus. 10. He quickly built the bridge and led his troops across. 11. Divitiacus, the Haeduan, brother of Dumnorix and friend of Liscus, came to Caesar. 12. Vesontio, the winter quarters of Labienus, was a town of the Sequani.

Suggestions on the Exercise.

1. Words not given in the special vocabularies may be found in the general vocabulary at the end of the book.

2. Words in parenthesis are not to be translated.

3. *in* : translate : *into.*

LESSON II.

AGREEMENT OF ADJECTIVES AND VERBS.

GRAMMATICAL REFERENCES.

1. Attributive and Predicate Adjectives. 233. 2; A. & G. 285. 1 and 2.

2. Agreement of Adjectives.* 234 and 1, 235 to bottom of p. 153; A. & G. 286 and *a*, 287. 1; H. 394, 395. 1, 2.

3. Agreement of Verbs. 254. 1–3, 255. 1–3, 5; A. & G. 316 and *b*; 317 and *b–d*; H. 388, 389. 1; 390, 391, 392. 1, 4.

EXAMPLES.

1. magna alacritās et studium, *great eagerness and zeal.* **(2)**
2. rēs multae operae ac labōris, *a matter of much effort and labor.* **(2)**
3. C. Volusēnus, vir magnī cōnsilī et virtūtis, *Gaius Volusenus, a man of great wisdom and valor.* **(2)**
4. locus castrōrum erat ēditus et acclīvis, *the site of the camp was elevated and sloping.* **(2)**
5. fīlius et frātris fīlius ā Caesare remissī sunt, *his son and his brother's son were sent back by Caesar.* **(3)**
6. equitātus nōndum vēnerat,[1] *the cavalry had not yet come.* **(3)**
7. mittitur[2] ad eōs C. Arpineius et Q. Jūnius, *Gaius Arpineius and Quintus Junius were sent to them.* **(3)**
8. quārum rērum magnam partem temporis brevitās et incursus hostium impediēbat,[3] *a great part of which things the shortness of the time and the onrush of the enemy prevented.* **(3)**

---

* Note that the principles for the agreement of adjectives cover also the use of participles in the compound tenses of the passive, as well as in the periphrastic conjugations.

6

9. **neque agricultūra neque ūsus bellī intermittitur,** *neither farm-ing nor the practice of war is interrupted.* **(3)**

Notes on the Examples.

1. When the subject is a collective noun, the verb usually stands in the singular.

2. The verb here agrees with the nearer subject.

3. The two subjects are here felt as constituting one idea; hence the singular verb.

VOCABULARY.

chieftain, **prīnceps, ipis,** *m.*

construct, **aedificō,** 1.*

consul, **cōnsul, is,** *m.*

district, **regiō, ōnis,** *f.*

either . . . or, **aut . . . aut.**

gate, **porta, ae,** *f.*

influence, **auctōritās, ātis,** *f.*

neither . . . nor, **neque (nec) . . . neque (nec).**

pilot, **gubernātor, ōris,** *m.*

praise, **laudō,** 1.*

prudence, **prūdentia, ae,** *f.*

rower, **rēmex, igis,** *m.*

see, **videō, ēre, vīdī, vīsus.**

send, **mittō, ere, mīsī, missus.**

ship, **nāvis, is,** *f.*; ship of war **nāvis longa,** *lit.* long ship.

steadfastness, **cōnstantia, ae,** *f.*

surround, **circumeō, īre, iī, itus.**

tear down, **dīruō, ere, ruī, rutus.**

wall, **mūrus, ī,** *m.*

wife, **uxor, ōris,** *f.*

EXERCISE.

1. Messala and Piso had been consuls. **2.** Neither the gate nor the wall will be torn down. **3.** We praise Sabinus, a man of the greatest prudence and steadfastness. **4.** In this district we saw many towns and villages. **5.** Either the father or the son was sent. **6.** Many ships of war had been constructed, and many rowers and pilots had been secured. **7.** The influence of these maritime tribes was very great. **8.** A large multitude of

---

* Regular verbs of the first conjugation are indicated by the numeral 1.

men had surrounded the town and was hurling stones and javelins.   9. The Senate and Roman people[1] decreed a thanksgiving.   10. The camp had been placed on a small hill.   11. The wife and daughter of this chieftain had been captured.   12. These two great wars had been completed in one summer.

Suggestion on the Exercise.

1. **Senātus populusque Rōmānus :** this phrase regularly takes a singular verb.

LESSON III.

RELATIVE PRONOUNS. POSSESSIVE PRONOUNS.

GRAMMATICAL REFERENCES.

1. Relative Pronouns. 250. 1–3, 251. 1, 5, 6; A. & G. 305 and *a*, 306, 308. *a, f* and N.; H. 396 and 2, 398 and 1.

2. Possessive Pronouns. 243 and 1, 233. 3; A. & G. 302 and *a, c*; H. 501.

EXAMPLES.

1. Allobrogēs, quī trāns Rhodanum vīcōs habent, *the Allobroges who have villages across the Rhone.* (**1**)

2. genus hōc erat pugnae quō sē Germānī exercuerant, *this was the sort of battle in which the Germans had trained themselves.* (**1**)

3. Casticus rēgnum occupāvit in cīvitāte suā quod pater ante habuerat, *Casticus seized the royal power in his own state which his father had held before him.* (**1, 2**)

4. Titūrius et Cotta quī in Menapiōrum fīnēs legiōnēs dūxerant, *Titurius and Cotta who had led their legions into the territory of the Menapii.* (**1, 2**)

5. sagittāriōs et funditōrēs mittēbat quōrum magnum numerum habēbat, *he sent archers and slingers, of whom he had a great number.* (**1**)

6. ūsus ac disciplīna quae ā nōbīs accēperant, *the experience and discipline which they had received from us.* (**1**)

7. Vesontiōnem vēnit, quod est oppidum maximum Sēquanōrum, *he came to Vesontio, which is the largest town of the Sequani.* (**1**)

8. Senonēs quae est cīvitās fīrma inter Gallōs, *the Senones who are a strong state among the Gauls.* (**1**)

9. auxilium suum pollicentur, *they promise their aid.* (**2**)

10. vestrae salūtis causā suum perīculum neglēxērunt, *for the sake of your safety they made light of their own danger* (**2**)

9

VOCABULARY.

ancestors, **majōrēs, um,** *m.,* *lit. elders.*

arrival, **adventus, ūs,** *m.*

before, *adv.,* **ante.**

freedom, **lībertās, ātis,** *f.*

grant, **concēdō, ere, cessī, cessus.**

guard, **servō,** 1.

hear, hear of, **audiō, īre, īvī, ītus.**

magnitude, **magnitūdō, inis,** *f.*

maintain, **retineō, ere, uī, tentus.**

pacify, **pācō,** 1.

pitch (a camp), **pōnō, ere, posuī, positus.**

remaining, **reliquus, a, um.**

reproach, **incūsō,** 1.

set out, **proficīscor, ī, profectus.**

set on fire, **incendō, ere, cendī, cēnsus.**

surrender, **dēdō, ere, dēdidī, deditus.**

throw into confusion, **perturbō,** 1.

EXERCISE.

1. You will set out for[1] your province, and I for mine. 2. The Nervii reproached the remaining Belgians who had surrendered themselves to the Roman people.   3. The Gauls were alarmed by the magnitude of the works which they had neither seen nor heard of before.[2]   4. We will remain in our own camp which we have pitched here. 5. They set on fire all the villages and buildings which they had seen.   6. The enemy were thrown into confusion by the suddenness of our arrival.   7. We shall maintain the glory and freedom which we received from our ancestors.   8. The mother and daughter whom you captured were guarded in our camp.   9. Sabinus will withdraw his forces to the nearest hill.   10. These are the tribes which we pacified.   11. The Suebi, who had come to the banks of the Rhine, returned into their own territory.   12. Ariovistus, king of the Germans, was holding abodes in Gaul which had been granted by[3] the Sequani.

Suggestions on the Exercise.

1. *for :* use **in** with the accusative.
2. The adverb regularly precedes the word which it modifies
3. *by :* use **ā** with the ablative.

LESSON IV.

THE ACCUSATIVE.

GRAMMATICAL REFERENCES.

(Accusative of Direct Object.)

1. Simple Uses. 175. 1, 176. 1; A. & G. 387; H. 404 and 1.

2. With Compound Verbs. 175. 2. *a*; A. & G. 388. *b*; H. 406.

3. Neuter Pronouns and Adjectives used as Accusative of Result Produced.' 176. 2; A. & G. 390. *c*; H. 409. 1.

4. Two Accusatives, — Direct Object and Predicate Accusative 177. 1; A. & G. 393; H. 410 and 1.

5. Adjective as Predicate Accusative. 177. 2; A. & G. 393. N.; H. 410. 3.

6. Passive Construction of the Foregoing Verbs. 177. 3; A. & G. 393. *a*; H. 410. 1.

EXAMPLES.

1. post eās legiōnēs impedīmenta collocāverat, *behind these legions he had placed the baggage.* (**1**)

2. mīlitēs nostrī Atrebātēs in flūmen compulērunt, *our soldiers drove the Atrebates into the river.* (**1**)

3. Caesar in Rhēnō pontem fēcit, *Caesar built a bridge over the Rhine.* (**1**)

4. Rēmōs reliquōsque Belgās adiit, *he visited the Remi and the rest of the Belgae.* (**2**)

5. complūrēs equitēs hunc ūnum peditem circumsistēbant, *several horsemen were surrounding this one foot-soldier.* (**2**)

6. hōrum auctōritās apud plēbem plūrimum[1] valēbat, *the influence of these was very powerful with the common people.* (**3**)

12

7. Sēquanī nihil[2] respondērunt, *the Sequani made no answer.* (**3**)

8. pauca[3] respondērunt, *they replied briefly.* (**3**)

9. summō magistrātuī praeerat, quem vergobretum appellant, *he was in charge of the highest office (the man) whom they called 'vergobret.'* (**4**)

10. hōc cōnsilium hostēs alacriōrēs ad pugnam effēcerat, *this plan had made the enemy more eager for battle.* (**5**)

11. amīcus ab senātū nostrō appellātus erat, *he had been called friend by our Senate.* (**6**)

Notes on the Examples.

1. **plūrimum valēbat**: lit. *availed very much;* Accusative of Result Produced.

2. **nihil respondērunt** : lit. *replied nothing.*

3. **pauca respondērunt**: lit. *replied a few things.*

VOCABULARY.

attack, **oppugnō**, 1.

avail, **valeō**, **ēre**, **uī**, **valitūrus**.

call (name), **appellō**, 1.

choose, **dēligō**, **ere**, **lēgī**, **lēctus**.

circumstance, **rēs**, **reī**, *f.*

comrade, **commīlitō**, **ōnis**, *m.*

courageous, **fortis**, **e**.

cross, **trānseō**, **īre**, **iī**, **itus**.

embankment, **agger**, **eris**, *m.*

fickleness, **levitās**, **ātis**, *f.*

fortification, **mūnītiō**, **ōnis**, *f.*

get ready, *trans.*, **comparō**, 1.

go around, **circumeō**, **īre**, **iī**, **itus**.

grain, **frūmentum**, **ī**, *n.*

high, **altus**, **a**, **um**.

precede, **antecēdō**, **ere**, **cessī**, **cessūrus**.

surpass, **praecēdō**, **ere**, **cessī**, **cessūrus**.

EXERCISE.

1. This circumstance made the troops more courageous. 2. The Morini went around the fortifications of the Romans. 3. We feared the fickleness of the Gauls, who are often changeable. 4. We got ready grain, chose horsemen, and[1] crossed the River Seine. 5. Near[2] the Ocean the Rhine makes many large[3] islands. 6. The enemy attacked the foot-soldiers who had preceded our army.	7. They had made the camp more extensive and the embankment higher.	8. Our efforts will avail very little.[4]	9. He called me friend and comrade.	10. The Arverni surpassed the remaining Gauls in courage[5] and steadfastness.	11. We were called friends and comrades.	12. This speech of Liscus was of no avail.[6]

Suggestions on the Exercise.

1. For the proper employment of connectives in enumerations, see 341. *a–c*; A. & G. 323. *c.* 1, 3; H. 657. 6 and N.

2. *near :* use **prope**, prep. with acc.

3. *many large :* the Latin says : *many and large.*

4. *very little :* compare the 6th example.

5. *in courage :* use the simple ablative.

6. *of no avail :* translate : *availed nothing.*

LESSON V.

THE ACCUSATIVE (*continued*).

GRAMMATICAL REFERENCES.

1. Two Accusatives, — Person Affected and Result Produced 178. 1. *a–e*; A. & G. 394, 396 and *a*; H. 411.

2. Passive Construction of these Verbs. 178. 2; A. & G. 393. *b*; H. 411. 1.

3. Two Accusatives with Compound Verbs. 179. 1–3; A. & G. 395 and N. 2; H. 413.

4. Accusative of Time and Space. 181. 1; A. & G. 423, 425; H. 417.

5. Accusative of Limit of Motion. 182. 1–4; A. & G. 426. 2, 427. 2, 428. *a, b, j*; H. 418 and 1, 419 and 1, 2.

6. Accusative as Subject of Infinitive. 184; A. & G. 397. *e*; H. 415.

7. Other Accusative Uses. 185; A. & G. 397. *a*; H. 416. 2, 3.

EXAMPLES.

1. interim cottīdiē Caesar Haeduōs frūmentum flāgitāre, *meanwhile Caesar daily demanded the grain of the Haedui.* (**1**)

2. mīlitēs nāvibus flūmen trānsportat, *he sets his troops across the river by boats.* (**3**)

3. Belgae sunt Rhēnum trāductī, *the Belgians were led across the Rhine.* (**3**)

4. ab Suēbīs complūrēs annōs bellō premēbantur, *for very many years they were harried in war by the Suebi.* (**4**)

5. Caesar bīduum in hīs locīs morātur, *Caesar tarried two days in these places.* (**4**)

6. erant duae fossae quīndecim pedēs lātae, *there were two ditches, fifteen feet broad.* (**4**)

15

7. hīc locus ab hoste sescentōs passūs aberat, *this place was six hundred paces distant from the enemy.* (**4**)

8. domōs redeunt, *they return to their homes.* (**5**)

9. in Galliam ulteriōrem contendit et ad Genavam pervēnit, *he hastened to Gaul and arrived in the vicinity of Geneva.* (**5**)

10. Bibracte īre contendit, *he hastened to go to Bibracte.* (**5**)

11. lēgātōs revertī jussit, *he ordered the envoys to return.* (**6**)

12. maximam partem lacte vīvunt, *they subsist for the most part on milk.* (**7**)

Remarks.

1. Verbs of demanding more commonly take ā with the ablative, instead of the accusative of the person. This is regularly true of petō, as tribūnātum ā Caesare petīvī, *I asked a tribuneship of Caesar.*

2. To denote duration of time for a small number of days or years, it is customary to use bīduum, trīduum, quadrīduum, *two days, three days, four days;* and biennium, triennium, quadriennium, *two years, three years, four years.*

VOCABULARY.

ask, petō, ere, petīvī or petiī, petītus.

auxiliaries, auxilia, ōrum, *n.*

delay, moror, 1.

demand, flāgitō, 1.

eight hundred, octingentī, ae, *a.*

extend, pateō, ēre, uī.

field, ager, agrī, *m.*

forest, silva, ae, *f.*

hasten, contendō, ere, tendī, tentum.

help, auxilium, ī, *n.*

legion, legiō, ōnis, *f.*

month, mēnsis, is, *m.*

of, *with verbs of asking,* ā (ab), *prep. with the abl.*

pace, passus, ūs, *m.*

part, pars, partis, *f.*

remain, maneō, ēre, mānsī, mānsūrus.

tarry, moror, 1.

transport, trānsportō, 1.

winter, hiems, mis, *f.*

EXERCISE.

1. These fields extended about eight hundred paces. 2. The Gauls are in large part fickle. 3. You had de-

layed many days in the vicinity of Tolosa. 4. The fortifications were forty feet high. 5. Sabinus ordered the auxiliaries to be sent home. 6. We asked help of the Britons. 7. Ariovistus had remained four months in these forests and swamps. 8. You had demanded money of us. 9. We transported these troops across the River Rhone and hastened to Geneva. 10. During the remaining part of the winter these legions remained in the vicinity of Aquileia. 11. The horsemen were led across the river. 12. We tarried two days near Tolosa and then came to Narbo. 13. Caesar informed Sabinus of[1] his departure. 14. Sabinus was informed of[1] Caesar's departure.

Suggestion on the Exercise.

1. *of:* use **dē** with the abl.

LESSON VI.

THE DATIVE.

GRAMMATICAL REFERENCES.

(Dative of Indirect Object.)

1. Indirect Object in Connection with a Direct Object after Transitive Verbs. 187. I and *a*; A. & G. 362; H. 424.

2. Indirect Object with Intransitive Verbs. 187. II; A. & G. 366, 367; H. 424, 426. 1, 2.

3. Indirect Object with Compound Verbs. 187. III. 1, 2; A. & G. 370; H. 429 and 1.

EXAMPLES.

1. ūnam legiōnem C. Fabiō dedit, *he gave one legion to Gaius Fabius.* (**1**)

2. id Caesarī nūntiātum est, *that was reported to Caesar.* (**1**)

3. Haeduōrum cīvitātī Caesar indulserat, *Caesar had favored the state of the Haedui.* (**2**)

4. neque mulieribus neque puerīs pepercit, *he spared neither women nor children.* (**2**)

5. Trēvirī ejus imperiō nōn pārēbant, *the Treviri did not obey his order.* (**2**)

6. aciem suam carrīs circumdedērunt, *they placed their line of battle around the wagons.* (**3**)

7. minus facile fīnitimīs bellum īnferre poterant, *they were less easily able to wage war against their neighbors.* (**3**)

8. eī mūnītiōnī quam fēcerat T. Labiēnum praefēcit, *he placed Titus Labienus in charge of that fortification which he had made.* (**3**)

9. Brūtus huic classī praeerat, *Brutus was in charge of this fleet.* (**3**)

VOCABULARY.

(account) on account of, **prop-ter**, *prep. with acc.*

arms, weapons, **arma, ōrum**, *n.*

bravely, **fortiter**.

bring upon, **īnferō, ferre, tulī, illātus**.

charge, be in charge of, **praesum, esse, fuī, futūrus**, *with dat. ;* put in charge, **praeficiō, ere, fēcī, fectus**, *with dat. of indirect object.*

favor, **faveō, ēre, fāvī, fautūrus**.

hand over, **trādō, ere, trādidī, trāditus**.

hostage, **obses, idis**, *m.*

lieutenant, **lēgātus, ī**, *m.*

obey, **pāreō, ēre, uī, pāritūrus**.

persuade, **persuādeō, ēre, suāsī, suāsum**.

place around, **circumdō, dare, dedī, datus**.

province, **prōvincia, ae**, *f.*

reduce, **redigō, ere, redēgī, redāctus**.

resist, **resistō, ere, restitī**.

spare, **parcō, ere, pepercī, parsūrus**.

trust, **cōnfīdō, ere, cōnfīsus**, *semi-dep.*

young man, **juvenis, is**, *m.*

EXERCISE.

1. The Roman people did not reduce to[1] a province those tribes which it had spared. 2. These young men obeyed the friend who had favored them. 3. The arms and hostages had already been handed over[2] to the lieutenant who was in command of these troops. 4. The Sequani had given lands and money to Ariovistus. 5. We placed a great multitude of horsemen around the foot-soldiers. 6. These Roman envoys persuaded the tribes to which they had been sent. 7. We saw Sabinus, who was in charge of the winter quarters near Vesontio. 8. You will spare this chieftain and his sons. 9. We put Galba in charge of this business. 10. We shall bravely resist those tribes which bring[3] war upon us. 11. The commander trusts this legion on account of (its) valor. 12. I favored neither you nor your brother.

Suggestions on the Exercise.

1. *to :* use **in** with the acc.

2. *handed over :* make the participle agree with the nearer subject.

3. *bring upon :* use the future tense.

LESSON VII.

THE DATIVE (*continued*).

GRAMMATICAL REFERENCES.

1. Dative of Agency. 189. 1, 2 ; A. & G. 374 ; II. 431

2. Dative of Possession. 190 and 1; A. & G. 373 and *a*; H. 430.

3. Dative of Purpose or Tendency. 191. 1, 2 ; A. & G. 382 and 1, 2 ; H. 433 and 3.

4. Dative with Adjectives. 192. 1, 2 ; A. & G. 383, 384 ; H. 434 and 2.

EXAMPLES.

1. omnēs cruciātūs Sēquanīs perferendī sunt, *all tortures must be endured by the Sequani.* (**1**)

2. Caesarī omnia ūnō tempore agenda erant, *all things had to be done by Caesar at one time.* (**1**)

3. praeter agrī solum nōbīs nihil est, *except the soil of the field, we have nothing,* lit. *nothing is to us.* (**2**)

4. mihi erit perpetua amīcitia tēcum, *I shall have everlasting friendship with you.* (**2**)

5. diēs colloquiō dictus est, *a day was set for a conference.* (**3**)

6. Germānī auxiliō ā Belgīs arcessītī sunt, *the Germans were summoned by the Belgians for aid.* (**3**)

7. ūna rēs nostrīs magnō ūsuī erat, *one thing was of great advantage to our men,* lit. *to our men for great advantage.* (**3**)

8. quīnque cohortēs castrīs praesidiō relīquit, *he left five cohorts as a guard for the camp.* (**3**)

9. proximī sunt Germānīs, *they are next to the Germans.* (**4**)

10. maximē plēbī acceptus erat, *he was especially acceptable to the common people.* (**4**)

Remarks.

1. Note the special neuter impersonal use of the second periphrastic conjugation in connection with the Dative of Agency, *e.g.* **nōbīs nōn exspectandum est**, *we must not wait*, lit. *it must not be waited by us;* **nōbīs resistendum est**, *we must resist.*

2. The chief verbs, besides **sum**, that take a Dative of Purpose or Tendency are : **relinquō, dēligō, dīcō, mittō, veniō.**

3. Among the commoner Datives of Purpose or Tendency are : **auxiliō, ūsuī, impedīmentō, praesidiō, subsidiō.**

VOCABULARY.

abode, **domicilium, ī,** *n.*
army, **exercitus, ūs,** *m.*
assistance, **auxilium, ī,** *n.*
at once, **statim.**
cavalry, **equitātus, ūs,** *m.*
do, **faciō, ere, fēcī, factus.**
javelin, **pīlum, ī,** *n.*
leave, **relinquō, ere, līquī, līctus.**
protection, **praesidium, ī,** *n.*

set, appoint, **cōnstituō, ere, uī, ūtus.**
suitable, **idōneus, a, um.**
undertake, **suscipiō, ere, cēpī, ceptus.**
use, **ūsus, ūs,** *m.*
wait, **exspectō, 1.**
where, **ubi.**

EXERCISE.

1. Labienus had set this day for the battle. **2.** The same thing must be done by all the Gauls which we have done. **3.** We have no place [1] which we call suitable for an abode. **4.** All these maritime tribes were near to the places where Publius Crassus had waged war. **5.** He has already sent one cohort as (for) assistance to us. **6.** Courageous soldiers ought to be praised by their leaders. **7.** These soldiers have neither javelins [1] nor swords. **8.** This embassy must be undertaken by your two sons. **9.** We shall order Galba to leave these two legions as (for) a protection to the camp. **10.** Our ships were nearest to the shore. 11 We must not wait, but must set out at once.[2] 12. The cavalry of the Haeduans was of (for) great use to the Roman army.

Suggestions on the Exercise.

1. *have no place; have neither javelins :* see Examples 3, 4.
2. See Remark 1.

The Belgae Conspire against Caesar.

Caesar had conquered the Helvetii and driven Ariovistus out of Gaul across the Rhine into Germany. He himself was in Hither Gaul, where he heard frequent rumors concerning the plans of the Belgians. These feared the army of the Roman people, and were conspiring and giving hostages to each other.[1] Caesar was alarmed by the letters and messages which he received and enrolled two new legions in Hither Gaul and sent Quintus Pedius (as) lieutenant with these into Farther Gaul. After a little[2] he set out himself and came to the borders of the Belgians in about fifteen days.[3]

Suggestions on the Exercise.

1. *to each other :* inter sē.
2. *after a little :* paulō post (*afterwards by a little*).
3. *in about fifteen days :* use the simple abl.

LESSON VIII.

THE GENITIVE.

GRAMMATICAL REFERENCES.

1. Genitive of Origin. 196.

2. Genitive of Possession. 198. 1, 3; A. & G. 343 and *b*; H. 440. 1.

3. Subjective Genitive. 199; A. & G. 343. N. 1; H. 440. 1.

4. Objective Genitive. 200; A. & G. 347, 348; H. 440. 2.

5. Genitive of the Whole ('Partitive Genitive'). 201 entire; A. & G. 346. *a*. 1–3, *c*, *e*; H. 440. 5 and N., 441, 442, 443.

6. Genitive of Quality. 203. 1–5; A. & G. 345. *a*, *b*; H. 440. 3.

EXAMPLES.

1. fīlius Galbae rēgis, *the son of King Galba.* **(1)**

2. Haeduōrum fīnēs, *the territory of the Haeduans.* **(2)**

3. signa decimae legiōnis, *the standards of the tenth legion.* **(2)**

4. Gallia est Ariovistī, *Gaul belongs to Ariovistus,* lit. *is of Ariovistus.* **(2)**

5. imperātōris est hōc facere, *it is the function of the commander to do this,* lit. *is of the commander.* **(2)**

6 fuga tōtīus exercitūs, *the flight of the entire army.* **(3)**

7. eōrum clāmor fremitusque, *their crying and shouting.* **(3)**

8. rēgnī cupiditāte inductus, *impelled by a desire of regal power.* **(4)**

9. domum reditiōnis spēs, *the hope of returning home.* **(4)**

10. Orgetorīgis fīlia atque ūnus ē fīliīs, *the daughter of Orgetoriχ and one of his sons.* **(1 and 5)**

11. quīnque mīlia passuum, *five miles,* lit. *five thousands of paces.* **(5)**

24

12. **castrīs satis praesidī relīquit,** *he left sufficient guard for the camp,* lit. *sufficient of guard.*   (**5**)

13. **quantum auctōritātis? quantum temporis?** *how much influence? how much time?*   (**5**)

14. **vir magnae auctōritātis,** *a man of great influence.*   (**6**)

15. **cōnsilia ejus modī,** *designs of that sort.*   (**6**)

16. **mūrus in altitūdinem sēdecim pedum,** *a wall sixteen feet high* lit. *of sixteen feet into height.*   (**6**)

17. **auxilī causā,** *for the sake of assistance.*   (**2**)

Remark

Causā is much commoner than **grātiā** in the sense : *on account of, for the sake of.*

VOCABULARY.

accomplish, **perficiō, ere, fēcī, fectus.**

capture, **capiō, ere, cēpī, captus.**

cut to pieces, **concīdō, ere, cīdī, cīsus.**

departure, **discessus, ūs, m.**

distant, be distant, **absum, abesse, āfuī, āfutūrus.**

enough, **satis,** *indecl.*

greatly, **magnopere.**

hate, **ōdī, ōdisse.**

kill, **occīdō, ere, cīdī, cīsus.**

lose, **āmittō, ere, mīsī, missus.**

mile, **mīlle passūs,** *lit.* thousand paces ; *plu.* **mīlia passuum.**

sake, for the sake of, **causā** (*abl.*) *with gen. ; the gen. always precedes.*

terrify, **terreō, ēre, uī, itus.**

thousand, **mīlle ;** *plu.* **mīlia.**

utter, **dīcō, ere, dīxī, dictus.**

warlike, **bellicōsus, a, um.**

EXERCISE.

1. Orgetorix was a man of the greatest influence among the Helvetii, but he had no prudence.[1]   **2.** By the departure of the Roman horsemen the barbarians were made more eager.   **3.** He had already accomplished all the things for the sake of which he had led his army across the Rhine into Germany.   **4.** Procillus was among the noblest men of the Gallic Province. 5. You have not sent enough assistance [2] to these cohorts. 6. There were two daughters of this chieftain, of whom one was captured, the other (was) killed. 7. The Usipetes were greatly terrified by the sudden arrival of the Romans; four thousand of them came into the power of Caesar. 8. The tribe of the Nervii was by far the largest and most warlike of all the Belgians. 9. The River Rhone was five miles distant from this town. 10. You see the fury of all those who hate the rule of the Roman people. 11. We cut to pieces three thousand Germans who had lost all hope of safety. 12. Some opinions of this kind were uttered.

Suggestions on the Exercise.

1. *had no prudence :* translate : *nothing of prudence was to him.*
2. *enough assistance :* see Example 12.
3. *from :* use **ab.**

LESSON IX.

THE GENITIVE (*continued*).

GRAMMATICAL REFERENCES.

1. Genitive with Adjectives. 204. 1–3; A. & G. 349 and *a,* *b,* 385. *c* and 2 ; H. 450, 451. 1, 2 and N. 1, 3.

2. Genitive with *meminī, reminīscor, oblīvīscor.* 206. 1, 2; A. & G. 350. *a, b, c, d* ; H. 454 and 1, 455.

3. Genitive with Verbs of Judicial Action. 208. 1, 2, *a* ; A. & G. 352 and *a,* 353. 1 ; H. 456 and 3, 4.

4. Genitive with Impersonal Verbs. 209. 1; A. & G. 354. *b, c* ; H. 457.

5. Genitive with *interest.* 210; 211. 1; A. & G. 355 and *a* ; H. 449. 1–4.

EXAMPLES.

1. **Dumnorīx erat cupidus rērum novārum,** *Dumnorix was desirous of a revolution,* lit. *of new things.* (**1**)

2. **agrī erant plēnissimī frūmentī,** *the fields were very full of grain.* (**1**)

3. **reminīscerētur prīstinae virtūtis Helvētiōrum,** *let him remember the pristine valor of the Helvetii.* (**2**)

4. **veteris contumēliae nōn oblīvīscitur,** *he does not forget the old insult.* (**2**)

5. **Vercingetorīx prōditiōnis īnsimulātus est,** *Vercingetorix was accused of treason.* (**3**)

6. **summae inīquitātis condemnātur,** *he is convicted of the greatest injustice.* (**3**)

7. **saepe cōnsilia ineunt, quōrum eōs paenitet,** *they often initiate plans which they repent of,* lit. *of which it repents them.* (**4**)

8. **hōc commūnis salūtis interest,** *this concerns the common safety.* (**5**)

VOCABULARY.

accuse, **īnsimulō**, 1.

blameless, **innocēns, entis.**

concerns, it concerns, **interest, esse, fuit,** *imp.*

confidence, **fīdūcia, ae,** *f.*

convict, **condemnō,** 1.

custom, **cōnsuētūdō, inis,** *f.*

eager for, **cupidus, a, um,** *with gen.*

entirely, **omnīnō.**

forget, **oblīvīscor, ī, oblītus.**

full, **plēnus, a, um.**

inexperienced in, **imperītus, a, um,** *with gen.*

military science, **rēs mīlitāris, reī mīlitāris,** *f.*

opinion, **sententia, ae,** *f.*

present, be present, **adsum, esse, adfuī, adfutūrus.**

remember, **reminīscor, ī.**

repent, it repents, **paenitet, ēre, uit,** *imp.*

republic, **rēs pūblica, reī pūblicae,** *f.*

versed in, **perītus, a, um,** *with gen.*

EXERCISE.

1. The Haedui repented of their fickleness and weakness. 2. This concerns the republic. 3. Your horsemen were all full of confidence and hope. 4. I shall never forget, comrades, the controversies and dissensions of which I was the cause. 5. These barbarians, inexperienced in our customs, had brought war on the Roman people. 6. We remember the great dangers which you undertook for the sake of our safety. 7. They will send you leaders versed in military science. 8. In the opinion[1] of all who were present you had been convicted of these wrongs. 9. These tribes were eager for horses and beasts of burden. 10. You were entirely inexperienced in this kind of battle. 11. Those men who are blameless will not be accused of avarice. 12. They have not forgotten the many wrongs they suffered.

Suggestion on the Exercise.

1. *in the opinion:* use the simple ablative.

The Remi alone Offer Aid to Caesar.

Of all the states of the Belgians, the Remi alone had not conspired against the Roman people. But all the remaining Belgae were in arms, and had even summoned the Germans who dwelt this side the Rhine. These Belgians had in ancient days[1] inhabited Germany, but they had been led across the Rhine and had settled on[2] the lands of the Gauls whom they had driven out. They were very brave and had kept from their borders the Cimbrians and Teutons, who once had ravaged Gaul. There were many Belgian tribes and all had promised troops for[3] this war.

Suggestions on the Exercise.

1. *in ancient days:* **antīquitus (adv.).**
2. *settle on:* **occupō, 1.**
3. *for:* **ad.**

LESSON X.

THE ABLATIVE.

GRAMMATICAL REFERENCES.

1. Ablative of Separation. 214 entire; A. & G. 400, 401, 402. *a*; H. 462, 465.

2. Ablative of Source. 215 entire; A. & G. 403. *a*; H. 467, 469. 1, 2.

3. Ablative of Agent. 216 entire; A. & G. 405; H. 468 and 1.

4. Ablative of Comparison. 217. 1–4; A. & G. 406 and *a*, 407 and *c*; H. 471 and 1, 4.

5. Ablative of Means. 218; A. & G. 409; H. 476.

EXAMPLES.

1. **Caesar Ubiōs obsidiōne līberāvit**, *Caesar freed the Ubii from oppression.* (**1**)

2. **mūrus dēfēnsōribus nūdātus,** *a wall stripped of its defenders.* (**1**)

3. **Caesar proeliō abstinēbat,** *Caesar refrained from battle.* (**1**)

4. **prīncipēs Britanniae frūmentō nostrōs prohibēbant,** *the chieftains of Britain kept our men from grain.* (**1**)

5. **ex castrīs discēdere coepērunt,** *they began to withdraw from camp.* (**1**)

6. **vir fortissimus amplissimō genere nātus,** *a very gallant man born of a very noble family.* (**2**)

7. **locō nātus honestō,** *born in an* (lit. *from an*) *honorable station.* (**2**)

8. **Belgae erant ortī ab Germānīs,** *the Belgae were descended from the Germans.* (**2**)

9. **haec ā Caesare geruntur,** *these things were done by Caesar.* (**3**)

10. **dē hīs rēbus per**[1] **nūntiōs certior factus est**, *he was informed of these things through messengers.*

11. **hī sunt cēterīs hūmāniōrēs**, *these are more civilized than the rest.* (**4**)

12. **nōn amplius octingentōs equitēs habuērunt**, *they did not have more than eight hundred cavalry.* (**4**)

13. **magnō dolōre afficiēbantur**, *they were afflicted with great distress.* (**5**)

14. **eōs frūmentō jūvit**, *he assisted them with grain.* (**5**)

Note on the Examples.

1. When a person is viewed not as an independent agent, but rather as one through whose instrumentality something is done, this relation is expressed by **per** with the accusative.

VOCABULARY.

ancient, **antīquus, a, um.**

born, be born, **nāscor, ī, nātus.**

cut off, **interclūdō, ere, clūsī, clūsus.**

dear, **cārus, a, um.**

desist, **dēsistō, ere, dēstitī.**

fortify, **mūniō, īre, īvī, ītus.**

free, *verb*, **līberō, 1.**

hold, regard, **habeō, ēre, uī, itus.**

keep from, **prohibeō, ēre, uī, itus.**

oppress, **premō, ere, pressī, pressus.**

pay, **pendō, ere, pependī.**

runaway slave, **fugitīvus, ī, *m.***

supplies, **commeātus, ūs, *m.***

tamper with, **sollicitō, 1.**

withdraw, **dēcēdō, ere, cessī, cessūrus.**

EXERCISE.

1. Caesar held the lives[1] of his soldiers dearer than his own safety. **2.** The Usipetes were oppressed in war[2] by the Suebi and were kept from agriculture. **3.** The Helvetii finally desisted from this attempt. **4.** The River Rhone was not more than five miles distant from the camp of Sabinus. **5.** Ariovistus cut off Caesar from grain and supplies. **6.** All withdrew from that part of the village which had been granted by Galba to the Gauls.

7 This young man was born of a most ancient family.
8. We lost less than seven hundred foot-soldiers.
9. They fortified this place with a wall and a ditch.
10. The Belgians were tampered with by some Gauls.
11. These soldiers had already fought with javelins and swords more than two hours. 12. This circumstance was announced to the enemy through runaway slaves of Sabinus. 13. By our help you were freed from the tribute which you had paid to the Germans (for) three years.

Suggestions on the Exercise.

1. *lives :* the Latin uses the sing. in such cases
2. *in war :* express by the Ablative of Means.

LESSON XI.

THE ABLATIVE (*continued*).

GRAMMATICAL REFERENCES.

1. Ablative with the Deponents, *ūtor, fruor, etc.* 218. 1; A. & G. 410; H. 477. I.

2. Ablative with *frĕtus.* 218. 3; A. & G. 431. *a*; H. 476. 1.

3. Ablative in Special Phrases. 218. 7; H. 476. 4.

4. Ablative with Verbs of *Filling* and Adjectives of *Plenty.* 218. 8; A. & G. 409. *a*; H. 477. II.

5. Ablative of Way by Which. 218. 9; A. & G. 429. *a*; H. 476.

6. Ablative of Cause. 219 entire; A. & G. 404; H. 475.

EXAMPLES.

1. Germānī jūmentīs importātīs nōn ūtuntur, *the Germans do not use imported horses.* (**1**)

2. ūsī sunt eōdem duce,[1] *they used the same man as leader.* (**1**)

3. hī omnibus commodīs fruuntur, *these enjoy all advantages.* (**1**)

4. eōdem ille mūnere fungēbātur, *he performed the same duty.* (**1**)

5. magnō pecoris numerō potītur, *he secures possession of a great quantity of cattle.* (**1**)

6. tuā amīcitiā frētus sum, *I rely on your friendship.* (**2**)

7. castrīs sē tenuit, *he kept himself in camp.* (**3**)

8. proeliō nostrōs lacessere coepērunt, *they began to provoke our men to battle* or *offer battle to our men*, lit. *harass by battle.* (**3**)

9. equestrī proeliō cottīdiē contendit, *he contended daily in a cavalry battle.* (**3**)

10. tōtum montem hominibus complērī jussit, *he ordered the whole mountain to be covered with men.* (**4**)

11. frūmentum flūmine Ararī nāvibus subvexerat, *he brought up the grain in boats by way of the Arar River.* (**5**)

12. levitāte animī novīs imperiīs student, *on account of their fickleness of disposition they desire a change of control.* (**6**)

13. reī frūmentāriae jussū Caesaris praeerat, *by Caesar's order he was in charge of the grain supply.* (**6**)

Note on the Examples.

1. Note that **ūtor** may take a second ablative in predicate relation to the first. The predicate ablative may be either a noun or an adjective.

VOCABULARY.

advance, **prōgredior, ī, gressus.**

arrogantly, **īnsolenter.**

baggage, **impedīmenta, ōrum,** *n., lit.* hindrances.

boast, **glōrior, 1.**

contend, **contendō, ere, tendī, tentum.**

fear, *noun,* **timor, ōris,** *m.*

fill, fill up, **compleō, ēre, ēvī, ētus.**

hurdle, **crātēs, is,** *f.*

keep, confine, **teneō, ēre, uī.**

(offer) offer battle, **proeliō lacessō, ere, cessīvī, cessītus,** *lit.* harass in battle.

perform, **fungor, ī, fūnctus.**

(possession) gain possession, **potior, īrī, ītus.**

why? **cūr.**

within, **intrā,** *prep. with acc.*

EXERCISE.

1. Why did these men boast so arrogantly on account of their victories? **2.** The enemy gained possession of all our arms and baggage. **3.** Who enjoys war and plunder? **4.** All these tribes use the same language, laws, and[1] customs. **5.** The Roman soldiers filled up the trenches of this camp with stones and hurdles. **6.** You performed the duty of a brave soldier. **7.** Relying on their own valor, these men advanced bravely into the forests. 8. The Haedui had contended in war with the Sequani more than five years. 9. On account of the fear of the Suebi the Ubii kept themselves in the swamps. 10. Why did these five hundred horsemen offer battle to two thousand of the enemy? 11. The arms of which we have gained possession will be carried by way of the Rhone River to Vesontio. 12. On account of their confidence in[2] the place, our soldiers remained within their fortifications.

Suggestions on the Exercise.

1. For the employment of conjunctions in enumerations, see Lesson IV, Suggestion 1.

2. *confidence in the place:* the Latin says: *confidence of the place.*

The Two Armies Take Positions.

Caesar encouraged the Remi and ordered them to bring hostages to him.[1] Meanwhile all the forces of the Belgians had assembled and were approaching the camp of the Romans, as Caesar learned from the scouts whom he had sent (out). They were not far away when Caesar pitched his camp near the River Aisne, which was between the territory of the Remi and the Suessiones. This camp he fortified with a rampart[2] and a ditch. The camp of the Belgians was less than two miles distant.

Suggestions on the Exercise.

1. Use the reflexive.

2. *rampart:* **vāllum, ī, *n.***

LESSON XII.

THE ABLATIVE (*continued*).

GRAMMATICAL REFERENCES.

1. Ablative of Manner. 220 entire; A. & G. 412 **and** *a*; H. 473. 3 and N.

2. Ablative of Attendant Circumstance. 221.

3. Ablative of Accompaniment. 222; A. & G. 413 and *a*; H. 473. 1; 474. N. 1.

4. Ablative of Degree of Difference. 223; A. & G. 414; H. 479; cf. B. 357. 1; A. & G. 424. *f*; H. 488.

5. Ablative of Quality. 224; A. & G. 415; H. 473. 2 and N. 1.

EXAMPLES.

1. **magnā fīdūciā ad nostrās nāvēs prōcēdunt,** *they advance with great confidence to our ships.* (**1**)

2. **mōribus suīs Orgetorīgem ex vinculīs causam dīcere coēgērunt,** *according to their customs they compelled Orgetorix to plead his cause in chains.* (**1**)

3. **eōs longō intervāllō sequēbātur,** *he followed them at a long interval.* (**2**)

4. **silentiō ēgressus est cum tribus legiōnibus,** *he set out silently with three legions.* (**3**)

5. **omnibus cōpiīs ad castra Caesaris contendērunt,** *with all their forces they hurried to Caesar's camp.* (**3**)

6. **haec gēns paucīs ante mēnsibus ad Caesarem lēgātōs mīserat,** *this tribe had sent envoys to Caesar a few months before.* (**4**)

7. **bīduō post,** *two days afterwards.* (**4**)

8. **carīnae aliquantō plāniōrēs,** *hulls somewhat flatter.* (**4**)

9. **nōndum bonō animō in populum Rōmānum vidēbantur,** *they did not yet seem of good disposition towards the Roman people.* (**5**)

36

10. **Germānī erant ingentī magnitūdine corporum,** *the Germans were of enormous size of body.* **(5)**

11. **vir summā auctōritāte,** *a man of the highest authority.* **(5)**

Remarks.

1. The Ablative of Manner is best regarded as restricted to abstract words such as **celeritās, dignitās, lēnitās, prūdentia,** *etc.*

2. The Ablative of Quality primarily designates qualities which are more or less transitory. The observation sometimes made that the genitive denotes *internal* qualities, and the ablative *external* ones, is not sufficiently exact. In the phrase **hortātur ut bonō animō sint,** *he urges them to be of good courage,* the quality is internal: yet the genitive could not here be used; for while the quality is internal, it is transitory. The theoretical distinction between the Genitive of Quality and the Ablative of Quality is that the genitive denotes *permanent,* the ablative *transitory,* qualities. Yet where ambiguity would not result, the ablative may be used to denote a permanent quality. Thus one may say **vir summae virtūtis** or **summā virtūte,** *a man of the highest character.*

In all numerical designations of *weight, dimension, etc.,* the genitive is used.

VOCABULARY.

almost, **paene.**

assemble, *intrans.,* **conveniō, īre, vēnī, ventum.**

boundless, **īnfīnītus, a, um.**

common people, **plēbs, is,** *f.*

disposition, **animus, ī,** *m.*

extent, **magnitūdō, inis,** *f.*

incredible, **incrēdibilis, e.**

infantry, *as adj.,* **pedester, tris, tre.**

later, *adv.,* **post.**

pains, **dīligentia, ae,** *f.*

popularity, **grātia, ae,** *f.*

preserve, **cōnservō, 1.**

towards, in, *prep. with acc.*

war chariot, **essedum, ī,** *n.*

EXERCISE.

1 This state was of the greatest power and influence among the maritime tribes 2. These forces which have assembled are much greater. 3. They made this wall ten feet higher 4. Three days[1] later we crossed

the valley and river with less danger.   5. Dumnorix was of the greatest boldness and of great popularity among the common people.   6. This stream is of incredible smoothness.   7. A few years before they were of friendlier disposition toward us.   8. They fortified this camp with greater pains.[2]   9. In accordance with his custom Caesar preserved this state.   10. They advanced with their cavalry and war chariots.   11. The woods which you saw are of almost boundless extent. 12. These men had advanced a little farther[3] for the sake of water.   13. He hastened to the camp with his infantry forces.

Suggestions on the Exercise.

1. See Lesson V, Remark 2.
2. *pains :* use the singular.
3. *farther :* **longius.**

LESSON XIII.

THE ABLATIVE (*continued.*)

GRAMMATICAL REFERENCES.

1. Ablative of Specification. 226 entire; A. & G. 418;
R. 480.

2. Ablative Absolute. 227. 1, 2; A. & G. 419 and *a*, 420;
H. 489 and 1.

3. Ablative of Place Where. 228 entire; A. & G. 426. 3,
427. 3, 429. 1, 2; H. 483; 485. 2.

4. Ablative of Place from Which. 229 entire; A. & G. 426. 1,
427. 1, 428. *a*, *b*; H. 461, 462 and 3, 4.

EXAMPLES.

1. fāmā nōbilēs erᴀnt potentēsque bellō, *they were eminent in
   fame and powerful in war.* (**1**)

2. equitātū superior, *superior in cavalry.* (**1**)

3. Helvētiī reliquōs Gallōs virtūte praecēdunt, *the Helvetii surpass the other Gauls in valor.* (**1**)

4. M. Messallā, M. Pīsōne cōnsulibus, *in the consulship of Marcus
   Messalla and Marcus Piso,* lit. *Marcus Messalla and
   Marcus Piso (being) consuls.* (**2**)

5. rē frūmentāriā comparātā equitibusque dēlēctīs iter facere
   coepit, *having got ready grain and chosen horsemen, he
   began to march,* lit. *grain having been got ready, etc.* (**2**)

6. Germānicō bellō cōnfectō, *having completed the German war,*
   or, *when the German war had been completed.* (**2**)

7. tōtīs castrīs, *in the whole camp;* omnibus locīs, *in all places;*
   in Galliā, *in Gaul.* (**3**)

8. multī virī fortēs Tolōsā et Narbōne ēvocātī sunt, *many brave
   men were summoned from Tolosa and Narbo* (**4**)

39

9. **expellitur ex** oppidō Gergoviā, *he is driven out of the town Gergovia.* (**4**)

10. **ā** Gergoviā **dēcessit,** *he withdrew from the neighborhood of Gergovia.* (**4**)

11. **ex aedificiīs** quae habuerant **dēmigrārunt,** *they moved out of the houses which they had had.* (**4**)

12. **iter ab Ararī** āvertit, *he turned his course away from the Arar.* (**4**)

13. **uxōrem domō sēcum** dūxerat, *he had taken his wife with him from home.* (**4**)

Remark

1. Observe that in Latin the Ablative Absolute largely occurs where in English we employ subordinate clauses. Of the various kinds of clauses thus occurring, temporal clauses introduced by *when* and *after* are by far the most frequent.

VOCABULARY.

achieve, **gerō, ere, gessī, gestus.**
break out, **coorior, īrī, coortus.**
citadel, **arx, arcis,** *f.*
excel, **praestō, āre, praestitī.**
flee, **fugiō, ere, fūgī, fugitūrus.**
knowledge, **scientia, ae,** *f.*
march forth, **ēgredior, ī, ēgressus.**

message, **nūntius, ī,** *m.*
only, **tantum.**
practice, **ūsus, ūs,** *m.*
seamanship, **rēs nauticae, rērum nauticārum,** *f.*
(sides) from all sides, **undique.**
subdue, pacify, **pācō,** 1.

EXERCISE.

1. In Vesontio there was a high hill which made a citadel. 2. The Veneti surpass the remaining maritime tribes in knowledge and practice of seamanship. 3. The number of those who marched forth from home was[1] ten thousand. 4. When hostages had been given and peace had been made,[2] Galba settled two cohorts among the Nantuates in a village of the Veragri which is called Octodurus. 5. There was a town of the Remi, Bibrax by name. 6. Only two states sent hostages from Britain

7. In the consulship of Lucius Domitius and Appius Claudius, Caesar withdrew from his winter quarters into Italy.   8. The Roman ships excelled in speed alone.[3] 9. A sudden war broke out in Britain.   10. We received these messages from those who had fled from the vicinity of Geneva.   11. When these things had been achieved and all Gaul had been subdued,[2] envoys were sent to Caesar from all sides.   12. Having received these messages,[2] we set out from Tolosa.

Suggestions on the Exercise.

1. Use a plural verb to agree with the number of the predicate noun.

2. Express by the Ablative Absolute.

3. Express *alone* by ūnus in agreement.

Defeat of the Belgians.

At first they contended in a cavalry battle.   After a few hours, the barbarians withdrew and Caesar led the Romans back to camp.   Then he led the cavalry, archers, and slingers, across the river by the bridge, and hastened toward a ford, where he found the enemy.   Our soldiers attacked and killed a great number of them crossing the river, and the cavalry surrounded[1] and slew those who had already crossed.   Finally grain began to fail them, and calling a council,[2] they decided to return home.

Suggestions on the Exercise.

1. *surround:* circumveniō, īre, vēnī, ventus.

2. *calling a council:* express by the Ablative Absolute; for *call* use the compound, convocō, 1.

LESSON XIV.

THE ABLATIVE (*continued*).

GRAMMATICAL REFERENCES.

1. The Locative Case. 232. 1, 2; 169. 4; A. & G. 427. 3 and
a; 282. *d*; H. 483; 484. 1, 2; 483. 2.

2. Ablative of Time at Which. 230. 1-3; A. & G. 423 and
1; H. 486.

3. Ablative of Time within Which. 231; A. & G. 423, 424.
a; H. 487 and 1.

4. Roman Dates. 371, 372; A. & G. 631; H. 754; 755.

EXAMPLES.

1. reliquī domī remanent, *the rest remain at home.* **(1)**
2. hōc proelium Alesiae factum est, *this battle took place at
   Alesia.* **(1)**
3. sex legiōnēs Agedinci collocāvit, *he stationed six legions at
   Agedincum.* **(1)**
4. prīma lūce Cōnsidius ad eum accurrit, *at daybreak Considius
   races towards him.* **(2)**
5. hieme nāvēs aedificāvit, *he built ships in the winter.* **(2)**
6. tēcum proximīs comitiīs contrōversiam habuimus, *we had a
   quarrel with you at the last election.* **(2)**
7. eō annō in Galliā nūllum frūmentum erat, *in that year there
   was no wheat in Gaul.* **(2)**
8. eōrum adventū equōs Germānīs distribuit, *at their arrival he
   distributed horses to the Germans.* **(2)**
9. bellō Cassiānō dux fuerat, *he had been leader in the Cassian
   war.* **(2)**
10. decem diēbus omne opus effectum est, *within ten days the
    whole work was finished.* **(3)**

11. Īdibus Aprīlibus, *on the Ides of April.* **(4)**

12. is diēs erat ante diem quīntum Kalendās Aprīlēs, *that day was March 28th.* **(4)**

VOCABULARY.

April, of April, **Aprīlis, e.**

arrive, **adveniō, īre, vēnī, ventum.**

break (camp), **moveō, ēre, mōvī, mōtus.**

few, **paucī, ae, a.**

happen, **fīō, fīerī, factus.**

learn, **comperiō, īre, comperī, compertus.**

memory, **memoria, ae,** *f.*

midnight, **media nox, mediae noctis,** *f.*

ravage, **vexō, 1.**

silently, **silentiō,** *adv.*

EXERCISE.

1. April 7th we arrived in the vicinity of Geneva. **2.** Having learned these things, the Gauls at midnight silently left the camp. **3.** Within a few days he had built a bridge and had led his army across. **4.** These things happened at Alesia in the consulship of Cn. Domitius and Marcus Cato. **5.** Within the memory of our fathers these tribes had ravaged the Province. **6.** There were great dissensions at Cenabum. **7.** At Bibracte, a large town of the Haedui, there was at this time neither grain nor water. **8.** We set out for Gaul March 31st. **9.** On March 1st at the third hour we broke camp. **10.** Who of you was at home that day? **11.** On the same night these runaway slaves fled from the vicinity of Cenabum. **12.** We shall return within four days.[1]

Suggestion on the Exercise.

1. See Lesson V, Remark 2.

LESSON XV.

SYNTAX OF ADJECTIVES.

GRAMMATICAL REFERENCES.

1. Adjectives used Substantively. 236–238; A. & G. 288 and *a, b*; 289. *a, b*; H. 494, 495.

2. Adjectives with the Force of Adverbs. 239; A. & G. 290; H. 497 and 1.

3. Special Uses of the Comparative and Superlative. 240. 1–4: A. & G. 291. *a, b*; 292; H. 498, 499.

4. Adjectives denoting a Special Part of an Object. 241. 1; A. & G. 293; H. 497. 4.

5. Prīmus = *first who;* ultimus = *last who; etc.* 241. 2; A. & G. 290; H. 497. 3.

EXAMPLES.

1. omnēs cōnservāvit, *he preserved all.* (**1**)
2. omnia perdidimus, *we lost all things.*[1] (**1**)
3. bona eōrum dīripiunt, *they plunder their goods.* (**1**)
4. Caesar nostrōs castrīs tenuit, *Caesar kept our men in camp.* (**1**)
5. trīstēs terram intuēbantur, *they gazed sadly at the ground.* (**2**)
6. ejus auctōritās fuit amplissima, *his influence was very great.* (**3**)
7. frūmentum angustius prōvēnerat, *the grain crop had turned out rather small,* lit. *smaller (than usual).* (**3**)
8. summus mōns, *the top of the mountain.* (**4**)
9. ad extrēmās fossās castella cōnstituit, *at the ends of the ditches he placed redoubts.* (**4**)

44

10. **hī prīmi mūrum ascendērunt,** *these climbed the wall first.* (**5**)

11. **quam maximīs itineribus,** *with as hard marches as possible.*

(**3**)

Note on the Examples.

1. In other cases than the nominative and accusative this idea is best expressed by means of **rēs,** *e.g.* **omnium rērum,** *of all things;* **omnibus rēbus,** *by all things.* **Omnium, omnibus, parvōrum, parvīs,** and similar forms would be ambiguous in gender.

VOCABULARY.

call together, **convocō, 1.**

(crowd), in crowds, **frequēns, entis,** *adj.*

(end), at end of, **extrēmus, a, um,** *lit.* last.

fight, **pugnō, 1.**

following, **posterus, a, um.**

(foot), at foot of, **īnfimus** or **īmus,** *superl. of* **īnferus.**

glad, **laetus, a, um.**

massed together, **cōnfertus, a, um.**

powerful, **potēns, entis.**

recount, **ēnumerō, 1.**

scattered, **rārus, a, um.**

seem, **videor, ērī, vīsus.**

EXERCISE.

1. The forces did not withdraw far from the foot of the hill. **2.** He built as many ships as possible at the end of the winter. **3.** All who were present at that time seemed rather fickle. **4.** The remainder, who heard this envoy, learned all things. **5.** Having called together his (adherents), he recounted his wrongs. **6.** The Germans assembled in crowds at[1] the camp on the following day. **7.** The friends whom we saw at Geneva were very powerful. **8.** They marched forth gladly from camp. **9.** You came first to this village. **10.** Our men were not fighting massed together, but scattered. **11.** The Remi handed over all their (property) to the Romans. **12.** A few of[2] our men were too

eager and (so) were killed by the enemy.   13. This
town was full of all things[3] which were of use[4] for war

Suggestions on the Exercise.

1. *at:* express by **ad** with the acc.
2. *of:* express by **dē** with abl.
3. *all things:* see Note on the Examples.
4. *of use:* see Lesson VII, Example **7.**
5. *for war:* **ad bellum.**

The Belgians Disperse.

On that night the whole multitude poured forth[1] from
their camp.   Caesar, not yet having learned[2] the cause
for[3] their departure, feared treachery[4] and remained in
camp, but on the following day he placed Quintus Pedius
and Lucius Cotta (as) lieutenants in charge of the cavalry and sent them (on) ahead.   Titus Labienus followed
with three legions.   The Romans pursued the enemy
many miles and, having slain a large multitude of them
without any danger, returned to camp.   More than five
thousand Belgians perished on that day.

Suggestions on the Exercise.

1. *pour forth:* sē ēicere (ēiciō, ere, ējēcī, ējectus).
2. *having learned:* use the Ablative Absolute.
3. *for:* translate: *of.*
4. *treachery:* īnsidiae, ārum, *f.*

REVIEW.

1. They refused no danger for the sake of (their)
common freedom.   2. When an oath had been given
by all who were present at[1] this council, we withdrew.
3. They slew Gaius Fufius. a Roman knight, who by

Caesar's order was in charge of the grain supply. 4. Vercingetorix was of the greatest influence among the Arverni. 5. They tarried here a few days, and then returned home. 6. Two days before, we came to Bibracte, a very large town.[2] 7. We know no one braver than Baculus. 8. This wall was twenty feet high and eight feet thick. 9. The Haedui sent forces of cavalry and infantry as help[3] to the Bituriges. 10. All the villages and buildings which each one had caught sight of[4] were set on fire. 11. They inflicted punishment on this man according to the custom[5] of (their) ancestors. 12. Two thousand horsemen were gathered by the Sugambri, who are nearest to the Rhine of all the Germans.

Suggestions on the Exercise.

1. *at :* use **in** with the abl.
2. Use the prep. **ad** with the appositional phrase.
3. *as help :* see Lesson VII, Example 6.
4. *catch sight of :* cōnspiciō, ere, spexī, spectus.
5. *according to the custom :* see Lesson XII, Example 2.

LESSON XVI.

PRONOUNS.

GRAMMATICAL REFERENCES.

1. Personal Pronouns. 242. 1, 2, 4; A. & G. 295. *a, b*; H. 500 and 4.

2. Reflexive Pronouns. 244 entire; A. & G. 299 and *a*, 300. 1, 2, 301. *a, b*; H. 503 and 3, 4; 504.

3. Reciprocal Pronouns. 245; A. & G. 301. *f*; H. 502. 1.

4. Hīc, Ille, Iste. 246. 1–5; A. & G. 297. *a–c*; 296. *a*; H. 505 and 1; 506. 1; 507 and 3, 4.

5. Is. 247. 1–4; A. & G. 297. *d*; H. 508 and 1, 2, 4.

6. Īdem. 248. 1, 2; A. & G. 298. *b*; 384. N. 2; H. 508. 3, 5.

7. Ipse. 249. 1, 2; A. & G. 298. *c* and N. 1, *f*; H. 509. 1, 3.

EXAMPLES.

1. tantā contemptiōne nostrī, *with so great scorn for us.* **(1)**

2. omnium vestrum cōnsēnsū, *by the agreement of all of you.* **(1)**

3. sēse dēfendunt, *they defend themselves.* **(2)**

4. differunt hae nātiōnēs inter sē, *these nations differ from each other,* lit. *between themselves* (reciprocal use). **(3)**

5. petēbant utī Caesar sibi[1] potestātem faceret, *they begged that Caesar would give them the opportunity.* **(2)**

6. hi rūrsus in armīs sunt, illī domī remanent, *the latter are in turn under arms, the former remain at home.* **(4)**

7. haec sī acerba videntur, multō graviōra illa sunt, *if these last things seem harsh, (yet) those former ones are much worse.* **(4)**

8. ejus bellī haec fuit causa, *the following was the cause of that war.* **(4)**

9. **in exercitū Sullae et posteā in M. Crassī fuerat,** *he had been in the army of Sulla, and afterwards in that of Marcus Crassus.* (**5**)

10. **legiōnem neque eam plēnissimam dēspiciēbant,** *they despised the legion, and that not a very full one.* (**5**)

11. **ejus adventū, eōrum adventū;** *by his arrival, by their arrival.* (**5**)

12. **id quod accidit suspicābātur,** *he was suspecting that which happened.* (**5**)

13. **eadem opiniō quam reliquae gentēs habent,** *the same opinion as the remaining tribes have.* (**6**)

14. **ipsō terrōre equōrum ōrdinēs perturbantur,** *the ranks are thrown into confusion by the very terror inspired by the horses.* (**7**)

15. **ipse erat Dumnorīx,** *Dumnorix was the very man.* (**7**)

Note on the Examples.

1. This illustrates the indirect reflexive.

VOCABULARY.

against, **in,** *prep. with acc.*

confer (with), **colloquor, ī, locū-tus.**

defend, **dēfendō, ere, fendī, fēn-sus.**

former . . . (latter), **ille, a, ud.**

go, **eō, īre, īvī, itum.**

good, **bonus, a, um.**

latter, of two already mentioned, **hīc, haec, hōc.**

(lend), be lent, be added, **accēdō, ere, accessī, accessūrus.**

protect, **prōtegō, ere, tēxī, tēctus.**

route, **iter, itineris,** *n.*

shield, **scūtum, ī,** *n.*

summit of, **summus, a, um.**

support, *noun,* **subsidium, ī, u**

EXERCISE.

1. Two legions were now fighting on the very bank of the river. 2. Three cohorts, and those the best of the tenth legion, were sent as a support[1] to these. 3. By their arrival hope was lent to our men. 4. Titurius

hastened to the bridge by the same route as the enemy had gone.[2]   5. He used the following words.   6. We shall always bravely defend ourselves and our possessions.   7. The town itself was on the summit of the hill.   8. Of these two soldiers, they protected the former with their shields; against the latter they hurled their javelins.   9. They withdrew on account of fear of you.   10. On that very day I saw what[3] you now see.   11. These chieftains conferred together.[4]   12. We did this for the sake of your safety and that of all of us.[5]

Suggestions on the Exercise.

1. See Lesson VII, Examples 6, 7, 8.

2. *as the enemy had gone:* translate: *by which the enemy had gone.*

3. *what:* translate: *that which.*

4. *together:* translate: *between themselves.*

5. See Example 2.

LESSON XVII.

PRONOUNS (*continued*).

GRAMMATICAL REFERENCES.

1. **Quis** (Indefinite).   252. 1; A. & G. 310 and *a*; H. 512 and 1

2. **Aliquis.**   252. 2; A. & G. 311; H. 512.

3. **Quīdam.**   252. 3 and *a*; A. & G. 310; H. 512. 6.

4. **Quisquam.**   252. 4; A. & G. 312; H. 513.

5. **Quisque.**   252. 5; A. & G. 313 and *a*; H. 515.

6. **Alius, Alter.**   253. 1–3; A. & G. 315 and *c*; H. 516 and 1

7. **Cēterī.**   253. 4; A. & G. 315.

8. **Reliquī.**   253. 5; A. & G. 315.

9. **Uterque.**   355. 2; A. & G. 313; H. 516. 4.

EXAMPLES.

1. sī quid animī in nōbīs est, *if there is any courage in us.*   **(1)**

2. hostēs ubi aliquōs ex nāvī ēgredientēs cōnspexerant, adoriēbantur, *when the enemy had seen some disembarking,
they attacked them.*   **(2)**

3. cum quibusdam adulēscentibus colloquitur, *he converses with
certain young men.*   **(3)**

4. quīdam ex hīs nocte ad Nerviōs pervēnērunt, *certain of these
came to the Nervii by night.*   **(3)**

5. neque vestītūs praeter pellēs habent quicquam, *nor do they
have any clothing except skins.*   **(4)**

6. neque quisquam locō cessit, *nor did any one withdraw from
his post.*   **(4)**

7. sibi quisque cōnsulēbat, *each one was looking out for himself.*   **(5)**

8. alii vāllum scindere, alii fossās complēre incēpērunt, *some began to tear down the rampart, others to fill the trenches.* (6)

9. legiōnēs aliae aliā in parte hostibus restitērunt, *the legions some in one quarter, others in another resisted the enemy.* (6)

10. alterius factiōnis prīncipēs erant Haeduī, alterius Sēquanī, *of the one faction, the Haedui were leaders, of the other the Sequani.* (6)

11. cēterōs amīcōs populī Rōmānī dēfendēmus, *we shall defend the other friends of the Roman people.* (7)

12. reliquum exercitum Sabīnō dedit, *he gave the rest of the army to Sabinus.* (8)

13. suās uterque cōpiās īnstrūxit, *each drew up his forces.* (9)

14. utrumque ōrant, *they entreat both,* or *each.* (9)

Remark.

1. Note that in Latin the singular of **uterque** is regularly used where in English we say *both*, if the reference is to two *individuals*, as **utrumque vīdī.** When the reference is to two *groups* the plural is used.

VOCABULARY.

abandon, **dēserō, ere, seruī, sertus.**	mountain, **mōns, montis,** *m.*
betake oneself, **recipiō, ere, cēpī, ceptus,** *with the reflexive.*	rashly, **temere.**
council, **concilium, ī,** *n.*	rise up, **cōnsurgō, ere, surrēxī, surrēctum.**
crowd, **multitūdō, inis,** *f.*	speak, **dīcō, ere, dīxī, dictus.**
fiercely, **ācriter.**	take possession, **occupō,** 1.
lead on, impel, **indūcō, ere, dūxī, ductus.**	

EXERCISE.

1. The Menapii had fields and buildings on[1] each bank of the river.   2. Both (sides) fought fiercely.   3. When any one speaks in the council, the rest rise up.   4. The

remainder of the crowd of children and women fled in[2] all directions.   5. The one general was forty miles distant, the other a little more.[3]   6. The one (party) betook themselves to the mountain, the other to their baggage. 7. The tenth legion took possession of a certain hill. 8. Some are led on by avarice, others by desire for power.   9. You took possession of one hill, we of another.   10. The Britons had surrounded the rest with their cavalry and war chariots.   11. The remainder betook themselves home.   12. Each held his own[4] place. 13. Why does any one so rashly abandon his duty ? 14. Both (persons) are present.

Suggestions on the Exercise.

1. *on :* use **ad**.
2. *in :* translate : *into*.
3. *a little more :* translate : *more by a little*.
4. Note that when **suus** and **quisque** are combined, **suus precedes**

Submission of the Suessiones and Bellovaci.

On the following day Caesar advanced more than twenty-seven miles by forced[1] marches to Noviodunum, the largest town[2] of the Suessiones, and at once attempted to take it by storm.   But the wall was very high and the town was surrounded[3] by a deep ditch.   The Romans therefore desisted from this attempt and were assaulting the town, when the Gauls asked (for) peace, and, on the petition of the Remi,[4] secured their request.   Having received the Suessiones[5] in surrender,[6] he then led his army against the Bellovaci, who were at Bratuspantium.   These also soon surrendered themselves to Caesar.

Suggestions on the Exercise.

1. *forced :* translate : *as great as possible ;* see Lesson **XV,** Example 11.

2. *the largest town :* see Review, p. 47, Sentence 6.

3. *surrounded :* cīnctus, a, um.

4. *on the petition of the Remi :* translate by the Ablative Absolute, — *the Remi requesting (it).*

5. *having received the Suessiones :* translate by the Ablative Absolute.

6. *in surrender :* translate : *into surrender.*

LESSON XVIII.

TENSES OF THE INDICATIVE.

GRAMMATICAL REFERENCES.

1. The Present. 259. 1–4; A. & G. 465, 466, 467, 469; H. 532 and 1, 2, 3; 533. 1; 530.

2. The Imperfect. 260. 1–4; A. & G. 470, 471. *a–c*; H. 534 and 1, 2, 3; 535. 1; 530.

3. The Future. 261. 1, 2; A. & G. 472 and *b*; H. 536.

4. The Perfect. 262. *A* and *B*; A. & G. 473, 476; H. 537. 1, 2; 538. 4.

5. The Pluperfect. 263 and *a*; A. & G. 477; H. 539.

6. The Future Perfect. 264 and *a. b*; A. & G. 478; H. 540 and 2.

EXAMPLES.

1. ferē libenter hominēs id quod volunt crēdunt, *men generally believe what they wish.* **(1)**

2. Caesar Haeduīs obsidēs imperat, *Caesar demands hostages of the Haeduans.* **(1)**

3. jam rūmōrēs adferēbantur, *already rumors were being brought.* **(2)**

4. crēbrās excursiōnēs faciēbant, *they kept making frequent sallies.* **(2)**

5. hostēs nostrōs intrā mūnītiōnēs prōgredī prohibēbant, *the enemy tried to prevent our men from advancing within the fortifications.* **(2)**

6. sē in currūs recipere cōnsuērunt, *they are wont* (lit. *have accustomed themselves*) *to return to the chariots.* **(4)**

7. Haeduōs appropinquāre cognōverant, *they knew that the Haedui were approaching.* **(5)**

VOCABULARY

body, **corpus, corporis,** *n.*

develop, nourish, **alō, ere, aluī, altus** *or* **alitus.**

dismount, **dēsiliō, īre, siluī** or **siliī, sultum.**

enormous, **immānis, e.**

fact, **rēs, reī,** *f.*

:familiar), am familiar with, *perf.* of **cognōscō, ere, nōvī, nitus,** *trans.*

harbor, **portus, ūs,** *m.*

know. I know *perf. of* **cognōscō, ere, nōvī, nitus.**

procure, **parō,** 1.

rouse, **sollicitō,** 1.

sail, *verb,* **nāvigō,** 1.

size, **magnitūdō, inis,** *f.*

strength, **vīrēs, ium,** *f.*

suspect, **suspicor,** 1.

visit, **adeō, īre, iī, itus.**

(wont), am wont, *perf.* of **cōn-suēscō, ere, suēvī, suētum.**

EXERCISE.

1. The Helvetii are wont to receive hostages, not to give them. **2.** We did not yet know your plans, but were suspecting them. **3.** This fact develops their strength and makes men of enormous size of body.[1] **4.** Meanwhile ships of war were being built, weapons were being procured, and[2] the neighboring tribes were being roused. **5.** The Britons used to dismount from their war chariots and to fight on foot.[3] **6.** We shall soon know all the things which he has heard. **7.** The Veneti were wont to sail with their ships[4] to Britain. **8.** They kept hurling stones and javelins from the wall against our men. **9.** I have visited this island and am familiar with its shore and harbors. **10.** The barbarians were trying to surround our camp

Suggestions on the Exercise.

1   *body:* use the plural.

2.   *and:* see Lesson IV, Suggestion 1.

3.   *on foot:* use the simple ablative, in the plural.

4.   *with their ships,* use the simple ablative of **Means.**

LESSON XIX.

PURPOSE CLAUSES.

GRAMMATICAL REFERENCES.

1. Purpose Clauses with *ut, nē, quō.* 282. 1. *a–e*; A. & G. 531. 1 and *a*; H. 568 and 7.

2. Relative Clauses of Purpose. 282. 2; A. & G. 531. 2; H. 590.

3. Relative Clauses with *dignus, indignus, idōneus* 282. 3; A. & G. 535. *j* ; H. 591. 7.

4. Sequence of Tenses. 267. 1–3; 268. 1, 3; A. & G. 482. 1, 2; 483; 485. *a, e*; H. 543–546.

EXAMPLES.

1. lēgātōs ad Dumnorīgem mittunt ut ā Sēquanīs impetrārent,[1] *they sent envoys to Dumnorix in order that they might obtain their request from the Sequani.* **(1)**

2. jubet portās claudī, nē castra nūdentur,[2] *he orders the gates to be closed in order that the camp may not be exposed.* **(1)**

3. portās clausit, nē quam oppidānī injūriam acciperent, *he closed the gates that the townspeople might not receive any injury.* **(1)**

4. quō parātiōrēs essent ad īnsequendum, *in order that they might be more prepared for pursuing.* **(1)**

5. equitātum omnem praemittit quī videant,[2] *he sends forward all the cavalry to see.* **(2)**

6. hunc idōneum jūdicāvit quem ad Pompeium mitteret, *he judged him suitable to send to Pompey.* **(3)**

Notes on the Examples

1 Note the secondary sequence after the historical present.

2 Note the primary sequence after the historical present.

Remark.

Note that the Latin uses **nē quis**, *in order that no one;* **nē quid**, *in order that nothing;* **nē ūllus**, **nē quī**, *in order that no;* similarly, **nē ūsquam**, *in order that nowhere;* **nē unquam**, *in order that never.*

VOCABULARY.

ambassador, **lēgātus, ī**, *m.*

attack, **impetus, ūs**, *m.*

bar, **obstruō, ere, strūxī, strūctus.**

before, in front of, **prō**, *prep. with the abl.*

beg for, **ōrō**, 1, *trans.*

better, *adv.*, **melius**

block, **interclūdō, ere, clūsī, clūsus.**

burn, **combūrō, ere, bussī, būstus.**

easily, **facile.**

occur, **fīō, fierī, factus.**

return, *noun*, **reditus, ūs**, *m.*

road, **iter, itineris**, *n.*

send ahead, **praemittō, ere, mīsī, missus.**

station, **collocō**, 1.

suitable, **idōneus, a, um.**

take away, **tollō, ere, sustulī, sublātus.**

withstand, **sustineō, ēre, uī, tentus.**

EXERCISE.

1. He stationed the legions before the camp, in order that no sudden attack might occur.   2. They sent envoys to ask help, in order that they might more easily withstand the attack of the enemy.   3. In order that no one might block the roads, he sent men to guard them. 4. They send ambassadors to him to beg for peace. 5. He set out for Aquitania, in order that help might not be sent from these districts into Gaul.   6. They burned all their grain in order that all hope of a return might be taken away.   7. He sent Crassus ahead to choose a suitable place for a camp.   8. There was no one suitable to be put in charge of the winter quarters.   9. He fled that he might not be captured.   10. Pompey barred the gates that he might better withstand the attack of Caesar.

11. Caesar made a bridge across the Rhine[1] in order to terrify the Germans.

Suggestion on the Exercise.

1. *across the Rhine :* the Latin says, *in the Rhine.*

Caesar Extends Clemency to the Bellovaci.

In order that Caesar might not inflict punishment on the Bellovaci, but might exercise his (usual) clemency towards them, Divitiacus, the Haeduan, spoke in their behalf.[1] For the Bellovaci had always been friends of the Haedui, and had revolted and waged war against the Romans not of their own accord,[2] but impelled by their chieftains, who had now fled to Britain. Caesar, therefore, in order to increase the influence of the Haedui among all the Belgians, received the Bellovaci under his protection[4] and spared them, but in order that they might not again revolt, he demanded six hundred hostages.

Suggestions on the Exercise.

1. *in their behalf :* translate : *for* (**prō**) *them.*
2. *of their own accord :* **suā sponte.**
3. *increase :* **amplificō**, 1.
4. *under his protection :* **in fidem.**

LESSON XX.

CLAUSES OF CHARACTERISTIC. CLAUSES OF RESULT.

GRAMMATICAL REFERENCES.

1. Simple Clauses of Characteristic. 283. 1, 2; A. & G. 535 and *a, b*; H. 591. 1, 5.

2. Clauses of Characteristic introduced by *quīn*. 283. 4; A. & G. 559. 2; H. 594. II. 2, end; 595. 4.

3. Clauses of Result introduced by *ut* and *ut nōn*. 284. 1; A. & G. 537 and 1; H. 570. — For Sequence of Tenses in Result Clauses, see 268. 6; A. & G. 485. *c*; H. 550.

4. Result Clauses introduced by *quīn*. 284. 3; A. & G. 559. 1; H. 594. II.

EXAMPLES.

1. repertī complūrēs nostrī mīlitēs quī in phalangem īnsilīrent, *very many of our soldiers were found who leaped into the phalanx.* (**1**)

2. neque adhūc repertus est quisquam quī mortem recūsāret, *nor as yet has any one been found who refused death.* (**1**)

3. nūlla fuit cīvitās quīn lēgātōs mitteret, *there was no state which did not send envoys.* (**2**)

4. nēmō fuit quīn vulnerārētur, *there was no one who was not wounded.* (**2**)

5. tantus timor omnem exercitum occupāvit, ut omnium mentēs perturbāret, *so great fear seized the whole army that it unsettled the minds of all.* (**3**)

6 multīs vulneribus cōnfectus est, ut sē sustinēre nōn posset, *he was exhausted by many wounds, so that he could no longer hold out.* (**3**)

7 nēmō est tam fortis quīn reī novitāte perturbētur, *no one is so steadfast as not to be confused by a strange occurrence,* lit. *by the strangeness of an occurrence.* (**4**)

60

VOCABULARY.

arise, spring up, **coorior, īrī, coortus.**

borders, **fīnēs, ium,** *m., lit.* ends.

bring about, **faciō, ere, fēcī, factus** ; be brought about, **fīō, fīerī, factus.**

convey, **perferō, ferre, tulī, lātus.**

change, **commūtātiō, ōnis,** *f.*

charioteer, **aurīga, ae,** *m.*

drive back, **repellō, ere, reppulī repulsus.**

equal, **adaequō, 1.**

only, **sōlus, a, um.**

report, **fāma, ae,** *f.*

retreat, **receptus, ūs,** *m.*

throw, **jaciō, ere, jēcī, jactus.**

EXERCISE.

1 There is no honor which he does not seek. 2. There was no one in this whole cohort who was not captured by the enemy. 3. So great a storm arose that very many of Caesar's ships[1] were lost. 4. The charioteers so station the war chariots that they have an easy retreat to their (friends). 5. There was no one left who surpassed him in steadfastness. 6. By the arrival of these so great a change of affairs was brought about that our men renewed the battle. 7. So many weapons were thrown into the ditch that the heaps of them almost equalled the height of the wall. 8. There is no one who does not know all these things 9. These were the only (ones) who in the memory of our fathers kept the Cimbrians and Teutons away from their borders. 10 The report of this victory was conveyed with incredible swiftness, so that it arrived at[2] the camp before midnight. 11. Our men fought so bravely that they drove back the enemy into the forests

Suggestions on the Exercise.

1. *very many of Caesar's ships:* translate : *very many ships of Caesar.*

2. *at :* translate : *to.*

LESSON XXI.

CAUSAL CLAUSES. TEMPORAL CLAUSES.

GRAMMATICAL REFERENCES.

1. **Causal Clauses.** 286. 1 and *b*; 286. 2; A. & G. 540. 1, 2; 549; H. 588. I, II, and 2; 598.

2. **Temporal Clauses** introduced by *postquam, ubi* etc., denoting a single past act. 287. 1; A. & G. 543; H. 602.

3. **Clauses** introduced by *ut, ubi, simul ac,* denoting a repeated act. 287. 2; H. 602. 2.

EXAMPLES.

1. in hīs locīs, quod omnis Gallia ad septentriōnēs vergit, mātūrae sunt hiemēs, *the winters are early in these places, because all Gaul stretches toward the north.* (**1**)

2. graviter eōs accūsat, quod ab eīs nōn sublevētur, *he bitterly accuses them because he is not assisted by them.* (**1**)

3. cum sē dēfendere nōn possent, lēgātōs ad Caesarem mittunt, *since they could not defend themselves, they sent ambassadors to Caesar.* (**1**)

4. postquam id animadvertit, cōpiās in proximum collem subdūcit, *after he noticed that, he withdrew his forces to the nearest hill.* (**2**)

5. id ubi audīvit, ad hostēs contendit, *when he learned that, he hastened toward the enemy.* (**2**)

6. simul atque sē ex fugā recēpērunt, statim ad Caesarem lēgātōs mittunt, *as soon as they recovered from flight, they sent envoys to Caesar.* (**2**)

7. ubi ex lītore aliquōs singulārēs ex nāvī ēgredientēs cōnspexerant, adoriēbantur, *whenever they saw any disembarking separately, they attacked them.* (**3**)

Remark.

Observe that where in English we use the pluperfect with *after*, *as soon as*, etc., the Latin regularly employs the perfect, not the pluperfect.

VOCABULARY.

approach, **adventus, ūs,** *m.*

arrest, **comprehendō, ere, hendī, hēnsus.**

arrive, **perveniō, īre, vēnī, ventum.**

believe, **crēdō, ere, didī, ditum,** *with dat.*

blame, **culpō, 1.**

complain, **queror, ī, questus.**

deep, **altus, a, um.**

demand, **poscō, ere, poposcī.**

depart, **dēcēdō, ere, cessī, cessū·rus.**

destroy, break down, **rescindō, ere, scidī, scissus.**

move out, *intr.,* **dēmigrō, 1.**

thither, **eō.**

EXERCISE.

1. Whenever they had come to a deep river, they made a bridge by means of boats.   2. Since they were alarmed by the approach of so great a multitude, they moved out from these buildings and crossed the river. 3. As soon as the envoys of the Germans had come to Caesar's camp, they were all arrested.   4. The Haedui were complaining because the Germans were ravaging their[1] territory.   5. Because the rest of the army is farther distant, we will not wait.   6. After Caesar had arrived there,[2] he demanded hostages, arms, and horses. 7. When this report arrived, there was no one who believed it.   8. As soon as they saw these horsemen, they became much more eager.[3]   9. After they had conferred with each other[4] more than two hours,[5] Ariovistus withdrew.   10. We blame you because you have deserted us.   11. Since these things are so, we must depart.[6] 12. As soon as he destroyed the bridge, he returned into Gaul.

Suggestions on the Exercise.

1. *their :* use the reflexive, suus.
2. *there :* the Latin says : *thither.*
3. *much more eager :* translate : *more eager by much.*
4. *with each other :* translate : *between themselves.*
5. *more than two hours :* see Lesson X, Example 12.
6. *we must depart :* see Lesson VII, Remark 1.

The Nervii and Their Allies Lay an Ambush for the Romans

The Nervii and their neighbors,[1] the Atrebates and Viromandui, were the only (ones) who were now in arms. These were the most distant[2] and were the bravest of all the Belgae. They had hidden their women, children, and old men in the swamps, and had encamped[3] across the River Sambre,[4] where they were awaiting the arrival of the Romans. Caesar had sent men ahead to choose a suitable place and to fortify a camp, and was himself following with all his forces, when suddenly the Nervii flew out[5] from the woods, where they were holding themselves in hiding.[6]

Suggestions on the Exercise.

1. *neighbors :* use the adjective *neighboring* as a substantive.
2. *were the most distant :* translate : *were farthest distant.*
3. *encamp :* cōnsīdō, ere, sēdī, sessum.
4. *Sambre :* Sabis, is.
5. *fly out :* ēvolō, 1.
6. *in hiding :* in occultō.

LESSON XXII.

TEMPORAL CLAUSES (*continued*).

GRAMMATICAL REFERENCES.

1. *Cum*-Clauses. 288. 1–3; 289; A. & G. 545 and *a*, 546 and *ı*, 547, 548; H. 600. *I* and 1, II, 601 and 2.

2. *Antequam* and *priusquam.* 291. 1, 2; 292, 1, 2; A. & G. 551. *a–c* ; H. 605. I, II.

3. *Dum, dŏnec, quoad.* 293. I–III ; A. & G. 553, 554, 555, 556; H. 603. 1, II, 1, 2.

EXAMPLES.

1. ad equōs sē celeriter, cum ūsus est, recipiunt, *they retreat swiftly to their horses, when there is need.* **(1)**

2. cum Caesar in Galliam vēnit, duae factiōnēs erant, *when Caesar came into Gaul, there were two factions.* **(1)**

3. jam Gallī fugere apparābant, cum mātrēs familiae repente procurrērunt, *the Gauls were making ready to flee, when suddenly the matrons rushed forth.* **(1)**

4. cum equitātus noster sē in agrōs ējēcerat, essedāriōs Britannī ex silvīs ēmittēbant, *whenever our cavalry rushed out into the country, the Britons would send their charioteers out from the woods.* **(1)**

5. cum ad oppidum accessisset castraque ibi pōneret, puerī mulierēsque pācem petiērunt, *when he had drawn near to the town and was pitching camp there, the women and children sought peace.* **(1)**

6. nōn prius fugere dēstitērunt quam ad Rhēnum pervēnērunt, *they did not cease fleeing before they reached the Rhine.* **(2)**

7. legiōnēs omnēs in ūnum locum coēgit prius quam dē ejus adventū nūntiārī posset, *he assembled all his legions in one place before his arrival could be announced.* **(2)**

8. **dum haec geruntur, cēterī discessērunt,** *while these things were being done, the rest departed.* **(3)**

9. **exspectāvit Caesar, dum nāvēs convenīrent,** *Caesar waited for the ships to assemble,* lit. *till the ships should assemble.* **(3)**

VOCABULARY.

attack, **adorior, īrī, ortus.**

drag, drag along, **trahō, ere, trāxi, trāctus.**

fall in with, **incidō, ere, incidī,** *construed with* **in** *and acc.*

go away, **abeō, īre, abiī, abitūrus.**

join (battle), **committō, ere,**

mīsī, missus.

land, *verb*, **expōnō, ere, posuī, positus.**

scarcely, **vix.**

there, **ibi.**

till, **dum, dōnec.**

while, **dum.**

EXERCISE.

1. While he was tarrying a few days in the vicinity of Geneva, envoys came to him.   2. Whenever this cohort had made an attack, the enemy were driven back.   3. They waited for their cavalry to return.   4. We went away before you arrived.   5. When the foot-soldiers had been landed from the ships and were hastening to camp, the Morini attacked them.   6. Our troops had scarcely marched out from the camp, when the Gauls joined battle.   7. As Procillus was being dragged along by the Germans, he fell in with Caesar.   8. When they had come to this river, they pitched their camp there.   9. We remained here three days till our friends should arrive.   10. I saw no one until you came.   11. They fled before he should capture their town.   12. When he saw this, he retreated to the hill.   13. While Caesar was conferring with Ariovistus, the German horsemen attacked the Romans.

LESSON XXIII.

SUBSTANTIVE CLAUSES.

GRAMMATICAL REFERENCES.

1. Substantive Clauses developed from the Jussive. 295.
1, 2, 4, 5, 6, 8; *cf.* A. & G. 563, and *c, d, e,* 565; H. 564. I, II
and 1.

2. Substantive Clauses developed from the Deliberative. 295
7; 298; *cf.* A. & G. 558. *a*; H. 595. 1, 591. 4.

3. Substantive Clauses after verbs of *hindering, preventing, etc.*
295. 3; A. & G. 558. *b*; H. 595. 2, 596. 2.

EXAMPLES.

1. **postulāvit ut locum colloquiō dēligerent,** *he demanded that they should choose a place for a conference* (i.e. *he demanded, let them choose a place*). **(1)**

2. **ōrant ut cīvitātī subveniat,** *they beg that he will come to the help of their state* (i.e. *they beg, let him come*). **(1)**

3. **mīlitēs cohortātus est nē suae prīstinae virtūtis oblīvīscerentur,** *he exhorted the soldiers not to forget their former valor* (*let them not forget*). **(1)**

4. **cīvitātī persuāsit ut dē fīnibus suīs exīrent,** *he persuaded the state to go forth from their territory* (*let them go forth*). **(1)**

5. **huic permīsit ut in hīs locīs legiōnem collocāret,** *he permitted him to station his legion in these districts.* **(1)**

6. **nōn dubitant quīn dē omnibus obsidibus gravissimum supplicium sūmat,** *they do not doubt that he will inflict the severest punishment on all the hostages,* lit. *take punishment from.* **(2)**

7. **hī multitūdinem dēterrent nē frūmentum cōnferant,** *these prevent the people from contributing the grain* **(3)**

8. Suessiōnēs dēterrēre nōn potuerant quin cum hīs cōnsentīrent, *they had not been able to prevent the Suessiones from siding with these.* (3)

9. eōs dēterruit quō minus hostēs īnsequerentur, *he prevented them from pursuing the enemy.* (3)

VOCABULARY.

avoid, **vītō**, 1.
bring (of persons), **addūcō, ere, dūxī, ductus.**
command, **imperō**, 1.
conference, **colloquium, ī,** *n.*
conquer, **vincō, ere, vīcī victus.**
doubt, **dubitō,** 1.
entreat, **obsecrō,** 1

exhort, **cohortor,** 1.
prevent, **dēterreō, ēre, uī, itus.**
punishment, **supplicium, ī,** *n.*
suspicion, **suspīciō, ōnis,** *f.*
take, **sūmō, ere, sūmpsi, sūmptus**
true, **vērus, a, um.**
warn, **moneō, ēre, uī, itus.**

EXERCISE.

1. We do not doubt that the Romans will conquer the Helvetii. 2. We prevented a greater multitude of Germans from being led across the Rhine. 3. No one will prevent us from freeing these states. 4. I demanded that you bring only six men to this conference. 5. We warn you to avoid suspicions. 6. They persuaded the Sequani not to delay longer in their territory. 7. I shall permit you to return these hostages. 8. Who doubts that these things are true? 9. I entreat that you will not inflict punishment on[1] my brother. 10. He commanded that these men be led back home. 11. I prevented him from doing this. 12. He exhorted his (followers) not to lose hope.

Suggestion on the Exercise.

1. For *inflict punishment on*, the Latin says: *take punishment from;* see Example 6.

The Battle on the Sambre.

The attack was sudden and time was lacking for drawing up[1] a line of battle.   Besides there were many hedges[2]
which obstructed[3] the view.[4]   Each legion, therefore, resisted those whom it met.[5]   The soldiers of the ninth
and tenth legions fell upon[6] the Atrebates and drove them
back, (all) out of breath[7] with running,[8] across the stream.
At the same time the eleventh and eighth legions drove
the Viromandui back from the camp, headlong[9] towards
the river   Accordingly there were left only two legions,
the seventh and the twelfth, to defend the camp.[10]

Suggestions on the Exercise.

1. *for drawing up a line of battle :* **ad aciem īnstruendam.**

2. *hedge :* **saepēs, is, f.**

3. *obstruct :* **impediō, īre, īvī, ītus**.

4. *view :* **prōspectus, ūs, m.**

5. *each legion resisted, etc. :* translate : *whom each legion me*
(**occurrō, ere, currī, cursum ;** with dat.), *those it resisted.*

6. *fall upon*   use the word for *attack.*

7. *out of breath :* **exanimātus, a, um.**

8. *running :* **cursus, ūs, m.**

9. *headlong :* **praeceps, praecipitis.**

10. *to defend the camp :* use Relative Clause of Purpose.

LESSON XXIV.

SUBSTANTIVE CLAUSES (*continued*).

GRAMMATICAL REFERENCES.

1. Substantive Clauses developed from the Optative. 296 entire; *cf.* A. & G. 563. *b*, 564; H. 565.

2. Substantive Clauses of Result. 297. 1–3; A. & G. 569. 1, 2, 570, 571; H. 571. 1–4.

3. Substantive Clauses introduced by *quod.* 299. 1, 2; A. & G. 572 and *a*; H. 588. 3.

EXAMPLES.

1. **verēbantur nē ad eōs exercitus noster addūcerētur,** *they feared that our army would be led against them.* (**1**)

2. **veritus est ut hostium impetum sustinēre posset,** *he feared that he would not be able to withstand the onset of the enemy.* (**1**)

3. **quae rēs efficiēbat ut commeātūs sine perīculō portārī possent,** *this circumstance brought it about that supplies could be brought without danger.* (**2**)

4. **est enim hōc Gallicae cōnsuētūdinis, ut viātōrēs invītōs cōnsistere cōgant,** *for this is (a feature) of the Gallic customs, that they compel travelers to stop against their will.* (**2**)

5. **acciderat, ut Gallī bellī renovandī cōnsilium caperent,** *it had happened that the Gauls formed the plan of renewing the war.* (**2**)

6. **ex eō quod obsidēs dare intermīserant,** *from the fact that they had ceased to give hostages.* (**3**)

7. **quod castra mōvī, factum est inopiā pābulī,** *as to the fact that I moved the camp, it was done on account of lack of forage.* (**3**)

VOCABULARY.

bring about, **efficiō, ere, fēcī, fectus.**

conspire, **conjūrō,** 1.

discover, **comperiō, īre, comperī, compertus.**

especially, **maximē.**

fear, **vereor, ērī, itus.**

(few), very few, **perpaucī, ae, a.**

hand, be at hand, **adsum, esse, adfuī, futūrus.**

happen, **accidō, ere, accidī;** *impers.* **accidit,** it happens.

injury, **injūria, ae,** *f.*

strengthen, **mūniō, īre, īvī, ītus.**

EXERCISE.

1. As to the fact that I have brought a multitude with me into Gaul, I have done it in order to strengthen myself.   **2.** It happened that very few ships were at hand. **3.** The enemy feared that all hope of safety would be taken away.   **4.** I fear that we shall be cut off from supplies.   **5.** He fears that he will not avoid suspicions. **6.** Caesar brought it about that he had the Germans in his own power.   **7.** He was especially alarmed by this circumstance, that they were conspiring and giving hostages to each other.[1]   **8.** He feared that he would be surrounded by a multitude of the enemy.   **9.** I shall not forget this injury, that you ravaged the lands of the Haedui.   **10.** He feared that we would not come. **11.** I shall bring it about that you discover these things. **12.** Another fact was [2] that the cavalry of the Usipetes had retreated into the territory of the Sugambri.

Suggestions on the Exercise.

1. *to each other:* see Lesson XXI, Suggestion **4.**
2. *another fact was:* translate: *it was added.*

LESSON XXV.

INDIRECT QUESTIONS.

GRAMMATICAL REFERENCES.

1. Simple Questions. 300. 1–3; A. & G. 574, 575. *b*, 576. *a*; H. 649. II.

2. Double Questions. 300. 4; *cf.* A. & G. 334, 335. *d*; H. 650. 1, 2.

EXAMPLES.

1. haud sciō mīrandumne sit, *I do not know whether it is to be wondered at.* (**1**)

2. dēmōnstrāvērunt quanta facultās praedae faciendae darētur, *they showed what an opportunity of securing plunder was offered.* (**1**)

3. quid fierī velit ostendit, *he shows what he wishes to be done.* (**1**)

4. ejus reī quae causa esset, quaesiit, *he asked what was the reason of that thing.* (**1**)

5. voluit intellegere utrum apud eōs pudor an timor plūs valēret, *he wished to know whether honor or fear had the mastery with them.* (**2**)

6. id eāne causā quam prōnūntiāverint an perfidiā fēcerint, incertum est, *it is uncertain whether they did this for the reason they stated or from treachery.* (**2**)

7. apud Germānōs cōnsuētūdō erat ut mātrēs familiae sortibus dēclārārent utrum proelium committī ex ūsū esset necne, *among the Germans it was the custom for the matrons to declare by lots whether it was advantageous for battle to be begun or not.* (**2**)

8. hanc palūdem sī nostrī trānsīrent, hostēs exspectābant, *the enemy were waiting (to see) whether our men would cross this marsh.* (**1**)

72

Remark.

To denote future time in indirect questions, periphrastic forms are used where ambiguity would otherwise result; as, **nōn quaerō quid dictūrus sīs,** *I do not ask what you will say.* **Nōn quaerō quid dīcās,** would naturally mean: *I do not ask what you are saying.*

VOCABULARY.

always, **semper.**

ask, **quaerō, ere, quaesīvī, sītus.**

headship, **prīncipātus, ūs,** *m.*

how, *in indir. questions*, **ut,** *when modifying the clause as a whole; to denote degree,* **quam.**

if, *with* **exspectō,** *etc.*, **sī.**

perceive, **sentiō, īre, sēnsī, sēnsus.**

report, **nūntiō, 1.**

scout, **explōrātor, ōris,** *m.*

show, **ostendō, ere, endī, entus.**

still, **adhūc.**

what nature, of what nature, **quālis, e.**

wonder, **mīror, 1.**

EXERCISE.

1. Caesar showed how the Haedui had always held the headship of Gaul. **2.** We were waiting (to see) what they would do.[1] **3.** These men reported to the enemy what things were done in our camp. **4.** We were wondering how soon they would break down the bridge. **5.** I asked what you had said in the council of the Gauls. **6.** I wonder why Ariovistus did not contend in battle on this day. **7.** I do not know whether Caesar is still in Germany or has returned into Gaul. **8.** He inquired of[2] the captives what states were in arms. **9.** They did not know whether these states were in arms or not. **10.** The scouts showed him of what nature the mountain was. **11.** Volusenus reported what tribes he had visited. **12.** I perceive what you will do.[1]

Suggestions on the Exercise.

1. See the Remark on the mode of expressing future time in indirect questions.

2. *of:* with **quaerō** this is expressed by the prep. **ab** or **ex**.

The Battle on the Sambre (*continued*).

It thus happened that the Roman camp was exposed[1] in front[2] and on the left side.   Then the Nervii, crowded together in a dense swarm, hastened up the hill[3] towards the camp and the two legions.   Caesar saw the danger at once.   The soldiers of the twelfth legion were huddled together[4] so (closely) that they could not use their swords; nearly all the centurions were either killed or wounded. Sextius Baculus, the first centurion,[5] was so weakened by wounds that he could no longer stand.

Suggestions on the Exercise.

1. *expose:* **nūdō**, 1.
2. *in front, on the side:* express by the ablative with **ā**.
3. *up the hill:* **colle adversō**, lit. *the hill being against* (*them*)
4. *huddled together:* use **cōnfertus** here also.
5. *first centurion:* **centuriō prīmī pīlī**.

LESSON XXVI.

CONDITIONAL SENTENCES.

GRAMMATICAL REFERENCES.

1. First Type. Nothing Implied. 302. 1–4; A. & G. 515 and *a*; 518. *a, b*; 516. *a*; H. 574 and 2, 580. 1.

2. Second Type. *Should . . . would* **Type.** 303; A. & G. 516. *b*; H. 576.

3. Third Type. Contrary to Fact. 304 entire; A. & G. 517 and *a, c, d*; H. 579 and 1, 582, 583.

4. Conditional Clauses of Comparison. 307. 1, 2; A. & G. 524 and N. 2; H. 584 and 1, 2.

5. Subordinate Adversative Clauses introduced by *etsī* **and** *cum*. 309. 2, 3; A. & G. 527. *c*; 549; H. 585; 598.

EXAMPLES.

1. sī hōc dīcis, errās, *if you say this, you are mistaken.* (**1**)
2. sī hōc dīcēbās, errābās, *if you were saying this, you were mistaken.* (**1**)
3. sī hōc dīcēs, errābis, *if you say* (i.e. *shall say*) *this, you will be mistaken.* (**1**)
4. sī hōc dīxistī, errāvistī, *if you said this, you were mistaken.* (**1**)
5. sī hōc dicās, errēs, *if you should say this* (*were you to say this*), *you would be mistaken.* (**2**)
6. sī hōc dīcerēs, errārēs, *if you were saying this, you would be making a mistake.* (**3**)
7. sī hōc dīxissēs, errāvissēs, *if you had said this, you would have made a mistake.* (**3**)
8. sī quis equitum dēciderat, peditēs circumsistēbant, *if any one of the horsemen fell, the foot-soldiers gathered around him.* (**1**)

9. Ariovistī absentis crūdēlitātem horrēbant, velut sī adesset, *they shuddered at the cruelty of Ariovistus at a distance, as though he were at hand.* (**4**)

10. etsī prope exācta aestās erat, in Morinōs exercitum addūxit, *although the summer was almost over, he led his army among the Morini.* (**5**)

11. hōs cum Suēbī expellere nōn potuissent, tamen vectīgālēs sibi fēcērunt, *though the Suebi had been unable to drive these out, yet they made them tributary to themselves.* (**5**)

VOCABULARY.

although, **etsī.**

as if, **velut sī.**

concerning, **dē**, *prep. with abl.*

if, **sī** ; if . . . not, **nisi.**

letter, **litterae, ārum,** *f.*

near, **prope**, *prep. with acc.*

news, **nūntiī, ōrum**, *m.*, *from* **nūntius**, message.

regard, **habeō, ēre, uī, itus.**

unless, **nisi.**

EXERCISE.

1. Unless the news concerning Caesar's victory had been brought at that time, this town would have been lost. 2. Unless you withdraw[1] from these districts, I shall regard you as an enemy.[2] 3. Although the winter was at hand, yet Caesar set out for Britain. 4. He spoke as if he had visited Britain. 5. If any one should announce these things to Ariovistus, he[3] would inflict[4] the severest punishment on us. 6. We should fear nothing, if he were present. 7. Unless you do[1] this, I shall not send the letter. 8. They would have come, if they had known this. 9. Were he to know this, he would send us aid at once. 10. He would have joined battle, if he had seen these forces near the camp of the enemy. 11. Unless help is at hand, we have no hope of safety 12. Although he did not know their plans, yet he suspected that which

happened.   13. If you do not come to us, we shall come to you.

Suggestions on the Exercise.

1. The pupil should observe when the English present has future force, and should make the Latin tenses conform to the actual time indicated.

2. *as an enemy :* **prō hoste.**

3. *he :* **hīc.**

4. Compare Lesson XXIII, Suggestion **1.**

LESSON XXVII.

INDIRECT DISCOURSE.

GRAMMATICAL REFERENCES.

Moods.

1. Declaratory Sentences. 314. 1, 3; 331. I; A. & G. 580;
H. 642, 643. 3, 4.

2. Interrogative Sentences. 315. 1–3; A. & G. 586, 587;
H. 642 and 2, 3.

3. Imperative Sentences. 316 and *a*; A. & G. 588 and *a*;
H. 642.

Tenses.

4. Of the Infinitive. 317 and *a*; A. & G. 584 and *a*; H. 644,
617.

5. Of the Subjunctive. 318 and *a*; A. & G. 585 and *a*;
H. 644.

EXAMPLES.

1. **Ariovistus respondit sēsē nōn esse ventūrum,** *Ariovistus replied
that he would not come.* (Direct: **nōn veniam.**) (**1**)

2. **referunt, esse silvam īnfīnītā magnitūdine, quae Bacēnis appellātur,** *they bring back word that there is a forest of
limitless extent, which is called Bacenis.* (The direct
statement here is **est silva**; the clause **quae appellātur** is
an addition of the writer.) (**1**)

3. **Caesar respondit, eō sibi minus dubitātiōnis darī, quod eās
rēs, quās lēgātī Helvētiī commemorāssent, memoriā tenē-
ret,** *Caesar answered that less hesitation was afforded him
because he remembered those things which the Helvetian
ambassadors had stated.* (**1**)

4. **Caesarī respondit sē prius in Galliam vēnisse quam populum
Rōmānum. Quid sibi vellet? Cūr in suās possessiōnēs**

78

veníret? *he answered Caesar that he had come into Gaul before the Roman people. What did he want? Why did he come into his domain?* (Direct: **ego prius vēnī Quid vīs? Cūr venīs?**) (**1** and **2**)

5. **sī veteris contumēliae oblīvīscī vellet, num etiam recentium injūriārum memoriam sē dēpōnere posse,** *if he were willing to forget the former indignity, could he also banish the recollection of recent wrongs?* (Direct: **sī velim, num possum?**) (**1** and **2**)

6. **sciō tē haec ēgisse,** {
I know you were doing this. (Direct: **agē-bās.**) (**4**)
I know you did this. (Direct: **ēgistī.**) (**4**)
I know you had done this. (Direct: **ēge-rās.**) (**4**)

7. **quid metueret,** *why should he fear?* (Direct: **quid metuam,** Deliberative Subjunctive.) (**2**)

Remarks.

1. Note that a dependent perfect infinitive is treated as an historical tense, whenever, if resolved into an equivalent indicative, it would be historical.

2. Note that for the sake of vividness a present tense of the direct discourse is not infrequently retained in the indirect after an historical tense. This is called **repraesentātiō,** 'a bringing back to the present.'

VOCABULARY.

cruelly, **crūdēliter.**	rule, **imperō, 1.**
follow, **sequor, ī, secūtus.**	think, **exīstimō, 1 ; putō, 1.**
know, **sciō, īre, scīvī, scītus.**	wish, **volō, velle, voluī.**

EXERCISE.

1. The envoys said that they would report these things to their (countrymen). 2. Volusenus said that he had visited Britain and seen many tribes and towns. 3. The chieftains of the Nervii said that they wished these things. 4. We thought that you were following us. 5. When Caesar thought that Gaul had been subdued, a

sudden war broke out. 6. They thought they would persuade the Romans to give them lands. 7. They thought the Romans were withdrawing from these places 8. He knew that they would return home if they wished. 9. He said that he had conquered all with whom he had contended. 10. He said that it would happen [1] in a few years that all the Germans would cross the Rhine. 11. We know that Ariovistus, after he conquered the Gauls, ruled cruelly. 12. Caesar perceived that all the Gauls were conspiring.

Suggestion on the Exercise.

1. *happen :* use the future inf. of **esse** to express this.

The Battle on the Sambre (*continued*).

Some at the rear [1] were abandoning their posts, withdrawing from the battle, and avoiding the spears of the enemy. Meanwhile the Nervii kept advancing in great numbers. Caesar, therefore, fearing that his men would be surrounded by so great a multitude, hastened to the first line, and exhorted the legions to be [2] of good courage. Thus new strength was added to them, and all strove valiantly to withstand the assault of the enemy. At the same time, the two legions which had been protecting the baggage [3] hastened toward the camp with the greatest speed.

Suggestions on the Exercise.

1. *at the rear :* ā novissimīs.

2. *to be :* Lesson XXIII, Example 3.

3. *had been protecting the baggage .* translate *had been for a protection to the baggage.*

LESSON XXVIII.

THE INFINITIVE.

GRAMMATICAL REFERENCES.

1. Infinitive without Subject Accusative, used as **Subject** 327. 1, 2 and *a*; A. & G. 452. N. 2, 455. *a*; H. 615, 612. 3.

2. Infinitive without Subject Accusative, used as Object. 328. 1, 2; A. & G. 456; H. 607 and 1, 2, 608. 4, 612 and 1.

3. Infinitive with Subject Accusative, used as Subject. 330; A. & G. 455. 2; H. 615.

4. Infinitive with Subject Accusative, used as Object. 331 entire; A. & G. 459; H. 613. 1–3.

5. Passive Construction of Verbs which in the Active are followed by the Infinitive with Subject Accusative. 332 entire; H. 611. 1, 2 and Notes 1, 3.

EXAMPLES.

1. necesse est nōbīs Gergoviam contendere, *it is necessary for us to hasten to Gergovia.* (**1**)

2. oportēbat frūmentum mīlitibus mētīrī, *it was his duty to measure out grain to the soldiers.* (**1**)

3. placuit castra dēfendere, *it was resolved* (lit. *it pleased them*) *to defend the camp.* (**1**)

4. licet id facere, *it is permitted to do that.* (**1**)

5. nēmō prōgredī ausus est, *no one dared to advance.* (**2**)

6. dēbētis adventum nostrum exspectāre, *you ought to await our arrival.* (**2**)

7. agrī nostrī vāstārī nōn dēbuērunt, *our lands ought not to have been laid waste.* (**2**)

8. Gallia dēbet lībera esse, *Gaul ought to be free.* (**2**)

9. **nōn aequum est Germānōs in Galliam trānsīre**, *it is not right for the Germans to cross over into Gaul.* (3)

10. **pollicitī sunt sē obsidēs datūrōs esse**, *they promised that they would give hostages.* (4)

11. **Orgetorīgem ex vinculīs causam dīcere coēgērunt**, *they compelled Orgetorix to plead his cause in chains.* (4)

12. **arma trādere jussī sunt**, *they were ordered to surrender their arms.* (5)

13. **Suēbī centum pāgōs habēre dīcuntur**, *the Suebi are said to have one hundred cantons.* (5)

VOCABULARY.

able, be able, **possum, posse, potuī.**

command. **mandātum, ī,** *n.*

compel, **cōgō, ere, coēgī, coāctus.**

dare, **audeō, ēre, ausus,** *semi-dep.*

difficult, **difficilis, e.**

duty, it is a duty, **oportet, ēre, oportuit,** *impers.*

forbid, **vetō, āre, uī, itus.**

inflict (something on somebody), **īnferō, ferre, intulī, illātus,** *with acc. of direct obj. and dat. of indirect.*

necessary, it is necessary, **necesse est.**

ought, **dēbeō, ēre, uī, itus.**

promise, **polliceor, ērī, itus.**

spear, **tēlum, ī,** *n.*

try, **cōnor, 1.**

EXERCISE.

1. You ought to remember my favors.   2. It was difficult to fortify the camp and at the same time to avoid the spears of the enemy.   3. He did not dare to confer with us concerning these plans.   4. The Treveri were said to be tampering with the Germans.   5. You ought to have[1] obeyed our commands.   6. It is necessary to depart at once for Britain.   7. I do not know who compelled you to do his.   8. It is our duty to defend this province.   9. I forbade him to do this, in order that he might not seem to inflict injuries on our allies. 10. They ought to promise that they will come to us.

11. Caesar seemed to be able to do all things.   12. The soldiers were ordered to tear down the bridge.   13. The Veneti tried to capture the Roman ships of war. 14. They thought that they could [2] drive us back.

Suggestions on the Exercise.

1. See Example 7.
2. *could drive : i.e.* were able to **drive.**

LESSON XXIX.

PARTICIPLES.

GRAMMATICAL REFERENCES.

1. Tenses of the Participle. 336. 1–5; A. & G. 489 and 491, H. 640 and 1.

2. Use of Participles. 337. 1–3, 5, 8, *a*, *b*. 1), 2); A. & G. 494; 496, 497 and *d*; 500 and 1, 2, 4; H. 638, 1–3, 639, 613. 5.

EXAMPLES.

1. audiō tē loquentem, *I hear you as you speak.* (**1**)
2. audīvī tē loquentem, *I heard you as you were speaking.* (**1**)
3. audiam tē loquentem, *I shall hear you as you speak,* i.e. *as you shall be speaking.* (**1**)
4. locūtus tacet, *he has spoken and is silent,* lit. *having spoken he is silent.* (**1**)
5. locūtus tacuit, *he had spoken and was silent.* (**1**)
6. locūtus tacēbit, *he will speak and then be silent.* (**1**)
7. haec flēns ā Caesare petiit, *he asked these things of Caesar, weeping.* (**1** and **2**)
8. in nostrōs venientēs tēla coniciēbant, *they hurled their spears against our men as they came on,* lit. *coming.* (**1** and **2**)
9. rēgnī cupiditāte inductus conjūrātiōnem fēcit, *impelled by a desire of regal power, he made a conspiracy.* (**1** and **2**)
10. perfidiam veritī, domum revertērunt, *fearing treachery, they returned home.* (**1** and **2**)
11. Ariovistus ferendus nōn vidēbātur, *Ariovistus did not seem endurable.* (**1** and **2**)
12. nōn putābat concēdendum esse, *he did not think that concession should be made,* lit. *that it* (impers.) *ought to be conceded.* (**2**)

13. **pontem faciendum cūrat**, *he had a bridge built*, lit. *cared for a bridge to be built.* (**2**)

14. **hōs Haeduīs cūstōdiendōs trādidit**, *he handed these over to the Haedui to be guarded.* (**2**)

VOCABULARY.

admire, **admīror**, 1.

attempt, **cōnor**, 1.

dismiss, **dīmittō, ere, mīsī, missus.**

fear, **timeō, ēre, uī.**

lead, **dūcō, ere, dūxī, ductus.**

repair, **reficiō, ere, fēcī, fectus.**

treachery, **īnsidiae, ārum,** *f.*

without, **sine,** *prep. with abl.*

wreck (of vessels), **frangō, ere, frēgī, frāctus.**

EXERCISE.

1. They did not dare to follow our men farther as they retreated.[1] 2. Having followed the enemy more than four miles, Sabinus led his soldiers back to camp. 3. Having given these commands,[2] he dismissed the ambassadors from him. 4. When Procillus attempted to answer, Ariovistus prevented[3] him. 5. He did not think that fear ought to be entertained[4] by himself[5] without cause. 6. Caesar, fearing treachery, not yet having learned the cause[6] of their departure, kept his (men) in camp. 7. We saw the Nervii crossing this river. 8. This circumstance is worthy of admiration.[7] 9. He had as many ships as possible[8] constructed in that winter. 10. He gave one legion to Gaius Fabius, a lieutenant, to be led against the Morini. 11. All the ships which had been wrecked, he found repaired 12. We shall have these prisoners guarded.

Suggestions on the Exercise.

1. *as they retreated:* translate: *retreating.*
2. Express by the Ablative Absolute.

3. *prevented :* use **prohibeō.**

4. *that fear ought to be entertained :* translate : *that it ought to be feared.* Compare Example 12.

5. *by himself :* see Lesson VII, Examples 1, 2.

6. *not yet having learned the cause :* express by the Ablative Absolute, — *the cause not yet having been learned.*

7. *worthy of admiration :* express by the Gerundive.

8. *as many as possible :* see Lesson XV, Example 11.

The Battle on the Sambre (*continued*).

Thus the battle was renewed, and although the Nervii fought most courageously, yet the Romans finally defeated them and reduced their tribe almost to extinction.[1] Within a few days came envoys from the old men of the Nervii to beg that Caesar would exercise clemency towards them. They said that out of sixty thousand men scarcely five hundred were left, and out of six hundred senators only three. Caesar spared these suppliants[2] and permitted them to retain[3] their towns and villages. On the following day he began to march against the Aduatuci, who were coming to the help of the Nervii.

Suggestions on the Exercise.

1. *extinction :* **interneciō, ōnis,** f.

2. *suppliant :* **supplex, icis,** m.

3. *to retain :* see Lesson XXIII, Example 5.

LESSON XXX.

THE GERUND; THE GERUNDIVE CONSTRUCTION; THE SUPINE.

GRAMMATICAL REFERENCES.

1. The Gerund. 338. 1–5; A. & G. 502; 504 and *b*; 505 and *a*; 506 and N. 2; 507; H. 624, 626, 627, 628 and footnote 2, 629.

2. The Gerundive Construction. 339. 1–5; A. & G. 503; 504 and *b*, 505, 506, 507; H. 621, 623 and 1, 628.

3. The Supine. 340 entire; A. & G. 509, 510 and N. 2; H. 632 and 1, 633, 635 and 1, 2, 4.

EXAMPLES.

1. fīnem ōrandī fēcit, *he made an end of entreating.* **(1)**
2. cupidus bellandī, *fond of waging war.* **(1)**
3. ea quae ad proficīscendum pertinēbant, *those things which had to do with their setting out.* **(1)**
4. reperiēbat etiam in quaerendō Caesar, *Caesar also found out upon inquiring.* **(1)**
5. Gallī subitō bellī renovandī legiōnisque opprimendae cōnsilium cēpērunt, *the Gauls suddenly formed the plan of renewing the war and crushing the legion.* **(2)**
6. in spem potiundōrum castrōrum venīre, *to come into the expectation of getting possession of the camp.* **(2)**
7. parātiōrēs ad omnia perīcula subeunda, *better prepared for undergoing all dangers.* **(2)**
8. suī colligendī [1] hostibus facultātem nōn relīquit, *he did not leave to the enemy the opportunity of collecting themselves.* **(2)**
9. lēgātōs ad Caesarem mittunt rogātum auxilium, *they sent envoys to Caesar to ask help.* **(3)**
10. horridiōrēs sunt aspectū, *they are wilder to look upon.* **(3)**

87

Note on the Examples.

1. **Colligendī** agrees merely in form with **suī** ; in sense it is plural.

VOCABULARY.

beginning, **initium, ī,** *n.*

Casticus, **Casticus, ī,** *m.*

difficulty, **difficultās, tātis,** *f.*

end, **fīnis, is,** *m.*

excuse, **pūrgō,** 1.

forage, procure forage, **pābulor,** 1.

gain possession of, **potior, īrī, ītus.**

matter, **rēs, reī,** *f.*

regal power, **rēgnum, ī,** *n.*

skilled in, **perītus, a, um ;** *with gen.*

such, **tālis, e.**

EXERCISE.

1. This day had been set for attacking[1] all the winter quarters of Caesar. **2.** He said that this thing was easy to do. **3.** Caesar says that the Germans came to his camp[2] on the following day for the sake of excusing themselves. **4.** Such were the difficulties of waging war in these places. **5.** They thought that there was enough time for accomplishing[?] all these matters. **6.** He sent me to ask that you spare him. **7.** These horsemen came to procure forage. **8.** They remained at home for the sake of preserving themselves. **9.** Casticus and Orgetorix formed a conspiracy for gaining possession[3] of the regal power. **10.** We finally made an end of following. **11.** As soon as our men made a beginning of crossing, the enemy attacked them. **12.** The Veneti were skilled in sailing.

Suggestions on the Exercise.

1. *for attacking :* use the dative.

2. *his camp :* 249. 3 ; A. & G. 300. 2. *b* ; H. 509. 6.

3. *for accomplishing ; for gaining possession :* express by **ad.**

REVIEW.

1. Having heard of the revolt[1] of the Haedui, the Bellovaci began to prepare for war.   **2.** In the third watch he ordered them to break camp and advance silently four miles and to await him there.   **3.** Caesar rebuked[2] the soldiers because they thought they knew what ought to be done.   **4.** It concerned the common safety that these forces be kept apart.[3]   **5.** The rest of the legions did not hear the sound[4] of the trumpet,[5] because wide valleys lay between.[6]   **6.** The cavalry followed the Suessiones before they should recover[7] from fear.   **7.** They made their departure seem[8] like a flight. **8.** He showed the lieutenants whom he had placed in charge of the separate[9] legions what he wished to be done.   **9.** Wondering[10] why they had withdrawn from the shore, Caesar inquired of captives the cause. **10.** When he ordered this man to be arrested, he learned that he had fled a little (while) before.   **11.** He said that the Haedui were the only state which interfered with[11] the most certain triumph[12] of Gaul.   **12.** It was resolved that Litaviccus should be placed in charge of these troops.

Suggestions on the Exercise.

1. *having heard of the revolt :* express by the Ablative Absolute ; for *revolt* use **dēfectiō, ōnis, f.**

2. *rebuke :* **reprehendō, ere, hendī, hēnsus.**

3. *keep apart :* **distineō, ēre, uī.**

4. *sound :* **sonus, ī, m.**

5. *trumpet :* **tuba, ae f.**

6. *lie between :* **intercēdō, ere, cessī, cessūrus.**

7. *recover :* **sē recipere (recipiō, ere, cēpī, ceptus).**

8. *made their departure seem :* translate : *made that their departure seemed.*

9. *separate :* **singulī, ae, a.**

10. *wondering :* see Lesson XXIX, Example 10.

11. *interfere with :* **distineō, ēre, uī,** lit. *put off.*

12. *triumph* **victōria, ae, f.**

SUPPLEMENTARY EXERCISES IN CONTINUED DISCOURSE.

13.*

Intrigues of Dumnorix.

When Caesar set out a second time [1] for Britain, he took with him all the chiefs whom he feared. Among these was Dumnorix, who, (just) as he was most popular [2] with [3] the common people of the Gauls, so was a most bitter [4] enemy of the Romans. A little while before, he had said to the Haedui that Caesar had decided to make him [5] king. Though this was not true, it stirred up great indignation [6] among the Haeduans; nor was it pleasing [7] to Caesar, who was unwilling to leave Gaul, unless the Haeduans should be [8] of a good disposition towards him ·

Suggestions on the Exercise.

1. *a second time :* iterum.
2. *popular :* acceptus, a, um.
3. *with :* translate: *to.*
4. *bitter :* acerbus, a, um.
5. *him :* ipsum.
6. *indignation :* dolor, ōris, m.
7. *pleasing :* grātus, a, um.
8. *should be :* this is a Subordinate Clause of Indirect Discourse and must stand in the subjunctive.
9. *him :* use the reflexive.

---

* Twelve passages of continued discourse have been interspersed among the preceding lessons.

14.

Intrigues of Dumnorix (*continued*).

Dumnorix was unwilling to go with Caesar, because he saw that he would never again find so good an opportunity of conspiring against the Roman people. Accordingly he begged that he might be permitted[1] to remain at home; (saying) that he was inexperienced in sailing and feared the sea; that besides there were religious observances[2] which he could not perform, unless he should remain in Gaul. When this had been refused by Caesar, Dumnorix then tried to persuade the other chiefs to remain at home against Caesar's wishes.[3]

Suggestions on the Exercise

1. *that he might be permitted:* translate: *that it might be permitted to him.*

2. *religious observances:* use the plural of **religiō**, **ōnis**, f.

3. *against Caesar's wishes:* translate: *Caesar being unwilling.*

15.

Intrigues of Dumnorix (*continued*).

In order to accomplish this purpose,[1] Dumnorix said that Caesar was taking[2] them all to Britain that he might put them to death, and that no one of those who went[3] would ever return to Gaul. All these things were reported to Caesar through spies.[4] Meanwhile the ships were detained by adverse[5] winds[6] in the Portus Itius.[7] When finally a favorable[8] wind sprang up[9] and Caesar was setting sail,[10] Dumnorix along with the cavalry of the Haeduans began to return home.

Suggestions on the Exercise.

1. *accomplish this purpose :* translate : *accomplish* (**impetrō, 1**) *these things.*

2. *take :* **addūcō, ere, dūxī, ductus.**

3. *went :* translate : *should have gone.*

4. *spy :* **speculātor, ōris, m.**

5. *adverse :* **adversus, a, um.**

6. *wind :* **ventus, ī, m.**

7. *Portus Itius :* **Portus Itius, Portūs Itiī, m.**

8. *favorable :* **secundus, a, um.**

9. *spring up :* **coorior, īrī, coortus.**

10. *set sail :* **nāvēs solvō, ere, solvī, solūtus,** lit., *loose* or *unmoor the ships.*

16.

Death of Dumnorix.

As Dumnorix and his horsemen began to flee, Caesar immediately stopped [1] the departure and sent cavalry to overtake him and kill (him) if he should attempt to resist. When Caesar's cavalry demanded that Dumnorix should surrender, he began to defend himself by violence [2] and to implore [3] the assistance of his (followers). When these hesitated [4] to bear him aid, he was cut down [5] by the Romans, shouting [6] that he was free and a citizen of a free state. The Haeduans then returned with the Roman cavalry to the Port.

Suggestions on the Exercise.

1. *stop :* **intermittō, ere, mīsī, missus.**

2. *violence :* **vīs (vis), f.**

3. *implore :* **implōrō, 1.**

4. *hesitate :* **dubitō, 1.**

5. *cut down :* translate : *killed.*

6. *shout :* **clāmitō, 1.**

17.

Conditions in Gaul in the Winter of 54 B.C.

In that year in which Caesar had crossed the second
time into Britain, the harvest had been poor.[1]   In order
therefore to secure enough grain, it was necessary to distribute the legions that winter in many places.   Fearing
an uprising, he decided to pass the winter among the
Belgae, and stationed one legion among the Morini, who
had recently [2] surrendered to Labienus.   Another, in
charge of which he had placed Quintus Cicero, brother
of Marcus, he stationed among the Nervii ; three others
he sent among the Bellovaci ; one was led to Aduatuca,
which [3] is a town of the Eburones.[4]

Suggestions on the Exercise.

1. See Lesson XV, Example 7.
2. *recently :* translate : *a little before*
3. See Lesson III, Example 7.
4. *Eburones :* Eburōnēs, um, m.

18.

Assassination of Tasgetius.

In those states in which the nobles had driven out the
kings, Caesar was wont [1] to reward with regal power the
chiefs who had lent help to him.   One of these, Tasgetius,[2] he made king of the Carnutes,[3] a tribe which [4]
dwelt between the Seine [5] and the Loire.[5]   How he used
his power, we do not know ; but soon after [6] Caesar returned from Britain, Tasgetius was assassinated.   As
soon as Caesar heard of this, he sent Plancus with one

legion to arrest all who had been participants[7] in[8] the deed and to prevent the rest from revolting.

Suggestions on the Exercise.

1. *be wont :* **soleō, ēre, solitus,** semi-dep.

2. *Tasgetius :* **Tasgetius, ī, m.**

3. *Carnutes :* **Carnutēs, um, m.**

4. *a tribe which dwelt :* translate : *which tribe dwelt.*

5. *Seine :* **Sēquana, ae, m. ;** *Loire,* **Liger, is, m.;** acc. sing., **Ligerim.**

6. *soon after :* translate : *after by a little.* Note that *after* is here the conj.

7. *participants :* **participēs, um, m.**

8. *in :* translate : *of.*

19.

Indutiomarus.

The murder of Tasgetius showed of what disposition the Carnutes were towards the Romans. There was also a chief of the Treveri, Indutiomarus by name, who already for a long time had been hostile to Caesar. Annually he called together all the Gallic chieftains in order that he might test[1] their temper.[2] Caesar, fearing that the state of the Treveri might revolt, having gathered a large force, marched into their territory before he set out for Britain, in order that he might restore the prestige of the Roman people.

Suggestions on the Exercise.

1. *test :* **temptō,** 1.

2. *temper :* **animus, ī, m.**

20.

Indutiomarus (*continued*).

When Caesar came among[1] the Treveri, he found two chieftains, Indutiomarus and Cingetorix,[2] who were con

tending with each other for the supremacy.[3]   The latter
at once came to Caesar and informed him what was being
done by Indutiomarus.   He[4] meanwhile had gathered
troops and was preparing to fight.   Many (of the) senators, however, induced[5] by the authority of Cingetorix,
because they knew how powerful the Roman legions
were,[6] came to Caesar's camp and put themselves under
his protection.[7]   Then Indutiomarus, since he saw that
no one lent him help, attempted to excuse himself.

Suggestions on the Exercise.

1. *among :* use in with the acc.

2. *Cingetorix :* **Cingetorīx, īgis, m.**

3. *supremacy :* **prīncipātus, ūs, m.**

4. *he :* **ille.**

5. *induced :* **adductus, a, um.**

6. *how powerful the Roman legions were :* translate : *how much
the Roman legions were able;* Lesson IV, Example 6.

7. *put oneself under the protection :* **sē dēdere in fidem (alicūjus).**

21.

Indutiomarus *(continued).*

Caesar, since he thought he ought to set out[1] at once,
demanded nothing except hostages from Indutiomarus.
At the same time he did all things which he could for
increasing the prestige[2] of Cingetorix.   The next winter,
after Caesar had returned from Britain, Indutiomarus,
who resented (the fact) that[3] his power among his (countrymen) had been impaired, began to seek an opportunity of avenging the injury.   This was easier because
the Roman camps which had been established among
the Belgians were far distant from each other so that
one[4] could not lend help to another.

Suggestions on the Exercise.

1. *that he ought to set out :* translate: *that it ought to be set out by him* (impersonal construction).

2. *for increasing the prestige :* use the gerundive construction with **ad.**

3. *resent (the fact) that :* **molestē ferō (ferre, tulī, lātus),** lit., *bear hard :* followed by the inf. with subj. acc.

4. *one . . . to another :* see Lesson XVII, Example 9.

22.

The Attack on Aduatuca.

Ten days after[1] the legions had fortified their camp at Aduatuca among the Eburones, Indutiomarus persuaded Ambiorix[2] and Catuvolcus,[2] each of whom held one half[3] of the lands of the Eburones, to attack the Roman camp. Caesar was more than two hundred miles away. In the camp, in charge of which were Sabinus and Cotta, there were scarcely six thousand soldiers, of whom the larger part had just[4] been enrolled. The Gauls thought therefore that an excellent opportunity[5] of securing possession of the camp[6] had been offered them.

Suggestions on the Exercise.

1. *ten days after :* translate: *after by ten days than* (**quam**).

2. *Ambiorix :* **Ambiorīx, īgis,** m. ; *Catuvolcus :* **Catuvolcus, ī,** m.

3. *one half :* **dīmidia pars, dīmidiae partis,** f.

4. *just :* **proximē.**

5. *excellent opportunity :* the Latin expresses this by **summa (or maxima) facultās.**

6. *of securing possession of the camp :* see Lesson XXX, Example 6.

23.

The Attack on Aduatuca (*continued*).

A few days afterwards Ambiorix and Catuvolcus, hav‑ing gathered a large band of their (tribesmen), sud‑denly attacked the camp of the Romans.   But the camp was strongly[1] fortified and had been placed on high ground.[2]   Our men quickly took arms and mounted[3] the rampart.[4]   Meanwhile (some) Spanish horsemen, having made a sally,[5] drove back the Gauls with great slaughter. Then their leaders begged that some one would come out from the camp to confer with them.   Two Roman knights were accordingly sent to them.

Suggestions on the Exercise.

1. *strongly :* ēgregiē, lit. *excellently.*
2. *on high ground :* superiōre locō.
3. *mount :* ascendō, ere, endī, ēnsus.
4. *rampart :* vāllum, ī, n.
5. *having made a sally :* translate : *a sally having been made.*

24.

Ambiorix's Speech to the Romans.

Three years before, Caesar had relieved Ambiorix from the tribute which he had been forced to pay to the Aduatuci, and had also restored to him his son and his brother's son, whom the Aduatuci held as hostages.   In the beginning of his speech Ambiorix mentioned these favors and declared that he desired to make a return[1] for[2] them.   He said that he had not[3] attacked the camp of his own accord, but forced by his tribesmen.   These he said would not have brought war on the Romans, unless they had been compelled by the common conspiracy of all the Gauls.

Suggestions on the Exercise.

1. *make a return :* grātiam referō (ferre, rettulī, relātus).

2. *for :* prō, prep. with abl.

3. *said that . . . not :* for 'say that not,' the Latin regularly uses negō, āre, āvī, ātus.

25.

Ambiorix's Speech (*continued*).

Ambiorix added[1]: That his very weakness[2] proved[3] that he was speaking the truth,[4] for he was not so foolish[5] as to think that his forces could resist the Romans; that the states of Gaul had leagued themselves together[6] for the recovery of their freedom;[7] that on that very day all the Roman camps would be attacked at one and the same time; let Sabinus therefore be on his guard;[8] a very large multitude of Germans also had crossed the Rhine and would attack him within a few days.

Suggestions on the Exercise.

1. *add :* addō, ere, addidī, ditus.

2. *weakness :* humilitās, ātis, f.

3. *prove :* probō, 1.

4. *speak the truth :* vēra dīcō (ere, dīxī, dictus), lit. *speak true things.*

5. *foolish :* stultus, a, um.

6. *league themselves together :* translate: *conspire among themselves.*

7. *for the recovery of the freedom :* translate: *for freedom to be recovered* (Gerundive Construction). For *recover* use recuperō, 1.

8. *let him be on his guard :* an Imperative Clause in Indirect Discourse; hence the subjunctive is to be used.

26.

Ambiorix's Speech (*continued*).

If the two generals would follow his advice, they would abandon their camp at once and hasten to the winter quarters of Cicero or Labienus He promised that no one would attempt to attack them on the march

After he had delivered this speech,[1] Ambiorix withdrew, and the two knights returned to the camp and reported to Sabinus and Cotta what they had heard. These thought that the words of Ambiorix ought not to be despised; and that one tribe would not have dared to make war on the Roman people,[2] unless it were relying upon the help of the others.[3]

Suggestions on the Exercise.

1. *after he had delivered this speech:* translate: *this speech having been delivered.*

2. *on the Roman people:* use the dat.

3. *the others: i.e.* the other tribes.

27.

A Council of War is Held.

Accordingly the tribunes and centurions of the first rank[1] were summoned to a council (of war), which was held[2] in the middle of the camp. Cotta spoke first, (saying) that without the order[3] of Caesar they ought not to leave the camp; that (protected) by their fortifications they could resist all enemies who could be led against them; that they had already repulsed those who had attacked the camp; that a large supply[4] of grain was on hand and that more was expected daily;[5] finally that nothing was more foolish than to follow the advice of an enemy.

Suggestions on the Exercise.

1. *of the first rank :* **prīmī pīlī** (gen.).
2. *hold :* **habeō, ēre, uī, itus.**
3. *without the order :* **injussū.**
4. *supply :* **cōpia, ae, f.**
5. *daily :* **cottīdiē.**

28.

The Council of War (*continued*).

Most (of the) tribunes and centurions were of the same opinion, but Sabinus said that the Eburones would not have attacked them unless they knew that Caesar had already gone back to Italy; that from him therefore no help could be expected; that the Germans, who dwelt near by,[1] and the Gauls desired to avenge the wrongs they had suffered; that he himself urged that they withdraw; that if Ambiorix had told the truth,[2] this was their one hope of safety; if he had spoken falsely, they incurred[3] no risk.

Suggestions on the Exercise.

1. *near by :* **prope.**
2. *tell the truth, speak falsely :* **vēra dīcere, falsa dīcere** (*say true things, say false things*).
3. *incur :* **subeō, īre iī, itus.**

29.

The Romans Decide to March Out.

Although Sabinus could not persuade the tribunes and centurions that this was best[1] to do,[2] yet the rest yielded to him, and the command was given[3] to march out from the camp at dawn.[4]   Meanwhile Ambiorix and the

Eburones, hearing the voices [5] from the camp, perceived that the Romans had decided to follow their advice, and prepared to attack them from an ambush, as they marched [6] (along). That night they hid [7] themselves in the woods [8] through which the road led,[9] and there awaited the approach of the Romans.

Suggestions on the Exercise

1. *that this was best :* express by the inf.
2. *to do :* Lesson XXX, Example 10.
3. *the command was given :* translate : *it was commanded.*
4. *at dawn :* **prīmā lūce,** lit. *at first light.*
5. *hearing voices :* translate by the Ablative Absolute: *voices having being heard.*
6. *as they marched :* translate : (*them*) *marching,* the participle.
7. *hide :* abdō, ere, didī, ditus.
8. *in the woods :* the Latin idiom is: *into the woods.*
9. *lead :* ferō, ferre, tulī, lātus.

30.

The Romans are Overwhelmed.

Sabinus had decided to go to the camp of Cicero. When they had marched about two miles, the Romans come to a defile.[1] The last cohort had entered this, when suddenly Ambiorix and the Eburones rushed forth [2] from the woods and attacked the Roman army So sudden was the onset and so crowded were the cohorts that they could not withstand the multitude of Gauls who pressed upon [3] them Most (of them) were killed ; a very few escaped through the woods to the camp of Labienus.

Suggestions on the Exercise.

1. *defile :* angustiae, ārum, f.
2. *rush forth :* sē ēicere (ēiciō, ere, ējēcī, ējectus).
3. *press upon :* urgeō, ere, ursī ; trans.

31.

The Attack on Quintus Cicero.

After this victory Ambiorix did not delay, but set out immediately with his horsemen for[1] the camp of Quintus Cicero, which was about forty-five miles away; the infantry he ordered to follow him. On the following day he came into the territory of the Nervii, who had not forgotten the battle in which, three years before, Caesar had reduced their tribe nearly to extinction.[2] Ambiorix told their chiefs that Cicero's camp was near by;[3] why should they not do[4] as he had done,[5] attack[4] the legion, and recover[4] their freedom?

Suggestions on the Exercise.

1. *for :* **ad.**

2. *extinction :* **interneciō, ōnis, f.**

3. *near by :* use the adjective, **fīnitimus, a, um.**

4. *why should they not do*, etc. : for the mood, see Lesson XXVII, Example 7.

5. *as he had done :* a Subordinate Clause in Indirect Discourse.

32.

The Attack on Quintus Cicero (*continued*).

Kindled[1] by these words of Ambiorix, the Nervii and other neighboring tribes joined[2] themselves with the Eburones, and the whole multitude set out for the Roman camp. Our men, as soon as they saw the Gauls approaching, quickly rushed[3] to arms and mounted the rampart[4] to ward off the enemy. Cicero immediately sent messengers to inform Caesar of the danger, and promised them large rewards, if they should deliver[5] the letters. Meanwhile to the Gauls, asking a conference, Cicero replied that the Romans never accepted terms from an enemy in arms.[6]

Suggestions on the Exercise.

1. *kindled :* incitātus, a, um.
2. *join :* conjungō, ere, jūnxī, jūnctus.
3. *rush :* concurrō, ere, currī, cursum.
4. *mount the rampart :* see Selection 23, Suggestions **3, 4.**
5. *deliver :* dēferō, ferre, tulī, lātus.
6. *in arms :* use the adj., armātus, a, um.

33.

The Message in the Spear-Shaft.

When the messengers whom Cicero had sent to Caesar had been captured in sight of the Romans, Cicero by promises of the largest rewards persuaded a Gaul whom he had in the camp, to try to make his way [1] to Caesar. The letter which Cicero gave him was concealed [2] in a spear. Carrying this the Gaul easily made his way [1] to Caesar, and informed him of the dangers of Cicero and the legion. On the following day Caesar set out with one legion and about four hundred [3] cavalry, and hastened to come to Cicero's aid.

Suggestions on the Exercise.

1. *make one's way :* perveniō, īre, vēnī, ventum.
2. *conceal :* cēlō, 1.
3. *four hundred :* quadringentī, ae, a.

34.

The Gauls Raise the Siege.

As soon as the Gauls heard that Caesar was approaching, they set out to intercept [1] his army and cut it to

pieces. That night Caesar was informed of their departure through a letter of Cicero, and encouraged his men
for the conflict.[2]   On the following day, having advanced
about four miles, he came to a small stream, on the opposite side of [3] which the enemy were waiting.   Soon their
horsemen crossed the stream and offered battle to our
men, who by Caesar's order at once retreated.

Suggestions on the Exercise.

1. *intercept :* **intercipiō, ere, cēpī, ceptus.**
2. *for the conflict :* **ad dīmicandum.**
3. *on the opposite side of :* **ultrā,** prep. with **acc.**

35.

The Gauls are Defeated.

Caesar had pitched his camp on the top of a hill,
and had ordered his men to remain within the fortifications in order to give [1] the appearance of panic.   Thus it
happened that the Gauls boldly advanced up hill [2] against
the camp, thinking that they would easily defeat the
Romans.   They had arrived at the ditch and were filling it up, when suddenly from all sides the Romans fell
upon [3] them and put them to rout.   About the ninth [4]
hour on that same day Caesar's legions arrived at Cicero's
camp.

Suggestions on the Exercise.

1. *give :* here use **praebeō, ēre, uī, itus.**
2. *up hill :* **colle adversō,** lit. *the hill being against.*
3. *fall upon :* **adorior, īrī, ortus.**
4. *ninth :* **nōnus, a, um.**

PART TWO.

BASED ON CICERO;

LESSON I.

AGREEMENT OF ADJECTIVES AND VERBS.

GRAMMATICAL REFERENCES.

1. Attributive and Predicate Adjectives. 233. 2; A. & G. 285. 1 and 2.

2. Agreement of Adjectives.* 234 and 235 entire; A. & G 286 and *a*, *b*, 287. 1–4; H. 394, 395. 1, 2 and N.

3. Agreement of Verbs. 254 and 255 entire; A. & G. 316 and *b*; 317. *a–d*; H. 388, 389. 1, 2; 390, 391, 392. 1–4.

EXAMPLES.

1. Aristotelēs, vir summō ingeniō et scientiā, *Aristotle, a man of the greatest endowment and knowledge.* (**1, 2**)

2. stultitia et timiditās fugienda sunt, *folly and timidity are to be shunned.* (**2**)

3. honōrēs et victōriae fortuīta sunt, *honors and victories are accidental.* (**2**)

4. populī prōvinciaeque līberātae sunt, *nations and provinces were freed.* (**2**)

5. nōn omnis error stultitia est dīcenda, *not every mistake is to be called folly.* (**2**)

6. omnēs rēs quās mihi aut nātūra aut fortūna dederat, *all things which either nature or fortune had given me.* (**3**)

7. tempus et necessitās postulat, *the occasion and need demand.* (**3**)

8. tū et ille vēnistis, *you and he came.* (**3**)

---

* Note that the principles for the agreement of adjectives cover also the use of participles in the compound tenses of the passive, as well as in the periphrastic conjugations.

VOCABULARY.

authority, **auctōritās, ātis,** *f.*

conflagration, **incendium, ī,** *n.*

despise, **contemnō, ere, tempsī, temptus.**

dignity, **dignitās, ātis,** *f.*

fruit, **frūctus, ūs,** *m.*

harmony, **concordia, ae,** *f.*

house, **domus, ūs,** *f.*

labor, **labor, ōris,** *m.*

law-court, **basilica, ae,** *f.*

murder, **caedēs, is,** *f.*

old, **vetus, eris.**

prevent, keep off, **arceō, ēre, uī.**

protect, **tueor, ērī.**

reap, **capiō, ere, cēpī, captus.**

temple, **templum, ī,** *n.*

to-morrow, **crās.**

virtue, **virtūs, ūtis,** *f.*

EXERCISE.

1. Either * your father or brother will come.   2. The Senate and the Roman people will easily protect their dignity.   3. Peace and harmony deserve[1] to be praised. 4. A great multitude of men and women had assembled here.   5. Your brother and I will return to-morrow. 6. Catulus reaped the fruit of his virtue and labor. 7. The consul, the Senate, and[2] the State have been preserved.   8. Neither night, Catiline,[3] nor the house of your friends confines the voices of your conspiracy. 9. An old temple and a law-court were torn down. 10. The murder of citizens and the conflagration of the city must be prevented.   11. A camp has been pitched in Italy against the Roman people.   12. The Senate, the consul, and[2] the people see these things.

Suggestions on the Exercise.

1. *deserve to be praised:* use the second periphrastic conjugation.

2. For the use of conjunctions in enumerations, see 341. 4. *a–c* ; A. & G. 323. *c.* 1, 3 ; H. 657. 6 and N.

3. The Vocative usually follows one or more words of the sentence.

* Words not found in the Lesson Vocabularies may be found in the General Vocabulary at the end of the book

LESSON II.

RELATIVE PRONOUNS. POSSESSIVE PRONOUNS.

GRAMMATICAL REFERENCES.

1. Relative Pronouns. 250. 1–4, 251. 1, 5, 6; A. & G. 305 and *a*, 306 and *b*, 307. *c*, 308. *a*, *f* and N.; H. 396 and 2, 397, 398 and 1, 399. 4.

2. Possessive Pronouns. 243. 1–3, 233. 3; A. & G. 302 and *a*, *c*, *e*; H. 501, 393, 6.

EXAMPLES.

1. ego, vehemēns ille cōnsul quī cīvīs in exsilium ēiciō, *I, that energetic consul, who drive citizens into exile.* (**1**)

2. agrī quī ēmptī sunt, *the lands which were bought.* (**1**)

3. artēs quae ad hūmānitātem pertinent, *the studies which make for culture.* (**1**)

4. Virtūs et Fidēs quārum Rōmae templa sunt, *Virtue and Faith to whom* (lit. *of whom*) *there are temples at Rome.* (**1**)

5. incōnstantia et temeritās quae digna nōn sunt deō, *fickleness and haste, which are not worthy of a god.* (**1**)

6. quī nātūram secūtī sunt, multa laudābilia fēcērunt, *those who have followed nature have done many praiseworthy things.* (**1**)

7. quā ratiōne factum est, *and in this way it happened.* (**1**)

8. haec tēcum patria loquitur, *your country thus pleads with you,* lit. *says this.* (**2**)

9. suā manū sorōrem interfēcit, *he slew his sister with his own hand.* (**2**)

10. compressī cōnātūs tuōs, *I checked your attempts.* (**2**)

111

VOCABULARY.

already, jam.

await, exspectō, 1.*

counsel, cōnsilium, ī, *n.*

foresight, prūdentia, ae, *f.*

fortune, property, **fortūnae**, ārum, *f.*

invite, invītō, 1.

perceive, **sentiō, īre, sēnsī, sēnsus.**

plot, īnsidiae, ārum, *f.*

plunder, spoliō, 1.

Quirites, Roman citizens, **Quirītēs, ium,** *m.*

report, dēferō, ferre, tulī, lātus.

send ahead, **praemittō, ere, mīsī, missus.**

serious, **gravis, e,** *lit.* heavy.

EXERCISF,

1. We saw all the men and women who were present. 2. We praise you, O Quirites, who defend the republic so courageously. 3. All my friends perceive these plots, Catiline. 4. Cicero preserved the republic by his own counsels and foresight. 5. There were many cities whose temples these men plundered. 6. You will lose all your fortune soon. 7. I have always been (one) who defended your cause, O friends. 8. These Roman knights have reported to me the dangers which they fear. 9. The war which has broken out will be most serious. 10. I shall not invite you, who have already sent ahead men who are awaiting your arrival. 11. You went to your own friends 12. Who will restore peace and concord, which we all wish? 13. (Those) who protect the state, will always be praised.

---

* Regular verbs of the first conjugation are indicated by tn
numeral 1.

LESSON III.

QUESTIONS.

GRAMMATICAL REFERENCES.

1. Word Questions. 162. 1; A. & G. 333; H. 378.

2. Sentence Questions. 162. 2. *a–d*; A. & G. 332 and *a–c*
H. 378. 1, 2.

3. Double Questions. 162. 4 and *a*; A. & G. 334 and 335;
H. 380 and 1.

EXAMPLES.

1. quis umquam illud templum aspexit, *who ever looked at that
temple ?* **(1)**

2. quid postulās, *what do you demand ?* **(1)**

3. ubi eōs convēnit, *where did he meet them ?* **(1)**

4. quō tandem accūsātor cōnfūgit, *whither, pray, did the accuser
flee ?* **(1)**

5. eundemne tū jūdicem sūmēbās, *did you take the same man as
judge ?* **(2)**

6. num noctū vēnērunt, *they didn't come at night, did they?* **(2)**

7. nōnne aliō scelere hōc scelus cumulāstī, *did you not augment
this crime by another crime ?* **(2)**

8. id utrum libentēs an invītī dabant, *did they give that willingly
or unwillingly?* **(3)**

9. stultitiamne dīcam an impudentiam singulārem, *shall I call
it folly or stupendous impudence?* **(3)**

10. cum homine nōbīs rēs est an cum immānī bēluā, *are we dealing with a man or a wild beast ?* **(3)**

11. tabulās habet annōn, *has he the tablets, or not ?* **(3)**

113

VOCABULARY.

bring, **addūcō, ere, dūxī, ductus.**

conspirators, **conjūrātī, ōrum,** *m.*

ever, at any time, **umquam.**

find, **reperiō, īre, repperī, repertus.**

how great? **quantus, a, um.**

how many? **quot,** *indeclinable.*

prefer, **mālō, mālle, māluī.**

retain, **retineō, ēre, uī, tentus.**

return, *trans.*, **reddō, ere, reddidī, redditus.**

severe, **gravis, e.**

slavery, **servitūs, ūtis,** *f.*

to-day, **hodiē.**

visit (with punishment), **afficiō, ere, fēcī, fectus.**

whither, **quō,**

witness, **testis, is,** *m.*

zeal, **studium, ī,** *n.*

EXERCISE.

1. Did not Publius Scipio slay Tiberius Gracchus with his own hand? **2.** How many witnesses have you brought with you? **3.** Whither will these ambassadors go? **4.** Will you not visit these conspirators with the severest punishments? **5.** Where was Sextus Roscius killed? **6.** You and your friends were not awaiting us, were you? **7.** Do you perceive the zeal of those who are present? **8.** How great a multitude of citizens assembled here to-day? **9.** Will you retain this money or return it to me? **10.** Have you found your friends? **11.** Do you perceive the plans of these conspirators or not? **12.** Do you prefer freedom or slavery? **13.** Have you ever seen more loyal citizens?

LESSON IV.

THE ACCUSATIVE.

GRAMMATICAL REFERENCES

(ACCUSATIVE OF DIRECT OBJECT.)

1. Simple Uses. 175. 1, 176. 1 ; A. & G. 387 ; H. 404.

2. With Compound Verbs. 175. 2. *a* ; A. & G. 388. *b* ; H. 406.

3. Neuter Pronouns and Adjectives used as Accusative of 'Result Produced.' 176. 2 ; A. and G. 390. *c* ; H. 409. 1.

4. Two Accusatives, — Direct Object and Predicate Accusative. 177. 1 ; A. & G. 393 ; H. 410 and 1.

5. Adjective as Predicate Accusative. 177. 2 ; A. & G. 393. N. ; H. 410. 3.

6. Passive Construction of the Foregoing Verbs. 177. 3 ; A. & G. 393. *a* ; H. 410. 1.

EXAMPLES.

1. omnia quae cūrant meminērunt, *they remember all things for which they care.* (**1**)

2. foedus ferīre, *to strike a treaty.* (**1**)

3. omnēs terrōrēs subībō, *I shall endure all terrors.* (**2**)

4. hortōs Epicūrī modo praeterībāmus, *we were just now going past the gardens of Epicurus.* (**2**)

5. Xenophōn eadem[1] ferē peccat, *Xenophon commits almost the same errors.* (**3**)

6. vellem idem[2] possem glōriārī, *would that I could make the same boast.* (**3**)

7. tē fēcit hērēdem, *he made you his heir.* (**4**)

8. tū hērēs factus es, *you were made heir.* (**6**)

9. Ennius poētās sānctōs appellat, *Ennius calls poets sacred.* (**5**)

10. **cupiditās eōs caecōs reddit,** *greed renders them blind.* (**5**)

11. **jūris perītus numerābātur,** *he was accounted skilled in the law.* (**6**)

Notes on the Examples.

1. **eadem peccat :** lit. *errs the same things,* *i.e.* makes the same errors.

2. **idem glōriārī,** lit. *boast the same thing.*

VOCABULARY.

contemplate, **cōgitō, 1.**

cruel, **crūdēlis, e.**

democratic, **populāris, e.**

elect, **creō, 1.**

empire, **imperium, ī,** *n.*

energetic, **vehemēns, entis.**

except, *after negs.,* **nisi,** *conj.*

intact, **integer, gra, grum.**

mistake, make a mistake, **peccō, 1.**

painstaking, **dīligēns, entis.**

reckon, **numerō, 1.**

scale, **trānscendō, ere, endī,** *trans.*

severe (of persons), **sevērus, a, um.**

stand around, **circumstō, āre, stitī,** *trans.*

sturdy, **fortis, e.**

think, regard, **exīstimō, 1.**

utterance, **vōx, vōcis, f.**

EXERCISE.

1. Do you see the other sturdy citizens who stand around the senate-house ?   2. The Romans called Jupiter the 'Stayer' of the city and empire.   3. I will reply briefly [1] to these utterances of my country.   4. Against those who have wished these things I shall show myself severe and energetic.   5. Julius Caesar was called democratic.   6. I preserved the citizens intact and unharmed.   7. Some thought Cicero not a most painstaking consul but a most cruel tyrant.   8. These men contemplate nothing except murder.   9. Catiline was reckoned a bold leader.   10. Cicero and Antonius were elected consuls.   11. The report of this conspiracy has

already crossed the Alps.   12. These conspirators made many other mistakes.[2]

Suggestions on the Exercise.

1. *replied briefly:* translate *replied a few (things)*, using neuter plural.

2. *made many other mistakes:* see Note 1 on the Examples.

LESSON V.

THE ACCUSATIVE (*continued*).

GRAMMATICAL REFERENCES.

1. Two Accusatives. — Person Affected and Result Produced
178. 1. *a–e*; A. & G. 394, 396 and *a*; H. 411.

2. Passive Construction of these Verbs. 178. 2; A. & G
396. *b*; H. 411. 1.

3. Accusative of Time and Space. 181. 1; A. & G. 423, 425;
H. 417.

4. Accusative of Limit of Motion. 182. 1–4; A. & G. 426. 2,
427. 2, 428. *a, b, j*; H. 418 and 1, 419 and 1, 2.

5. Accusative in Exclamations. 183; A. & G. 397. *d*; H. 421.

6. Accusative as Subject of Infinitive. 184; A. & G. 397. *e*;
H. 415.

EXAMPLES.

1. **ea quae scīmus, aliōs docēmus,** *we teach others those things
   which we know.* **(1)**

2. **eōs hōc moneō,** *I give them this warning,* lit. *warn them
   this.* **(1)**

3. **id quod monēbātur,** *that which he was warned of.* **(2)**

4. **ea quae rogātī erant,** *those things which they had been
   asked.* **(2)**

5. **ducenta mīlia passuum ab urbe aberat,** *he was two hundred
   miles away from the city.* **(3)**

6. **biennium prōvinciam obtinuit,** *he held his province two
   years.* **(3)**

7. **multōs annōs rēgnāvit,** *he reigned many years.* **(3)**

8. **Rōmam rediit,** *he returned to Rome.* **(4)**

9. **domum revertērunt,** *they returned home.* **(4)**

10. **quam ob rem meam domum vēnistis?** *Why did you come to
    my house?* **(4)**

11. **tibi ad Forum Aurēlium praestōlābantur,** *they were waiting for you near Forum Aurelium.* (**4**)

12. **ad Tarentum profectus sum,** *I set out for the neighborhood of Tarentum.* (**4**)

13. **sē contulit Tarquiniōs, in urbem flōrentissimam,** *he betook himself to Tarquinii, a most flourishing city.* (**4**)

14. **Catilīnam ex urbe ēgredī jussī,** *I ordered Catiline to go forth from the city.* (**6**)

15. **eum prehendī jussimus,** *we ordered him to be arrested.* (**6**)

16. **Ō nōs beātōs!** *O happy we!* (**5**)

Remarks.

1. **Poscō, postulō, flāgitō,** while admitting the construction of two accusatives, more commonly take the accusative of the thing asked and the ablative with ab of the person. **Petō** *regularly* takes only the latter construction, as **tribūnātum ā Caesare petīvī,** *I asked a tribuneship from Caesar.*

2. **Rogō,** *inquire,* besides neuter pronouns and adjectives, admits only **sententiam** as accusative of the thing.

3. **Doceō** may take an infinitive in place of the accusative of the thing, as **tē doceō sentīre,** *I teach you to perceive.* The compound **ēdoceō** is the only verb of teaching that is freely used in the passive.

4. A favorite way of saying *so many years old* was by means of the phrase **annōs nātus,** as **sexāgintā annōs nātus,** *sixty years old,* lit. *born sixty years.*

5. To denote duration for a small number of days or years it is customary to use **bīduum, trīduum, quadrīduum,** *two days, three days, four days;* and **biennium, triennium, quadriennium,** *two years, three years, four years.*

VOCABULARY.

allow, **sinō, ere, sīvī, situs.**

ask, **rogō, 1.**

beg, **ōrō, 1.**

betake oneself, **recipiō, ere, cēpī, ceptus,** *with the reflexive pronoun.*

consulship, **cōnsulātus, ūs,** *m.*

deliver, **habeō, ēre, uī, itus.**

Faesulae, **Faesulae, ārum,** *f.*

fortunate, **fēlīx, īcis.**

letter (of the alphabet), **littera, ae,** *f.*

recollection, **memoria, ae,** *f.*

teach, **doceō, ēre, uī, doctus.**

EXERCISE.

1. Cicero delivered his first speech (when) twenty-five years old.[1]   2. O fortunate city, if all these things are true!   3. I ask these men their opinion concerning the republic.   4. These men have been asked their opinion concerning the republic.   5. Manlius, the centurion, a friend of Catiline, has pitched his camp near Faesulae. 6. I beg nothing of you except the recollection of my consulship.   7. Did Catiline betake himself to Marseilles or to the camp of Manlius at Faesulae?[2]   8. We taught this boy his letters.   9 We remained three years near Marseilles.   10. We shall allow him to go four miles.   11. They demanded money of us.   12. You order this man to be called king.   13. Had you been taught your letters?   14. We shall go first to Gaul, then into Germany.

Suggestions on the Exercise.

1. *twenty-five years old:* see Remark 4.

2. *to the camp of M. at Faesulae:* translate, *to Faesulae, to the camp of M.*

LESSON VI.

THE DATIVE.

GRAMMATICAL REFERENCES.

(DATIVE OF INDIRECT OBJECT.)

1. Indirect Object in Connection with a Direct Object after Transitive Verbs. 187. I and *a*; A. & G. 362; H. 424.

2. Indirect Object with Intransitive Verbs. 187. II; A. & G 366, 367; H. 424, 426. 1, 2.

3. Passive Construction of the Last Class of Verbs. 187. II. *b*; A. & G. 372; H. 426. 3.

4. Indirect Object with Compound Verbs. 187. III. 1, 2; A. & G. 370; H. 429 and 1.

5. Dative of Reference. 188. 1; A. & G. 376; H. 425. 4. and N.

6. Dative of Separation. 188. 2. *d*; A. & G. 381; H. 429. 2.

EXAMPLES.

1. haec studia adversīs rēbus perfugium praebent, *these pursuits afford a refuge to adversity.* **(1)**

2. omnibus aedificiīs pepercit, *he spared all the buildings.* **(2)**

3. laudī meae invīdērunt, *they envied my glory.* **(2)**

4. illa invidia tibi nōn nocuit, *that envy did not harm you.* **(2)**

5. per fīlium eī nocēbātur, *he was injured through his son,* lit. *it was injured to him.* **(3)**

6. nōn mihi persuādētur, *I am not persuaded,* lit. *it is not persuaded to me.* **(3)**

7. mihi invidētur, *I am envied;*
tibi invidētur, *you are envied;*
eī invidētur, *he is envied;*
nōbīs invidētur, *we are envied;*
vōbīs invidētur, *you are envied;*
eīs invidētur, *they are envied.* **(3).**

121

8. **Asia ūbertāte agrōrum omnibus terrīs antecellit,** *Asia sur-passes all countries in the fertility of its lands.* (**4**)

9. **amīcitiam omnibus rēbus hūmānīs antepōnimus,** *we set friendship before all human things.* (**4**)

10. **versātur mihi ante oculōs aspectus Cethēgī,** *the sight of Cethegus hovers before my eyes,* lit. *to me, before the eyes.* (**5**)

11. **multum tuīs operibus diūturnitās dētrahet,** *time will take away much from your achievements.* (**6**)

Remarks.

1. **Persuādeō** and **noceō,** besides the dative of the person, may take the Accusative of Result Produced. This construction, however, is confined to narrow limits; the chief accusatives so used are **hōc, illud, id, quod, quid** (interrogative and indefinite), **aliquid, nihil.** Examples are:

hōc Anaximandrō nōn persuāsit, *he did not persuade Anaximander to this effect.*

quid mihi istīus inimīcitiae nocēbunt, *what harm will that fellow's hostility do me?*

2. In the passive construction of these verbs the accusative of the thing is retained, *e.g. :*

hōc ipsīs Siculīs persuāsum est, *the Sicilians themselves were persuaded to this effect.*

3. With **mittō** and **scrībō** one may use either the accusative with **ad** or the dative, according as the idea of *motion* is or is not predominant. Thus either **mihi** or **ad mē scrīpsistī,** *you wrote to me.*

VOCABULARY.

bestow upon, **impertiō, īre, īvī, ītus.**

decide, **cōnstituō, ere, uī, ūtus.**

entire, **tōtus, a, um.**

envy, **invideō, ēre, vīdī, vīsum.**

fire, **īgnis, is,** *m.*

harm, **noceō, ēre, uī, itūrus.**

good fortune, **fortūna, ae,** *f.*

lay upon, **īnferō, ferre, intulī, illātus,** *with dat. of indir. obj.*

rank, **dignitās, ātis,** *f.*

support, **dēfendō, ere, endī, ēnsus.**

thwart, **obsistō, ere, obstitī,** *with dat. of indir. obj.*

whole, **tōtus, a, um.**

wrest, **extorqueō, ēre, torsī, tortus,** *with dat. of person from whom.*

EXERCISE.

1. Your dagger will be wrested from you.   2. The senators almost laid hands on Catiline himself in the senate-house.   3. I was envied on account of my glory. 4. Fires had been placed around the whole city, the temples of the gods, and the dwellings of the citizens. 5. Praise was bestowed on my colleague, Antonius. 6. Did they not envy your glory and rank?   7. The Allobroges placed your safety before their own advantages.   8. I shall obey your decrees and support those things which you decide.   9. The good fortune of the Roman people thwarted the designs of Catiline and the conspirators.   10. The entire ruin of your fortunes threatens you.   11. Who was persuaded of this? 12. No one was injured through us.

LESSON VII.

THE DATIVE (*continued*).

GRAMMATICAL REFERENCES.

1. Dative of Agency. 189. 1, 2; A. & G. 374; H. 431.

2. Dative of Possession. 190 and 1; A. & G. 373 and *a*, 430 and 1.

3. Dative of Purpose. 191. 1, 2; A. & G. 382 and 1, 2; H. 433 and 3.

4. Dative with Adjectives. 192. 1, 2; A. & G. 383, 384; H. 434 and 2.

EXAMPLES.

1. **nōbīs crūdēlitātis fāma subeunda est,** *we must suffer the reputation of being cruel,* lit. *the reputation must be undergone by us.* (**1**)

2. **quō animō tibi hōc ferendum esse putās ?** *with what feeling do you think this should be borne by you ?* (**1**)

3. **erit verendum mihi,** *I shall have to fear,* lit. *it will have to be feared by me* (impersonal use). (**1**)

4. **hī tibi ad caedem cōnstitūtī sunt,** *these have been marked for murder by you.* (**1**)

5. **necessitūdō quae mihi est cum illō ōrdine,** *the connection which I have with that class.* (**2**)

6. **fōns cui nōmen Arethūsa est,** *a fountain which has the name "Arethusa."* (**2**)

7. **novīs nūptiīs domum vacuēfēcistī,** *you cleared your house for a new marriage.* (**3**)

8. **illīus salūs cūrae plūribus fuit,** *his safety was an anxiety to many,* lit. *for anxiety.* (**3**)

9. **cui bonò est,** *to whom is it of advantage?* lit. *for an advantage.* (**3**)

10. hōc mihi dētrīmentō est, *this is a disadvantage to me.* (**3**)

11. genus litterārum meīs studiīs aptum, *a kind of literature suited to my studies.* (**4**)

12. mentēs improbōrum mihi sunt adversae, *the minds of the wicked are hostile to me.* (**4**)

Remarks.

1. Note that for the purpose of avoiding ambiguity the ablative with ā (ab) is used even with the gerundive, as, — hostibus ā nōbīs parcendum est, *we must spare our enemies.*

2. With nōmen est the name is very rarely attracted into the Dative in Cicero's writings, though quite commonly so attracted in later authors. Either construction, therefore, is quite idiomatic.

3. The chief verbs that take a Dative of Purpose besides sum are : relinquō, dēligō, dīcō, mittō, veniō, habeō, dūcō.

4. Among the commonest Datives of Purpose used with esse are : auxiliō, cūrae, dētrīmentō, salūtī, impedīmentō, odio, praesidiō.

VOCABULARY.

die, morior, morī, mortuus.

equal, pār, paris.

fertile, ferāx, ācis.

for, in behalf of, prō.

hostile, inimīcus, a, um.

lack, dēsum, dēesse, dēfuī, dē- futūrus

nowhere, nūsquam.

often, saepe.

pirate, praedō, ōnis, *m.*

suited, accommodātus, a, um.

undertake, suscipiō, ere, cēpī, ceptus.

welcome, grātus, a, um.

EXERCISE.

1. A good cause has been undertaken by us. **2.** These conspirators had neither weapons nor leaders. **3.** We were nowhere a match (equal to) for the pirates. **4.** I, who have so often been a help to many, will not be lacking to you. **5.** This plan is suited to the safety of all **6.** I must either live [1] with these men or die for [2] them **7.** We must not harm those [3] who are a help to us

8. All gods and all men are hostile to you.   **9.** He alone deserved [4] to be feared by us.   **10.** The lands which we have near Rome are most fertile.   **11.** Your favors were most welcome to me.   **12.** The state must be bravely defended by all who have arms.

Suggestions on the Exercise.

1. *I must live :* see Example 3.

2. *for :* use the prep. **prō** with the ablative.

3. *we must not harm those :* see Remark 1.

4. *deserved to be feared :* express by the second periphrastic conjugation.

Cicero's Birthplace.

Marcus Tullius Cicero was born at Arpinum,[1] which was a small town of the Volscians.[2]   Here for many years, among the mountains which divide [3] Latium [4] from Campania,[5] his ancestors had dwelt.   The Volscians were a brave race and had waged many long wars with the Romans, but were finally subdued.   Another famous man of the Volscians [6] was Gaius Marius,[7] who defeated and captured Jugurtha [8] and later drove back the Cimbrians and Teutons.   He [9] also was born at Arpinum.

Suggestions on the Exercise.

1. *at Arpinum :* **Arpīnī** (locative of **Arpīnum**).

2. *Volscians :* **Volscī, ōrum,** m.

3. *divide :* **dīvidō, ere, vīsī, vīsus.**

4. *Latium :* **Latium, ī,** n.

5. *Campania,* **Campānia, ae,** f.

6. *of the Volscians :* express by **ex** with the abl.

7. *Marius :* **Marius, ī,** m.

8. *Jugurtha :* **Jugurtha, ae,** m.

9. *he :* the pronoun (**ille**) should here be expressed.

LESSON VIII.

THE GENITIVE.

GRAMMATICAL REFERENCES.

1. Genitive of Material. 197; A. & G. 344.

2. Genitive of Possession. 198. 1, 3; A. & G. 343 and *b*; **H.** 440. 1.

3. Subjective Genitive. 199; A. & G. 343. N. 1; H. 440. 1.

4. Objective Genitive. 200; A. & G. 347, 348; H. 440. 2.

5. Genitive of the Whole ('Partitive Genitive'). 201 entire ; A. & G. 346. *a*. 1–3, *c*, *e*; H. 440. 5 and N., 441, 442, 443.

6. Genitive of Quality. 203. 1–5; A. & G. 345. *a*, *b*; H. 440. 3.

7. Appositional Genitive. 202; A. & G. 343. *d*; H. 440. 4.

EXAMPLES.

1. lībertātis causā, *for the sake of freedom.* **(2)**
2. amīcitiae grātiā, *for the sake of friendship.* **(2)**
3. stultī est haec spērāre, *it is (the part) of a fool to hope this.* **(2)**
4. maeror parentum, *the mourning of parents.* **(3)**
5. memoria bene factōrum, *the recollection of good deeds,* lit. *of things well done.* **(4)**
6. quīnque mīlia passuum, *five miles,* lit. *five thousands of paces.* **(5)**
7. quis nostrum, *who of us ?* **(5)**
8. quid est causae, *what reason is there ?* **(5)**
9. vir animī magnī, *a man of high purpose.* **(6)**
10. hūjus modī cōnsilia, *plans of this sort.* **(6)**
11. porticus trecentōrum pedum, *a portico three hundred feet long,* lit. *of three hundred feet.* **(6)**
12. quantī aestimābat, tantī vēndidit, *he sold it for as much as he valued it at.* **(6)**

127

13. **illae omnēs dissēnsiōnēs erant ejus modī,** *all those dissensions were of this kind.* **(6)**

14. **nōmen pācis dulce est,** *the name of peace is sweet.* **(7)**

Remarks.

1. **Causā** is much commoner than **grātiā** in the sense, *on account of, for the sake of.*

2. The Objective Genitive occurs most frequently in combination with nouns derived from verbs that govern the accusative; yet by an extension of usage we sometimes find the genitive used with nouns derived from verbs that govern other cases, *e.g.* **cōnsuē-tūdō hominum,** *intercourse with men* (*cf.* **cōnsuēscere cum hominibus,** *to associate with men*) ; **excessus vītae,** *departure from life* (*cf.* **excēdere ē vītā,** *to depart from life*).

3. Observe that the Genitive of Quality, when applied to persons, is properly used only of *permanent* characteristics ; *incidental* or *transitory* qualities cannot be indicated except by the ablative. See Lesson XII, Remark 3.

4. Note that the adjectives most frequently employed in connection with a genitive to denote quality are adjectives of amount (*e.g.* **magnus, maximus, summus, tantus,** and numerals) ; **ejus, hūjus,** *etc.*, in combination with **modī,** also occur frequently.

VOCABULARY.

bring out, **efferō, ferre, extulī, ēlātus.**

death, **mors, mortis,** *f.*

enact, **statuō, ere, uī, ūtus.**

fountain, **fōns, fontis,** *m.*

fresh, **dulcis, e.**

higher price, at a higher price, **plūris.**

highest (of qualities), **summus, a, um.**

penalty, **poena, ae,** *f.*

permanent, **sempiternus, a, um.**

refuse, **recūsō, 1.**

sell, **vēndō, ere, vēndidī, itus.**

tenor, sentiment, **sententia, ae,** *f.*

value, **aestimō, 1.**

EXERCISE.

1. On this small island near Syracuse there is a fountain of fresh water. 2. Among the praises of all these men what place [1] will my glory have? [2] 3. Who of all

those men [3] saluted him ?   4. Other letters of the same tenor were found.   5. The praetor brought out whatever (of) weapons there were.[4]   6. All these wars were of the same kind.   7. The memory of Cicero's consulship will be permanent.   8. This senator demanded the penalty of death.   9. The citizens will not refuse what [5] you enact for the sake of the safety of all.   10. We shall scarcely have enough protection.[1]   11. We sold these lands at a higher price.   12. At how much did the senate value these buildings ?   13. These men were of the highest authority.

Suggestions on the Exercise.

1 Use the Genitive of the Whole.
2. *will my glory have:* translate : *will be to my glory.*
3. *of those men:* express by the abl. with **ex.**
4. *were:* the verb will be in the singular.
5. *what:* translate : *those things which,* using neuter.

LESSON IX.

THE GENITIVE (continued).

GRAMMATICAL REFERENCES.

1. Genitive with Adjectives. 204. 1–3; A. & G. 349 and *a*, *b*, 385. *c* and 2; H. 450, 451. 1, 2 and N. 1, 3.

2. Genitive with *memini, reminiscor, oblīvīscor.* 206. 1, 2; A. & G. 350. *a, b, c, d*; H. 454 and 1, 455.

3. Genitive with Verbs of Judicial Action. 208, 1, 2, *a*, *b*; A. & G. 352 and *a*, 353. 1; H. 456 and 3, 4.

4. Genitive with Impersonal Verbs. 209. 1; A. & G. 354. *b, c*; H. 457.

5. Genitive with *misereor, miserescō.* 209. 2; A. & G. 354. *a*; H. 457.

6. Genitive with *interest* and *rēfert.* 210; 211. 1–4; A. & G. 355 and *a*; H. 449 1–4.

EXAMPLES.

1. semper appetentēs glōriae atque avidī laudis fuistis, *you were always desirous of glory and eager for praise.* **(1)**

2. vir bellōrum perītissimus, *a man most experienced in wars.* **(1)**

3. omnia plēna lūctūs et maerōris fuērunt, *all things were full of mourning and sorrow.* **(1)**

4. fuit hōc quondam proprium populī Rōmānī, *this was formerly characteristic of the Roman people.* **(1)**

5. tuī similis, *like you.* **(1)**

6. tuī meminī, *I remember you.* **(2)**

7. Cinnam meminī, *I recall Cinna.* **(2)**

8. Epicūrī nōn licet oblīvīscī, *we cannot forget Epicurus.* **(2)**

9. numquam oblīvīscar noctis illīus, *I shall never forget that night.* **(2)**

10. multa meminī, *I remember many things.* **(2)**

11. **īnsimulat Verrem avāritiae et audāciae,** *he accuses Verres of avarice and insolence.* **(3)**

12. **tē avāritiae coarguō,** *I convict you of greed.* **(3)**

13. **mē tuī miseret,** *I pity you.*

14. **mē stultitiae meae pudet,** *I am ashamed of my folly.* **(4)**

15. **quem nōn paenitēbat hōc facere,** *who did not repent of doing this.* **(4)**

16. **miserēminī ejus,** *pity him!* **(5)**

17. **hōc reī pūblicae interfuit,** *this concerned the commonwealth.* **(6)**

18. **meā interest,** *this concerns me.* **(6)**

Remarks.

1. With **meminī** and **oblīvīscor,** personal pronouns regularly stand in the genitive.

2. While **meminī** and **oblīvīscor** take either the accusative or the genitive of the thing remembered or forgotten, yet

3. Note that neuter nouns, neuter pronouns (as **haec, illa, ea, ista, quae,** *etc.*), and adjectives used substantively (as **multa, pauca, omnia**) regularly stand in the accusative.

4. **Recordor** always takes the accusative.

VOCABULARY.

acquit, **absolvō, ere, solvī, solūtus.**

ashamed, it shames, **pudet, ēre, puduit,** *impersonal.*

charge, **crīmen, inis,** *n.*

class, **genus, eris,** *n.*

cruelty, **crūdēlitās, ātis,** *f.*

fond, **studiōsus, a, um.**

ignorant, **ignārus, a, um.**

mindful, **memor, oris.**

pity, it causes pity, **miseret, ēre, uit,** *impersonal.*

purpose, **cōnsilium, ī,** *n.*

remember, **meminī, isse.**

repent, it causes repentance, **paenitet, ēre, uit,** *impersonal.*

EXERCISE.

1. When have you ever repented of your acts or your purposes? **2.** Will you forget our safety? **3.** Cethegus had always been fond of good weapons. **4.** These men are all like Catiline. **5.** Many accused Cicero of

the greatest cruelty.   6. You have a consul, Quirites,
who forgets his own safety and is mindful only of you.
7 The Vestal virgins were acquitted of this charge.
8. Are you not ashamed to remain in this city ?   9. We
pity the wives and children of these conspirators whom
we have arrested.   10. It concerns us to remember all
these things.   11. This whole class of citizens was most
desirous of peace.   12. We were not ignorant of these
reasons.   13. This concerns the safety of all our friends.

Cicero's Early Years.

Cicero spent his earliest [1] years partly at Arpinum,
partly in the City.   His father, whose health [2] was delicate, [3] was wealthy, had a large villa, [4] and was devoted to
liberal [5] pursuits. Hence his son from his earliest boyhood [6]
was fond of books and read as many as possible. [7]   When
only seven years old, he had (as) teacher, Archias, [8] a poet, [9]
who had been brought to Rome a few years before [10] by
Lucullus.   Forty years afterwards [11] he defended this
teacher, who had been accused by enemies.

Suggestions on the Exercise.

1. *earliest :* **prīmus, a, um.**
2. *health :* **valētūdō, inis, f.**
3 *delicate :* **tenuis, e,** lit. *thin.*
4. *villa :* **vīlla, ae, f.**
5. *liberal :* **līberālis, e.**
6. *boyhood :* **pueritia, ae, f.**
7. *as many as possible :* **quam plūrimī.**
8. *Archias :* **Archiās, ae, m.,** acc. **Archiam.**
9. *poet :* **poēta, ae, m.**
10. *a few years before :* translate : *before a few years.*
11 *forty years afterwards :* translate : *after forty years.*

LESSON X.

THE ABLATIVE.

GRAMMATICAL REFERENCES.

1. **Ablative of Separation.** 214 entire; A. & G. 400, 401, 402. *a*; H. 462, 465.

2. **Ablative of Source.** 215 entire; A. & G. 403. *a*; H. 467, 469. 1, 2.

3. **Ablative of Agent.** 216 entire; A. & G. 405; H. 468 and 1.

4. **Ablative of Comparison.** 217. 1–4; A. & G. 406 and *a*, 407 and *c*; H. 471 and 1, 4.

5. **Ablative of Means.** 218; A. & G. 409; H. 476.

EXAMPLES.

1. lībera rem pūblicam metū, *free the commonwealth from fear!* (**1**)
2. nōs omnīs vītā prīvāre cōnātī sunt, *they tried to deprive us all of life.* (**1**)
3. carēre aspectū cīvium māllem, *I should prefer to be deprived of the view of my fellow-citizens.* (**1**)
4. mihi nōn campus, nōn cūria umquam vacua mortis perīculō fuit, *for me not the campus, not the Curia were ever free from the danger of death.* (**1**)
5. hunc et hūjus sociōs ā tuīs templīs ārcēbis, *keep off this man and his associates from your temples!* (**1**)
6. ex urbe dēpulsus est, *he has been driven from the City.* (**1**)
7. parentibus humilibus nātī, *born of humble parents.* (**2**)
8. Archiās ibi nātus est locō nōbilī, *there Archias was born in a noble station* (lit. *from a noble station*). (**2**)

133

9. ēdūcuntur ab illīs gladiī, *swords were drawn by them.* (**3**)

10. quid est in homine ratiōne dīvīnius, *what is there in man diviner than reason?* (**4**)

11. nihil rārius perfectō ōrātōre invenītur, *nothing is more rarely found than a finished orator.* (**4**)

12. Lepidus quō multī fuērunt ducēs meliōrēs, *Lepidus than whom there were many better leaders.* (**4**)

13. cōntiōnibus accommodātior quam jūdiciīs, *better adapted for public meetings than for courts.* (**4**)

14. tēcum plūs annum vīxit, *he lived with you more than a year.* (**4**)

15. lātius opīniōne malum dissēminātum est, *the evil is more widely diffused than is thought.* (**4**)

16. compressī cōnātūs tuōs amīcōrum praesidiō, *I thwarted your attempts by the support of my friends.* (**5**)

Remark.

1. Cicero in his *Orations* (and probably also in his other works) confines the use of the Ablative of Comparison mainly to negative sentences and interrogative sentences implying a negative. No other writer, however, observes so strict a canon, and even in Cicero there is quite a percentage of exceptions. The ablative *must* be used in case of relative pronouns, *i.e.* always quō, quibus, — not quam quī. On the other hand, when the comparative is an *attributive* modifier of a noun in an oblique case, quam is used, and the proper form of the verb esse is expressed, as verba Varrōnis, hominis doctiōris quam fuit Claudius, *the words of Varro, a more learned man than Claudius.*

VOCABULARY.

deliver, līberō, 1.

deprive, prīvō, 1.

formerly, ōlim.

free from, *adj.*, vacuus, a, um.

guard, cūstōs, ōdis, *m.*

immortal, immortālis, e.

just, jūstus, a, um.

keep off, keep away, arceō, ēre, uī.

lack, careō, ēre, uī.

leading man, prīnceps, ipis, *m*

owe, dēbeō, ēre, uī, itus.

right, jūs, jūris, *n.*

sea, mare, is, *n.*

EXERCISE.

1. He owes more money[1] to me than to you. 2. More than a thousand Roman citizens saw this. 3. Very courageous[2] opinions were expressed[3] by the leading men. 4. This state lacked good leaders. 5. These two sons were born of me.[4] 6. I delivered the city from conflagration, the citizens from murder, Italy from war. 7. Juster honors than these were never paid[5] to the immortal gods. 8. Cicero was born of an equestrian family. 9. Who is more considerate than I? 10. These guards kept away from Cicero's house the men who had been sent by Catiline 11. We praise Pompey, than whom no one is more skilled in military matters. 12. That man ought to be deprived of life by you. 13. This sea, which was formerly full of dangers, is now free from pirates. 14. We remained here more than four years. 15. Shall those who have revolted from the republic, have the rights of citizens?

Suggestions on the Exercise.

1. *more money :* use the Genitive of the Whole.

2. *very courageous :* express by the superlative.

3. *express :* **dīcō, ere, dīxī, dictus.**

4. *of me :* use **ex** to denote source when the source is indicated by a pronoun.

5. *pay (honors) :* **habeō, ēre, uī, itus,** lit. *hold.*

LESSON XI.

THE ABLATIVE (continued).

GRAMMATICAL REFERENCES.

1. Ablative with the Deponents, *ūtor, fruor, etc.* 218. 1. A. & G. 410; H. 477. I.

2. Ablative with *opus est.* 218. 2; A. & G. 411 and *a*; H. 477. III.

3. Ablative with *nītor, innīxus, frētus.* 218. 3; A. & G. 431 and *a*; H. 476. 1, 3.

4. Ablative with Verbs of *Filling* and Adjectives of *Plenty* 218. 8; A. & G. 409. *a*; H. 477. II.

5. Ablative of Way by Which. 218. 9; A. & G. 429. *a*; H. 476.

6. Ablative of Cause. 219 entire; A. & G. 404; H. 475.

EXAMPLES.

1. eā lēnitāte senātus est ūsus, *the senate exercised this indulgence.* (**1**)

2. hāc eximiā fortūnā fruitur, *he enjoys this noteworthy fortune.* (**1**)

3. celeritāte opus est, *there is need of speed.* (**2**)

4. homō nōn grātiā nītitur, *the man does not depend on influence.* (**3**)

5. frētus hūmānitāte vestrā, *relying upon your kindness.* (**3**)

6. deus bonīs omnibus explēvit mundum, *God has filled the universe with all blessings.* (**4**)

7. forum armātīs mīlitibus refertum vīderat, *he had seen the Forum filled with armed soldiers.* (**4**)

8. Aurēliā Viā profectus est, *he set out by the Aurelian Way.* (**5**)

136

9. **ārdet dēsīderiō,** *he burns with longing.* (**6**)

10. **meō jussū conjūrātī per forum ductī sunt,** *at my bidding the conspirators were led through the Forum.* (**6**)

Remark.

1. Note that **ūtor** may take a second ablative (either noun or adjective) in the predicate relation, as **quō duce ūtēmur,** *whom shall we employ as leader?* **eō placidō ūtēris,** *you will find* (lit. *use*) *him tranquil.* The second ablative here bears the same relation to the first as a predicate accusative to the direct object.

VOCABULARY.

answer, **respōnsum, ī,** *n.*

at least, **saltem.**

consular, **cōnsulāris, e.**

depend on, **nītor, ī, nīxus** *or* **nīsus.**

find (good, bad, etc.), **ūtor, ī, ūsus,** *lit.* use.

game, **lūdus, ī,** *m.*

loyalty, **fidēs, eī,** *f.*

need, (there is) need, **opus (est)**

outrage, *verb,* **abūtor, ī, ūsus.**

overflow, **redundō,** 1.

patience, **patientia, ae,** *f.*

relying on, **frētus, a, um.**

support, **subsidium, ī,** *n.*

too, **nimium,** *adv.*

trusty, **fidēlis, e.**

wisdom, **sapientia, ae,** *f.*

EXERCISE.

1. We shall now find[1] these (men) better citizens.[1] 2. They will come to Rome by the Appian Way. 3. There will always be need of your advice and support. 4. The Senate depends on the loyalty and bravery of the people. 5. These men deserved to be feared (the) more by us on this account.[2] 6. That colony was fortified at my order. 7. All the Forum overflowed with the blood of citizens. 8. Cicero promised this, relying not on his own wisdom and counsels, but on the immortal gods alone. 9. I used the courageous and trusty assistance of these two praetors. 10. In consequence of their answers games were celebrated[3] during

ten days.   11. My voice at least has performed its consular duty.   12. Catiline has outraged the patience of
all of you too long.   13. Shall we never enjoy peace
and harmony ?

Suggestions on the Exercise.

1. *find :* see Remark 1.
2. *on this account :* translate : *on account of this* (neuter).
3. *celebrated :* use **faciō, ere, fēcī, factus.**

Cicero Serves in the Social War.

At the age of sixteen, Cicero came to Rome and spent
several months in the city.   He wished especially to hear
the great orators of that time, but the Social War [1] had
broken out, and the most famous of these orators, Hortensius, Rufus, and Antonius, [2] had taken arms and were
with the army.   Yet there were certain minor magistrates
to whose harangues he listened daily.   Before the end of
the war, Cicero himself also served, [3] first under Pompeius
Strabo, [4] later under Lucius Sulla. [4]

Suggestions on the Exercise.

1. *Social War :* **Bellum Sociāle.**
2. *Hortensius, Rufus, Antonius :* **Hortēnsius, Rūfus, Antōnius.**
3. *serve :* **stīpendia mereor** (ērī, itus), lit. *earn wages* (**stīpendia, ōrum,** n.).
4. *Strabo :* **Strābō, ōnis,** m.; *Sulla,* **Sulla, ae,** m.

LESSON XII.

THE ABLATIVE (*continued*).

GRAMMATICAL REFERENCES.

1. Ablative of Manner. 220 entire; A. & G. 412 and *a*; H. 473. 3 and N.

2. Ablative of Attendant Circumstance. 221.

3. Ablative of Accompaniment. 222; A. & G. 413 and *a*; H. 473. 1; 474. N. 1.

4. Ablative of Degree of Difference. 223; A. & G. 414; H. 479; *cf*. B. 357. 1; A. & G. 424. *f*; H. 488.

5. Ablative of Quality. 224; A. & G. 415; H. 473. 2 and N. 1.

6. Ablative of Price. 225 entire; A. & G. 416, 417 and *c*; H. 478.

EXAMPLES.

1. **aequō animō moriar,** *I shall die with calm spirit.* **(1)**

2. **ēgit causam summā cum gravitāte,** *he conducted the case with the greatest dignity.* **(1)**

3. **vetere prōverbiō,** *according to the old proverb.* **(1)**

4. **hīsce ōminibus, Catilīna, proficīscere,** *under these omens, Catiline, depart!* **(2)**

5. **lēgātī magnō comitātū pontem ingrediēbantur,** *the ambassadors with a large retinue were just setting foot on the bridge.* **(3)**

6. **cum exercitū accessit,** *he drew near with his army.* **(3)**

7. **ūnō diē longiōrem mēnsem faciunt,** *they make the month one day longer,* lit. *longer by one day.* **(4)**

8. **paucīs post diēbus,** *a few days afterwards.* **(4)**

9. **post quadriduum,** *four days afterwards.* **(4)**

10. **paucōs ante annōs,** *a few years before.* **(4)**

139

11. fuit īnfīrmō corpore, *he was of feeble body.*   (**5**)

12. hīc tribūnus plēbis erat audāciā singulārī, *this tribune of the people was of exceptional boldness.*   (**5**)

13. haec omnia signa sēstertium sex mīlibus vēndita sunt, *all these statues were sold for six thousand sesterces.*   (**6**)

14. hī agrī magnō vēneunt, *these lands are sold for a high price.*   (**6**)

15. multō plūris frūctūs Siciliae vēnīre potuērunt, *the harvests of Sicily might have been sold at a much higher price.*   (**6**)

Remarks.

1. The Ablative of Manner is best restricted to abstract words, such as **celeritās, dignitās, virtūs, prūdentia**, etc.

2. The Ablative of Accordance (see Example 3) appears also in such expressions as **meā sententiā, suīs mōribus, suā sponte**, etc.

3. The Ablative of Quality primarily designates qualities which are more or less transitory. The observation sometimes made that the genitive denotes *internal* qualities, and the ablative *external* ones, is not sufficiently exact. In the phrase **hortātur ut bonō animō sint**, *he urges them to be of good courage*, the quality is internal : yet the genitive could not here be used ; for while the quality is internal, it is transitory. The theoretical distinction between the Genitive of Quality and the Ablative of Quality is that the genitive denotes *permanent*, the ablative *transitory*, qualities. Yet where ambiguity would not result, the ablative may be used to denote a permanent quality. Thus one may say **vir summae virtūtis** or **summā virtūte**, *a man of the highest character.*

In all numerical designations of *weight, dimension*, etc., the genitive is used.

VOCABULARY.

arise, **surgō, ere, surrēxī, surrēctum.**

auspices, **auspicia, ōrum,** *n.*

buy, **emō, ere, ēmī, ēmptus.**

greed, **avāritia, ae,** *f.*

how high, at how high a price, **quantī.**

institution, **īnstitūtum, ī,** *n.*

overtake, **cōnsequor, ī, secūtus**

propose, **prōpōnō, ere, posuī, positus.**

provincials, **sociī, ōrum,** *m., lit.* allies.

uprightness, **probitās, ātis,** *f.*

wickedness, **scelus, eris,** *n.*

EXERCISE.

1. Was not this plan much more considerate than that which Caesar proposed?   2. Manlius will soon come against us with his army.   3. Gnaeus Pompey was of the greatest uprightness.   4. A little later we arose and went away.   5. We overtook your friends with the greatest speed.   6. We sold these lands for a little less than we bought (them).   7. We set out under the best auspices.   8. We shall defend the freedom of the Roman people according to the customs and institutions of our ancestors.   9. At how high a price did you buy this grain? I bought it at a very low price. 10. Three days before, the consul, with a great force,[1] had attacked the place which Catiline had chosen for a camp.   11. Verres plundered the provincials with incredible greed and wickedness.   12. You have, Quirites, a consul of the greatest steadfastness.

Suggestion on the Exercise.

1. *force:* use the plural, **cōpiae.**

LESSON XIII.

THE ABLATIVE (*continued*).

GRAMMATICAL REFERENCES.

1. Ablative of Specification. 226 entire; A. & G. 418; H. 480.

2. Ablative Absolute. 227. 1, 2; A. & G. 419 and *a*, 420; H. 489 and 1.

3. Ablative of Place Where. 228 entire; A. & G. 426. 3. 427. 3, 429. 1, 2; H. 483; 485. 2.

4. Ablative of Place from Which. 229 entire; A. & G. 426. 1, 427. 1, 428. *a*, *b*; H. 461, 462 and 3, 4.

EXAMPLES.

1. tū temporibus errāstī, *you made a mistake as to the time.* (**1**)

2. impudentiā, quā omnīs superābat, *shamelessness in which he surpassed all.* (**1**)

3. hominem majōrem nātū nōlēbās appellāre, *you were unwilling to address an older man*, lit. *a man greater as to birth.* (**1**)

4. tertiā ferē vigiliā exāctā, *when the third watch was almost finished.* (**2**)

5. hōc ūnō interfectō, intellegō hanc reī pūblicae pestem paulisper reprimī, *if this man alone is put to death, I realize that this disease of the commonwealth can be checked for a little.* (**2**)

6. Lepidō et Tullō cōnsulibus, *in the consulship of Lepidus and Tullus.* (**2**)

7. num dubitās id mē imperante facere, *do you hesitate to do that at my command ?* (**2**)

8. in urbe, *in the city.* (**3**)

9. in Graeciā, *in Greece.* (**3**)

10. Athēnīs, *at Athens.* (**3**)

11. hīs locīs, *in these places.* (**3**)

12. tōtā prōvinciā, *in the whole province.* (**3**)

13. ē prōvinciā rediit, *he returned from his province.* (**4**)

14. dēcēdēns ex Asiā, *departing from Asia.* (**4**)

15. domō fugientēs, *fleeing from home.* (**4**)

16. Teānum abest ā Lārīnō xviii mīlia passuum, *Teanum is eighteen miles distant from Larinum.* (**4**)

17. ā Brundisiō, *from the neighborhood of Brundisium.* (**4**)

18. Tusculō, clārissimō ex mūnicipiō, *from Tusculum, a famous municipal town.* (**4**)

VOCABULARY.

defeat, **superō**, 1.

depart, **dēcēdō, ere, cessī, cessūrus.**

enter upon, **ineō, īre, iī, itus.**

establish, **collocō**, 1.

form, make, **faciō, ere, fēcī, factus.**

hand over, **trādō, ere, trādidī, ditus.**

hatred, **odium,** *i, n.*

seal, **signum, ī,** *n.*

station, **collocō**, 1.

strong, **validus, a, um.**

surpass, **superō**, 1.

unbroken, **integer, gra, grum.**

worthy, **dignus, a, um.**

EXERCISE.

1. All the leading men whose murder Catiline was plotting have departed from Rome.   **2.** Have you seen the camp which has been established in Italy against the Roman people ?   **3.** Those who formed this conspiracy are worthy of the greatest hatred.   **4.** You almost surpass me in zeal.   **5.** With the gods as leaders[1] I entered upon this hope and purpose.   **6.** When all the forces of the enemy had been defeated[2] on land and sea, in the consulship of Cicero and Antonius, Catiline formed a conspiracy.   **7.** These letters were handed over to me with their seals unbroken.[3]   8. How many miles distant from Rome is Faesulae ?   9. He has already been at Faesulae, where he saw Manlius.   10. Three days later he went away from home.   11. Strong guards have been stationed in many places by us.   12. When will you set out from Italy ?

Suggestions on the Exercise.

1. *with the gods as leaders :* translate : *the gods (being) leaders.*

2. *when the forces had been defeated :* translate by the Ablative Absolute.

3. *with their seals unbroken :* translate by the Ablative Absolute.

Cicero's Oratorical and Philosophical Studies.

After the social war was finished,[1] Cicero returned to Rome and there devoted himself to the study of oratory[2] under the Rhodian[3] rhetorician,[4] Molo,[5] who was then staying[6] in the City.   Philosophy[7] he pursued[8] under Philo,[9] who had fled to Rome from the dangers of the Mithridatic War, and later under Diodotus.[9]   The latter lived for many years at Cicero's house[10] and died there at last in the consulship of Caesar and Bibulus, leaving Cicero as his only heir.

Suggestions on the Exercise.

1. *finish :* cōnficiō, ere, fēcī, fectus.

2. *oratory :* ars ōrātōria, artis ōrātōriae, f.

3. *Rhodian :* Rhodius, a, um.

4. *rhetorician :* rhētor, ŏris, m.

5. *Molo :* Molō, ōnis, m.

6. *stay :* moror, 1.

7. *philosophy .* philosophia, ae, f.

8. *pursue :* studeō, ēre, uī, with dat.

9. *Philo, Diodotus :* Philō, ōnis, m.; Diodotus, ī, m.

10. *at :* in, with the abl.

LESSON XIV.

THE ABLATIVE (*continued*).

GRAMMATICAL REFERENCES.

1. The Locative Case. 232. 1, 2; 169. 4; A. & G. 427. 3 and *a*; 282. *d*; H. 483; 484. 1, 2; 483. 2.

2. Ablative of Time at Which. 230. 1–3; A. & G. 423 and 1; H. 486.

3. Ablative of Time within Which. 231; A. & G. 423, 424. *a*; H. 487 and 1.

4. Roman Dates. 371, 372; A. & G. 631; H. 754; 755.

EXAMPLES.

1. Rōmae, *at Rome.* (**1**)

2. Corinthī, *at Corinth.* (**1**)

3. Rhodī, *at Rhodes.* (**1**)

4. domī, *at home.* (**1**)

5. humī, *on the ground.* (**1**)

6. Antiochīae, celebrī quondam urbe, *at Antioch, once a famous city.* (**1**)

7. Albae, in urbe opportūnā, *at Alba, a convenient city.* (**1**)

8. Nōnis Februāriīs Rōmae fuit, *he was at Rome on the Nones of February.* (**2, 4**)

9. hās ōrātiōnēs Lūdīs scrīpsī, *I wrote these speeches at the time of the Games.* (**2**)

10. Lūcullī adventū cōpiae Mithridātis fuērunt maximae, *at the arrival of Lucullus the forces of Mithridates were very great.* (**2**)

11. in bellō, *in time of war.* (**2**)

12. prīmō bellō Pūnicō, *in the First Punic War.* (**2**)

13. tribus hōrīs nūntiī vēnērunt, *the messengers came within three hours.* (**3**)

145

14. Rōscius multīs annīs Rōmam nōn vēnit, *in many years Ros-cius did not come to Rome.*   (**3**)

15. bis in diē, *twice a day.*   (**3**)

16. quadriduō mors Rōscī Chrȳsogonō nūntiātur, *within four days Roscius's death was reported to Chrysogonus.*   (**3**)

17. ante diem octāvum Īdūs Novembrēs, *on the 6th of November,* lit. *on the eighth day before the Ides* (strictly the seventh day before the Ides, which were the 13th).   (**4**)

Remarks

1. Observe that words not primarily denoting a period of time, as pāx, *peace,* bellum, *war,* commonly require the preposition in to denote time *at which,* unless they are accompanied by a modifier (adjective, demonstrative, or genitive). Thus, in bellō, *in war,* but prīmō bellō Pūnicō, *in the First Punic War.*

2. In bellō, *in war,* is to be distinguished in meaning and use from bellī. The former phrase is essentially *temporal* in meaning, — *in time of war,* while bellī is rather *local,* and means *in the field;* it occurs almost exclusively in combination with domī, *at home,* as domī bellīque, *at home and in the field.*

3. To denote time *within which, in the course of which,* the prepo-sition in is almost invariably employed when the clause contains a distributive numeral (bis, bīnī; ter, ternī) or saepe.

4. Bīduō, trīduō, quadriduō, and bienniō, trienniō, quadrienniō, are regularly used instead of duōbus diēbus, duōbus annīs, etc Compare Lesson VII, Remark 4.

VOCABULARY.

ancient, antīquus, a, um.

arrive, adveniō, īre, vēnī, ven-tum.

commit, committō, ere, mīsī, missus.

crime, scelus, eris, *n.*

departure, discessus, ūs, *m.*

exhaust, cōnficiō, ere, fēcī, fectus.

happen, fīō, fīerī, factus.

last, most recent, proximus, a, um.

March, of March, Mārtius, a, um.

Nones, Nōnae, ārum, *f.*

set up, collocō, 1.

short, brevis, e.

statue, signum, ī, *n.*

three times, ter, *adv.*

EXERCISE.

1. This statue was set up at that time.　**2.** In a short time you will be exhausted by these labors.　**3.** These things[1] happened on the 31st of December.　**4.** On the departure of my friends, I returned home.　**5.** At home I found these letters, which had arrived on the 2d of March.　**6.** Within three days, on March 10, I set out from the city, and returned on the 24th.　**7.** No crime has been committed at Rome within six months. **8.** Three times a month I sent him[2] letters.　**9.** At the last election you almost killed me with your dagger. **10.** These men assembled last night at your home.[3]　**11.** I said these things in the Senate, April 5.　**12.** At that time he was at Tusculum, a very ancient town.

Suggestions on the Exercise.

1. *these things :* haec.

2. *him :* see Lesson VI, Remark 3.

3. *at your home :* translate as though *to your home*

LESSON XV.

SYNTAX OF ADJECTIVES AND PRONOUNS.

GRAMMATICAL REFERENCES.

1. Adjectives used Substantively. 236–238; A. & G. 288 and *a, b*; 289. *a, b*; H. 494, 495.

2. Adjectives with the Force of Adverbs. 239; A. & G. 290; H. 497 and 1.

3 Special Uses of the Comparative and Superlative. 240. 1–4; A. & G. 291. *a, b*; 292; H. 498; 499.

4. Adjectives denoting a Special Part of an Object. 241. 1; A. & G. 293; H. 497. 4.

5. Prīmus = *first who;* ultimus = *last who;* etc. 241. 2; A. & G. 290; H. 497. 3.

6. Personal Pronouns. 242. 1, 2, 4; A. & G. 295. *a, b*; H. 500 and 4.

7. Reflexive Pronouns. 244 entire; A. & G. 299 and *a*, 300. 1, 2, 301. *a, b*; H. 503 and 3, 4; 504.

8. Reciprocal Pronouns. 245; A. & G. 301. *f*; H. 502. 1.

9. *Hīc, Ille, Iste.* 246. 1–5; A. & G. 297. *a–c*; 296. *a*; H. 505 and 1; 506. 1; 507 and 3, 4.

EXAMPLES.

1. sēcēdant improbī, sēcernant sē ā bonīs, *let the bad withdraw, let them separate themselves from the good.* **(1)**

2. omnēs stultī, *all the foolish.* **(1)**

3. omnia, *all things.*[1] **(1)**

4. nihil novī, *nothing new.*[2] **(1)**

5. maestus rediit, *he returned sadly.* **(2)**

6. **nēmō** in scaenā levior et **nēquior**, *no one on the stage more trifling and worthless* (*than usual*). (**3**)

7. **hūjus** domus est vel optima, *his home is the very best.* (**3**)

8. in **hāc īnsulā** extremā est fōns, *at the farthest part of this island is a fountain.* (**4**)

9. **quī** mihi prīmus fidem porrēxit, *who was the first to extend help to me.* (**5**)

10. **quis vestrum,** *who of you?* (**6**)

11. **dux** memor **vestrī,** *a leader mindful of you.* (**6**)

12. **fortūna** omnium **nostrum,** *the fortunes of us all.* (**6**)

13. **puerōs** mīsit quī haec **uxōrī suae**[3] nūntiārent, *he sent slaves to announce these things to his wife.* (**7**)

14. **contrōversiās** inter **sē** habuērunt, *they had disputes with one another.* (**8**)

15. **nōn** est ista[4] mea culpa, *that is not my fault.* (**9**)

16. **haec** fuērunt maxima in illō, in **hōc nūlla,** *these* (*defects*) *were very great in the former, non-existent in the latter.* (**9**\

Notes on the Examples.

1. In other cases than the nominative and accusative this idea is best expressed by means of **rēs**, *e.g.* **omnium rērum,** *of all things;* **omnibus rēbus,** *by all things.* **Omnium, omnibus, parvōrum, parvīs,** and similar forms would be ambiguous in gender.

2. Lit. *nothing of new,* — Genitive of the Whole.

3. **Suae** illustrates the use of the indirect reflexive.

4. **Ista** is here attracted from **istud** to the gender of the predicate noun ; such attraction of the pronoun is the rule in Latin.

Remarks.

1. **Suī** is regularly employed like **meī** and **tuī** as an Objective Genitive. To indicate the whole of which a part is taken, the Latin may use either **ex sē, ex suīs,** or **suōrum,** *e.g.* **multōs ex sē** or **multōs suōrum mīsērunt,** *they sent many of their own number.*

2. Observe that in such expressions as **inter sē amant,** *they love each other,* no direct object is expressed.

VOCABULARY.

discover, **comperiō, īre, comperī, compertus.**

distinguished, **clārus, a, um.**

end of, last part of, **extrēmus, a, um,** *limiting a noun.*

former . . . (latter), **ille, a, ud.**

glad, **laetus, a, um.**

latter (of two), **hīc, haec, hōc.**

meet, encounter, **oppetō, ere, īvī, ītus.**

one another, *use the proper reflexive pronoun.*

philosopher, **sapiēns, entis,** *m.*

unwilling, **invītus, a, um.**

EXERCISE.

1. Philosophers have never met death unwillingly.
2. Catiline did not lead forth all his (followers) with him. 3. There is authority in the Senate and harmony among all the good. 4. Many very distinguished men of the state had gathered in great numbers on this day. 5. We gladly suffered many things for your sake. 6. Whom of us all have you spared? 7. Cicero sent these letters April 2 from Greece to his dearest friends. 8. That was not my opinion. 9. We shall visit these enemies of the good with the very severest punishments. 10. He withdrew from his province at the end of the winter. 11. I was the first to discover all these things. 12. These witnesses were conferring with one another. 13. The former letter did not arrive; the latter I have lost.

Cicero's Legal Studies.

Cicero learned civil law from Quintus Mucius Scaevola,[1] the augur,[2] the most distinguished lawyer[3] of that time. Cicero himself uses the following[4] words concerning him: "As soon as I put on[5] the dress of manhood,[6] my father conducted me to Scaevola, and forbade me ever to withdraw from his side. Accordingly I committed[7]

to memory his discourses[8] and wise[9] sayings[10] and en·
joyed his wisdom." After his death, Cicero attended
(on) another Scaevola, the pontifex maximus,[11] whom he
calls the most eminent in talent of the Roman state.

Suggestions on the Exercise.

1. *Mucius Scaevola :* **Mūcius Scaevola ; Mūcī Scaevolae, m.**

2. *augur :* **augur, uris,** m.

3. *lawyer :* **jūris cōnsultus, ī,** m., lit. *versed in the law.*

4. *following :* use **hīc.**

5. *put on :* **sūmō, ere, sūmpsī, sūmptus.**

6. *dress of manhood :* **toga virīlis, togae virīlis,** f., lit. *toga of manhood.*

7. *commit :* **mandō,** 1.

8. *discourse :* **sermō, ōnis,** m.

9. *wise :* **sapiēns, entis.**

10. *saying :* **dictum, ī,** n.

11. *pontifex maximus :* **pontifex (-icis) maximus, m.**

REVIEW.

1. These tribes were driven out from their lands on
account of dissensions.   **2.** Our men were frightened
by the great multitude of these ships.   **3.** We shall
hurl our javelins into the midst of the camp.   **4.** He
came from Athens to Geneva, March 9.   **5.** After these
letters had been read aloud,[1] we consulted with each
other.[2]   **6.** Who is more eminent than he in nobility,[3]
or rank, or honor ?   **7.** We were of much better cour·
age after your arrival.   **8.** We sold our house for more
than we bought (it at).   **9.** Did you gain possession of
the swords and daggers which Gabinius left at his house ?
10. By our labors we have delivered the republic from
the very greatest dangers.   **11.** He has forgotten all

those things.　　12.　Did you come at once to his aid ?[4]
13. We must contend[5] with the greatest bravery and
resist these enemies[6] of the state.

Suggestions on the Exercise.

1. *after these letters had been read aloud :* express by the Ablative Absolute.

2. *with each other :* the reflexive must be that for the *first* person.

3. *nobility :* nōbilitās, ātis, f.

4. *to his aid :* translate : *to him for aid :* see Lesson VII.
Example 8.

5. *we must contend :* see Lesson VII, Example 3.

6. *resist these enemies :* Lesson VII, Remark 1.

LESSON XVI.

PRONOUNS (*continued*).

GRAMMATICAL REFERENCES.

1. Is. 247. 1–4; A. & G. 297. *d*; H. 508 and 1, 2, 4.

2. Idem. 248. 1, 2; A. & G. 298. *b*; 384. N. 2; H. 508. 3, 5

3. Ipse. 249. 1, 2; A. & G. 298. *c* and N. 1, *f*; H. 509. 1, 3.

4. Quis, Aliquis. 252. 1, 2; A. & G. 310; 311; H. 512 and 1

5. Quisquam. 252. 4; A. & G. 312; H. 513.

6. Quisque. 252. 5; A. & G. 313 and *a*; H. 515.

7. Alius, Alter. 253. 1–3; A. & G. 315 and *c*; H. 516 and 1.

8. Uterque. 355. 2; A. & G. 313; H. 516. 4.

EXAMPLES.

1. sī nōs, id quod dēbet, nostra patria dēlectat, *if our country pleases us, a thing which it ought.*

2. flēbat pater dē fīlī morte, dē patris fīlius, *the father was weeping over the impending death of his son; the son over (that) of the father.* (**1**)

3. exempla quaerimus et ea nōn antīqua, *we are seeking precedents, and those not ancient.* (**1**)

4. dīcēbant idem quod[1] ego, *they were saying the same thing as I.* (**2**)

5. ā multīs ipsa virtūs contemnitur, *by many even Virtue is scorned.* (**3**)

6. ipsae dēfluēbant corōnae, *the garlands fell down of their own accord.* (**3**)

7. Vēritās sē ipsa dēfendit, *Truth defends itself.* (**3**)

8. sī quī exīre volunt, possum cōnīvēre, *if any wish to go forth, I can shut my eyes to it.* (**4**)

9. aliquis dīcet, *some one will say.* (**4**)

10. nōn eguit cōnsiliō cūjusquam, *he did not need the advice of any one.* (**5**)

11. neque quicquam est optātius, *nor is anything more desirable.* (**5**)

12. pecūnia semper ā clārissimō quōque contempta est, *money has ever been despised by all the most distinguished men,* lit. *by each most distinguished man.* (**6**)

13 tertiō quōque verbō, *at every other word.* (**6**)

14. tribūnum aliī gladiis adoriuntur, aliī fūstibus, *some attack the tribune with swords, others with clubs.* (**7**)

15. alter absolūtus est, alter sē ipse condemnāvit, *the one was acquitted, the other condemned himself.* (**7**)

16. alius in aliā rē est magis ūtilis, *one person is more useful in one thing, another in another.* (**7**)

17. quōs ego utrōsque in eōdem genere praedātōrum pōnō, *both of whom* (i.e. *both groups*) *I place in the same class of plunderers.* (**8**)

18. uterque hōrum, *both of these.* (**8**)

Note on the Examples.

1. The English 'same as' is regularly expressed in Latin by **īdem quī**, less frequently by **īdem ac (atque)**.

Remark.

1. **Aliquis,** as well as **quisquam,** is used in negative sentences, though much less frequently, and with its regular force of *some one.* Thus nōn eget cōnsiliō alicūjus means : *he does not need the advice of some one, i.e.* some individual. This sentence is the negation of **eget cōnsiliō alicūjus,** *he needs the advice of some individual.* **Nōn eget cōnsiliō cūjusquam,** on the other hand, constitutes a more general denial, — *he does not need the advice of anybody (at all).*

VOCABULARY.

all the best, *the superlative with* quisque.

deny, **negō**, 1.

encourage, **cōnfīrmō**, 1.

fault, **culpa, ae,** *f.*

found, **condō, ere, condidī, itus.**

hope, **spērō**, 1.

lead, lead on, **dūcō, ere, dūxī, ductus.**

oration, **ōrātiō, ōnis,** *f.*

prepare, **parō**, 1.

read, **legō, ere, lēgī, lēctus.**

wall, of a house, **pariēs, etis** *m.*

wealth, **dīvitiae, ārum,** *f.*

well, **bene.**

EXERCISE.

1. Murder and conflagration are being prepared for this city and that, too, through citizens. 2. There were two opinions, the one of Silanus, the other of Caesar. 3. The temple of Jupiter, the Stayer, was founded at the same time as Rome itself. 4. We saw the letters which had been written by each one. 5. Both of us heard the same things as you. 6. To some he promised wealth, to others power. 7. All the best men have ever been led on by love of glory. 8. This camp has been well fortified, that which we hoped. 9. Does any one of those who are present deny these things? 10. Some have feared you, Caesar, but that is not your fault. 11. The very walls of houses do not confine the voices of your conspiracy. 12. I read no orations except (those) of Cicero. 13. Pompey's mere arrival encouraged the provincials.

LESSON XVII.

TENSES OF THE INDICATIVE.—SUBJUNCTIVE IN INDE-PENDENT SENTENCES.

GRAMMATICAL REFERENCES.

1. The Present. 259. 1–4; A. & G. 465, 466, 467, 469; H. 532 and 1, 2, 3; 533. 1; 530.

2. The Imperfect. 260. 1–4; A. & G. 470, 471. *a–c*; H. 534 and 1, 2, 3; 535. 1; 530.

3. The Future. 261. 1, 2; A. & G. 472 and *b*; H. 536.

4. The Perfect. 262. *A* and *B*; A. & G. 473, 476; H. 537. 1, 2, 538. 4.

5. The Pluperfect. 263; A. & G. 477; H. 539.

6. The Future Perfect. 264 and *a*; A. & G. 478; H. 540 and 2.

7. Hortatory Subjunctive. 274; A. & G. 439; H. 559. 1.

8. Jussive Subjunctive. 275; A. & G. 439; H. 559. 2.

9. Prohibitions. 276 and *b*; A. & G. 450; H. 561. 1, 2.

10. Deliberative Subjunctive. 277 and *a*; A. & G. 444; H. 559. 4.

EXAMPLES.

1. tē jam dūdum hortor, *I have long been urging you.* (**1**)

2. aliīs mortem parentum pollicēbātur, *to others he used to promise the death of parents.* (**2**)

3. ībis quō tē jam prīdem ista tua cupiditās rapiēbat, *you will go whither your desire had long been hurrying you.* (**2**)

4. num dubitās id facere quod jam faciēbās, *do you hesitate to do that which you were already doing ?* (**2**)

5. multās C. Caesaris virtūtēs cognōvī, *I am acquainted with many virtues of Gaius Caesar.* (**4**)

156

6. **quem ad modum cōnsuēvērunt,** *as they are accustomed.* (**4**)

7. **omnia nōrat,** *he knew all things.* (**5**)

8. **amēmus patriam, pāreāmus senātuī,** *let us love our country, let us obey the Senate.* (**7**)

9. **nē difficilia optēmus,** *let us not wish for what is difficult.* (**7**)

10. **dēsinant furere ac prōscrīptiōnēs et dictātūrās cōgitāre,** *let them cease to rage and think of proscriptions and dictatorships.* (**8**)

11. **nē attingant rem pūblicam,** *let them not touch the state!* (**9**)

12. **nōlī haec putāre,** *do not think this!* (**9**)

13. **quid faciās,** *what are you to do?* (**10**)

14. **quid facerēs,** *what were you to do?* (**10**)

15. **cūr C. Cornēlium nōn dēfenderem,** *why was I not to defend Gaius Cornelius?* (**10**)

VOCABULARY.

advantage, **ūtilitās, ātis,** *f.*

air, **spīritus, ūs,** *m.,* *lit.* breath.

consideration, **ratiō, ōnis,** *f.*

courage, **fortitūdō, inis,** *f.*

go out, **exeō, īre, iī, itūrus.**

leave, **relinquō, ere, līquī, lictus.**

live, **vīvō, ere, vīxī, vīctūrus.**

long, **diū** ; (already) for a long time, **jam diū** *or* **jam prīdem.**

loyal, **fidēlis, e.**

military, **mīlitāris, e.**

neglect, **neglegō, ere, lēxī, lēctus.**

pass over, **omittō, ere, mīsī, missus.**

picked, **dēlēctus, a, um.**

prevail over, **vincō, ere, vīcī, victus.**

standard, **signum, ī,** *n.*

EXERCISE.

1. Why should I pass over these loyal Roman knights? 2. Let the advantage of the republic prevail over all considerations of my safety. 3. For a long time, O senators,[1] you have been living among these dangers and plots. 4. Why should these men enjoy life and this common air for one hour? 5. Do not spare me. 6. He used to have picked men for[2] all labors. 7. Let him go out; let him set forth; let him not leave Manlius

alone in his camp at Faesulae! 8. Are we to neglect the lives[3] of our (fellow-) citizens on account of fear of dangers? 9. Those who had fought against the pirates knew Pompey's courage and uprightness. 10. Catiline had for a long time been preparing troops, weapons, and military standards 11 Whom are we to choose as leader? 12. You kept asking him his opinion.

Suggestions on the Exercise.

1. *O senators :* in the vocative, the Latin uses **patrēs cōnscrīptī.**
2. *for :* ad.
3. *lives :* the Latin uses the singular.

Cicero's First Oration.

For several years Cicero was devoted to these studies of his profession.[1] He was present constantly in the courts and listened to the most distinguished advocates.[2] (When) about twenty-five years old, he began to conduct[3] cases himself at Rome. His first oration was delivered in behalf of a certain Publius Quinctius, whose brother had died, leaving him (as) his heir. In this case, Cicero spoke against Hortensius, the most eminent orator of that time, and was in great fear on account of the latter's reputation.

Suggestions on the Exercise.

1. *profession :* ars, artis, f
2. *advocate :* ōrātor, ōris, m.
3. *conduct :* agō, ere, ēgī, āctus.

LESSON XVIII.

INDEPENDENT SUBJUNCTIVE (*continued*). — PURPOSE
CLAUSES.

GRAMMATICAL REFERENCES.

1. The Optative Subjunctive. 279. 1, 2; A. & G. 441, 442
H. 558 and 1, 2.

2. The Potential Subjunctive. 280. 1, 2, 3; A. & G. 446
447. 1–3; H. 552, 555.

3. The Imperative. 281 and 1; A. & G. 448, 449; H. 560
and 4.

4. Purpose Clauses with *ut, nē, quō*. 282. 1. *a–e*; A. & G.
531. 1 and *a*; H. 568 and 7.

5. Relative Clauses of Purpose. 282. 2; A. & G. 531. 2;
H. 590.

6. Relative Clauses with *dignus, indignus, idōneus*. 282. 3;
A. & G. 535. *f*; H. 591 7.

7. Sequence of Tenses. 267. 1–3; 268. 1, 3; A. & G. 482.
1, 2, 483, 485. *a, e*; H. 543–546.

EXAMPLES.

1. quod dī ōmen āvertant, *may the gods avert this omen!* **(1)**

2. utinam rēs pūblica stetisset, *would that the republic had
stood!* **(1)**

3. utinam Quirītēs, virōrum fortium cōpiam tantam habērētis,
*would, O Romans, that you had so great an abundance
of brave men!* **(1)**

4. dīxerit aliquis, *some one may say.* **(2)**

5. vix vērīsimile videātur, *it would hardly seem likely.* **(2)**

6. hōc sine ūllā dubitātiōne cōnfīrmāverim, *this I should affirm
without any hesitation.* **(2)**

7. in exsilium proficīscere, *go forth into exile.* **(3)**

8. rem vōbīs prōpōnam : vōs eam penditōte, *I will lay the matter before you : do you consider it.* **(3)**

9. cōnsulēs summum jūs habentō, *let the consuls have supreme power.* **(3)**

10. Lentulus in ea loca missus est, ut prīvātōs agrōs coëmeret, *Lentulus was sent to those places to purchase private lands.* **(4)**

11. pecūniam dedit nē condemnārētur, *he gave money that he might not be condemned.* **(4)**

12. ūnum annum ēligam quō facilius explicāre possim, *I will select one year that I may be able to explain more easily.* **(4)**

13. illum dēlēgistis quem bellō praepōnerētis, *you chose him to put in charge of the war.* **(5)**

14. dignī sunt quī cīvitāte dōnentur, *they are worthy to be presented with citizenship.* **(6)**

Remarks.

1. Note that the Latin uses nē quis, *in order that no one;* nē quid, *in order that nothing;* nē ūllus, nē quī, *in order that no.*

2. Observe the occasional use of purpose clauses, as in English, to denote the purpose with which a statement is made, as, nē timeās, incolumis est, *that you may have no fears,* (*I will say*) *he is safe.*

VOCABULARY.

absent, be absent, absum, esse, āfuī, āfutūrus.

briefly, breviter.

change, mūtō, 1.

diligence, dīligentia, ae, *f.*

extinguish, exstinguō, ere, īnxī, īnctus.

harm, dētrīmentum, ī, *n.*

set forth, *trans.*, expōnō, ere, posuī, positus.

vote, sententia, ae, *f.*

wound, vulnus, eris, *n.*

EXERCISE.

1. I sent the praetor to the house of Cethegus to find the swords and daggers. 2. Would that we had not returned to the City ! 3. May the immortal gods change

that [1] purpose of yours.   4. Some senators were absent on that day, in order that they might not cast their votes [2] concerning the punishment of the conspirators. 5. Would that all the leading men whom we have lost were now living!   6. No one would defend this man better than you.   7. Are those men worthy to enjoy our friendship?   8. He gave the ambassadors these letters that they might have more confidence.   9. I will set forth these things briefly that you may know them.   10 We received severe wounds in order that the republic might suffer no harm. [3]   11. You found faithful friends to deliver you from that fear.   12. Guard your homes with the greatest diligence!   13. Not to say more, [4] all these dissensions have been extinguished.

Suggestions on the Exercise.

1. *that of yours :* **iste.**

2 *cast a vote :* **sententiam ferō (ferre, tulī, lātus),** lit. *bear a vote.*

3. *that the republic might suffer no harm :* the Latin idiom is *lest the republic take anything of harm.*

4 *not to say more :* translate : *lest I say more (things).*

LESSON XIX.

CLAUSES OF CHARACTERISTIC. — CLAUSES OF RESULT.

GRAMMATICAL REFERENCES.

1. Simple Clauses of Characteristic. 283. 1, 2; A. & G. 535 and *a, b*; H. 591. 1, 5.

2. Clauses of Characteristic denoting Cause (*since*) or Opposition (*though*). 283. 3; A. & G. 535. *e*; H. 592 and 1; 593. 2.

3. Clauses of Characteristic introduced by *quīn*. 283. 4; A. & G. 559. 2; H. 594. II. 2, end, 595. 4.

4. Idiomatic Expressions. 283. **5**; A. & G. 535. *d*; H. 591. 3.

5. Clauses of Result introduced by *ut* and *ut nōn*. 284. 1; A. & G. 537 and 1; H. 570. — For Sequence of Tenses in Result Clauses, see 268. 6; A. & G. 485. *c*; H. 550.

6. Relative Clauses of Result. 284. 2; A. & G. 537. 2; H. 591. 2.

7. Result Clauses introduced by *quīn*. 284. 3; A. & G. 559. 1; H. 594. II.

EXAMPLES.

1. multī inventī sunt, quī summum malum dolōrem dīcerent, *many have been found who declared pain the greatest ill.* (**1**)
2. sapientia est ūna quae maestitiam pellat, *philosophy is the only thing that dispels sorrow.* (**1**)
3. quid est enim quod tē dēlectāre possit, *for what is there that can delight you ?* (**1**)
4. ō magna vīs vēritātis quae sē ipsa dēfendat, *oh the mighty power of truth, since it defends itself!* (**2**)
5. nēmō est quīn intellegat, *there is no one who does not know.* (**3**)
6. Epicūrus sē ūnus, quod sciam, sapientem professus est, *Epicurus alone, so far as I know, set up for a philosopher.* (**4**)

162

7. sīc enim tēcum loquar ut nōn odiō permōtus esse videar, *for 1 will so speak with you as not to seem to be moved by hatred.* (**5**)

8. nēmō tam improbus erit quī id nōn jūre factum esse fateātur, *there will be no one so wicked as not to admit it was done justly.* (**6**)

9. nēmō erit tam injūstus quīn dē meīs praemiīs putet, *no one will be so unjust as not to think of my rewards.* (**7**)

VOCABULARY.

crush, **opprimō, ere, pressī, pressus.**
deed, **factum, ī,** *n.*
foolish, **stultus, a, um.**
immediately, **statim.**
manage, **administrō, 1.**

plan, **cōgitō, 1.**
present, be present, **adsum, esse, adfuī, adfutūrus.**
prestige, **auctōritās, ātis,** *f.*
threaten, **immineō, ēre.**

EXERCISE.

1. There was no time at which I did not think of[1] the freedom of the Roman people. 2. I so managed matters that you were all preserved. 3. There was no one in the whole province who did not know these things. 4. For four years there was no crime which Catiline had not planned. 5. The conspirators did nothing which was not immediately announced to the consul. 6. Who is there who forgets the brave deeds of our fathers? 7. There was so great prestige in the Senate and so great harmony among all good citizens that this conspiracy was crushed. 8. There are some in this council who do not see the dangers which threaten us. 9. So far as I know, there is no one present who is not loyal. 10. No one is so foolish as not to see this conspiracy. 11. Who was there who defended you? 12. You assembled in so great numbers that I easily saw your zeal.

Suggestion on the Exercise.

1. *of:* dē.

Cicero's Defence of Roscius.

In the following year Cicero undertook a case by the defence[1] of which he won[2] the greatest glory. During[3] the dictatorship[4] of Sulla murders had occurred almost daily at Rome. Some had been killed by the order of the dictator, that he might take vengeance on his enemies; others were killed by those who wished to avenge personal[5] wrongs. Among these (last) was a certain Sextus Roscius, a wealthy citizen of Ameria,[6] who had been murdered by hostile neighbors.

Suggestions on the Exercise.

1. *defence:* dēfēnsiō, ōnis, f.
2. *win:* adipīscor, ī, adeptus.
3. *during:* **per**, prep. with acc.
4. *dictatorship:* dictātūra, ae, f.
5. *personal:* **proprius, a, um.**
6. *of Ameria:* use the adj.. **Amerīnus, a, um.**

LESSON XX.

CAUSAL CLAUSES. — TEMPORAL CLAUSES.

GRAMMATICAL REFERENCES.

1. **Causal Clauses.** 286. 1 and *b*; 286. 2; A. & G. 540. 1, 2; 549; H. 588. I, II, and 2; 598.

2. **Temporal Clauses** introduced by *postquam, ut, etc.,* denoting a single act. 287. 1; A. & G. 543; H. 602.

3. Clauses introduced by *ut, ubi, simul ac,* denoting a repeated act. 287. 2; H. 602. 2.

4. Pluperfect Indicative with *postquam.* 287. 3; H. 602. 1.

EXAMPLES.

1. **Gallia laudētur, quod sē nōn trādidit,**[1] *let Gaul be praised because it did not surrender.* (**1**)

2. **laudātur prōvincia quod resistat**[2] **Antōniō,** *the province is praised because it resists Antony.* (**1**)

3. **quae cum ita sint,** *since these things are so.* (**1**)

4. **mĕ accūsās nōn quod tuīs ratiōnibus nōn assentiar, sed quod nūllīs,** *you accuse me, not because I do not agree with your arguments, but because (I agree) with none.* (**1**)

5. **postquam ea diēs vēnit, incipit simulāre,** *after that day came, he began to pretend.* (**2**)

6. **ut Rōmam rediit, praetor factus est,** *when he returned to Rome, he was made praetor.* (**2**)

7. **quod ubi Verrēs audīvit, cupiditāte īnflammātus est,** *when Verres heard that, he was kindled with desire.* (**2**)

8. **simul ac tē aspexī, hōc sēnsī,** *as soon as I set eyes on you, I observed this* (**2**)

. post diem tertium gesta rés est, quam hōc dīxerat,[3] *the deed was done three days after he had said this.* (4)

Notes on the Examples.

1 The speaker's own reason, — hence the indicative.

2. Not the reason of the writer, but of those who bestow the praise, — hence the subjunctive

3. Note the pluperfect indicative after a phrase denoting a definite interval of time (post diem tertium)

VOCABULARY.

accomplice, socius, ī, *m.*

affect, afficiō, ere, fēcī, fectus.

between, inter, *prep. with acc.*

bring into, intrōdūcō, ere, dūxī, ductus.

distress, dolor, ōris, *m.*

guard, be on one's guard against, caveō, ēre, cāvī, cautūrus, *trans.*

inasmuch as, quoniam.

intervene, intersum, esse, fuī, futūrus.

let go, ēmittō, ere, mīsī, missus.

(longer), no longer, jam nōn, *lit.* already not.

receive, accipiō, ere, cēpī, ceptus

recognize, cognōscō, ere, nōvī, nitus.

render (thanks), agō, ere, ēgī, āctus.

since, *causal,* cum.

thanks, grātiae, ārum, *f.*

wall, mūrus, ī, *m.*

EXERCISE.

1. He is affected with great distress because he did not kill us all. 2. As soon as he perceived this, he returned to Rome. 3. Some accused Cicero because he had let Catiline go and had not arrested him. 4. Because a wall intervenes between us and Catiline, I no longer fear him. 5. When I came to Geneva, I found there the letters which you had sent me. 6. Since he had left his accomplices at Rome, I was always on my guard against them 7. After the conspirators were arrested, they were brought into the Senate. 8. Inasmuch as you have not yet heard the decree of the Senate, I will set it forth to you. 9. As soon as Cicero showed the letter to Lentulus, he recognized the seal 10. Thanks were rendered to me because I had preserved the state. 11. They accused you because you had received that money. 12. I am glad because you remained here.

LESSON XXI.

TEMPORAL CLAUSES (*continued*).

GRAMMATICAL REFERENCES.

1. *Cum*-Clauses. 288. 1–3; 289; A. & G. 545 and *a*, 546 and *a*, 547, 548; H. 600. I and 1, II, 601 and 2.

2. *Antequam* and *priusquam.* 291. 1, 2; 292, 1, 2; A. & G 551. *a–c*; H. 605. I, II.

3. *Dum, dōnec, quoad.* 293. I–III; A. & G. 553, 554, 555, 556; H. 603, 1, II, 1, 2.

. EXAMPLES.

1. an tum erās cōnsul, cum in Palātiō mea domus ārdēbat, *or were you then consul, when my house burned up on the Palatine?* (**1**)

2. quō cum Catilīna vēnisset, quis senātor salūtāvit eum, *when Catiline had come there, what senator saluted him?* (**1**)

3. neque, cum aliquid mandārat, cōnfectum putābat, *nor when he had allotted any task, did he think it finished.* (**1**)

4. cum mē violāre volent, sē ipsī indicābunt, *when they desire to harm me, they will bear testimony against themselves.* (**1**)

5. antequam ad causam redeō, dē mē pauca dīcam, *before I come back to the case, I will say a few things concerning myself.* (**2**)

6. quod ego, prius quam loquī coepistī, sēnsī, *which I perceived before you began to speak.* (**2**)

7. antequam veniat, litterās mittet, *before he comes, he will send a letter,* i.e. *he will send a letter in anticipation of his coming.* (**2**)

8. antequam verbum facerem. abiit, *he left before I uttered a word.* (**2**)

9. dum haec geruntur, Quīnctius ex agrō dētrūditur, *while these things were being done, Quinctius was driven from his land.* (**3**)

10. **ille erat timendus, dum urbis moenibus continēbātur,** *he was a man to be feared only as long as he was confined within the walls of the city.* **(3)**

11. **num exspectātis dum Metellus de istīus scelere testimōnium dīcat,** *are you waiting for Metellus to give his testimony concerning that villain's rascality?* **(2)**

VOCABULARY.

aid, **subsidium, ī,** *n.*

affair, **rēs, reī,** *f.*

as long as, **dum.**

bench, **subsellium, ī,** *n*

constantly, **semper.**

draw near, **appropinquō, 1.**

empty, **inānis, e.**

enter, **ingredior, ī, gressus sum.**

eye, **oculus, ī,** *m.*

November, **November, bris,** *e.*

open, **aperiō, īre, uī, ertus.**

read (aloud), **recitō, 1.**

several, **complūrēs, a** *or* **ia.**

towards, of direction, **ad,** *prep.* *with acc.*

turn, **convertō, ere, vertī, versus.**

until, **dum, dōnec.**

EXERCISE.

1. As long as I live, I shall remember this place and this day.   **2.** When Cicero entered the senate-house on the 8th of November, the eyes of all the senators were turned towards him.   **3.** When the ambassadors of the Allobroges had drawn near, the praetors arrested them.   **4.** Let us not wait for him to arrive.[1]   **5.** When the senators saw Catiline, they left the benches empty.   **6.** Cicero did not open the letters before the Senate assembled.   **7.** I shall say nothing concerning this matter before he comes.   **8.** At the time when I was managing these affairs, death was constantly threatening me.   **9.** Whenever we had found a suitable place, we tarried there several days.   **10.** While the letters were being read, some withdrew from the senate-house.   **11.** We were fearing death, until you came to our aid.[2]   **12.** When you come, you will find me at home.

Suggestions on the Exercise.

1. *for him to arrive:* translate : *till he arrive.*
2. *to our aid:* translace : *to us for aid;* see Lesson VII, **Ex. 8.**

The Defence of Roscius (*continued*).

Those who had killed Roscius approached Chrysogonus,[1] a freedman[2] of Sulla, who added the name of Roscius to the number of the proscribed.[3]   Roscius' property[4]
was then confiscated[5] and sold at a pretended[6] auction.[7]
Chrysogonus bought it for a trifle,[8] and then drove out
from his father's house the young Roscius,[9] who had
meanwhile remained on his farm[10] near Ameria.[11]   Chrysogonus and his accomplices now divided the property
between them.[12]   But they still feared Roscius, and so
accused him of the murder of his own father.

Suggestions on the Exercise.

1. *Chrysogonus:* **Chrȳsogonus, ī, m.**
2. *freedman:* **lībertus, ī, m.**
3. *the proscribed:* **prōscrīptī, ōrum, m.**
4. *property:* **bona, ōrum, n.**
5. *confiscate:* **pūblicō, 1.**
6. *pretend:* **simulō, 1.**
7. *auction:* **auctiō, ōnis, f.** ; use the **abl.**
8. *trifle:* translate: *for very little.*
9. *the young Roscius:* **Rōscius adulēscēns (-entis), m.**
10. *farm:* **praedium, ī, n.**
11. *Ameria:* **Ameria, ae, f.**
12. *between them:* *them* is reflexive.

LESSON XXII.

SUBSTANTIVE CLAUSES.

GRAMMATICAL REFERENCES.

1. Substantive Clauses developed from the Jussive. 295. 1, 2 4, 5, 6, 8; *cf.* A. & G. 563, and *c, d, e,* 565; H. 564. I, II and 1

2. Substantive Clauses developed from the Deliberative. 295 7; 298; *cf.* A. & G. 558. *a*; H. 595. 1, 591. 4.

3. Substantive Clauses after verbs of *hindering, preventing, etc* 295. 3; A. & G. 558. *b*; H. 595. 2, 596. 2.

4. Substantive Clauses developed from the Optative. 296 entire; *cf.* A. & G. 563. *b*, 564; H. 565.

5. Substantive Clauses of Result. 297. 1–3; A. & G. 569 1, 2, 570, 571; H. 571. 1–4.

EXAMPLES.

1. vōs ōrō nē id faciātis, *I beg you not to do that.* **(1)**

2. populus Rōmānus permittit ut cīvitāte dōnentur, *the Roman people allows them to be presented with citizenship.* **(1)**

3. senātus dēcernit ut frūmentum emātur, *the Senate decrees that grain be purchased.* **(1)**

4. labōrābam nē testēs dīcerent, *I strove that the witnesses should not speak.* **(1)**

5. hōc dīcās licet, *you may say this.* **(1)**

6. multa oportet dīcāt, *he ought to say many things.* **(1)**

7. cōnfiteāre necesse est, *it is necessary that you confess* **(1)**

8. nōn fuit causa cūr postulārēs, *there was no reason why you should ask.* **(2)**

9 dubitābit quisquam quīn ab Siculīs pecūniam cēperint, *will any one doubt that they took money from the Sicilians ?* **(2)**

10. plūra nē dīcam tuae lacrimae mē impediunt, *your tears pre-vent me from saying more.* **(3)**

11. **formīdō impedit quō minus causam dīcere velint,** *fear pre-vents them from being willing to plead the case.* **(3)**

12. **optō ut hōc audiātis,** *I desire that you hear this* **(4)**

13. **velim** [2] **scrībās,** [1] *I wish you would write.* **(4)**

14. **vellem** [3] **adesset,** [1] *I wish he were present.* **(4)**

15. **vellem** [3] **dī immortālēs fēcissent,** [1] *I wish the immortal gods had brought it to pass.* **(4)**

16. **vereor nē quis audeat dīcere,** *I fear that some one will venture to say.* **(4)**

17. **verentur ut habeam satis praesidī,** *they fear that I have not enough protection.* **(4)**

18. **persaepe accidit ut mīrēmur,** *it happens very often that we marvel.* **(5)**

Notes on the Examples.

1. Note the absence of **ut,** as regularly after **vīsne, velim, vellem.**

2. **Velim** is potential subjunctive ; the present implies that the wish contained in the object clause is one capable of realization.

3. **Vellem** is likewise a potential subjunctive ; the imperfect implies regret at the unreality of the object clause.

Remarks.

1. **Licet** and **oportet** take either the infinitive, or the subjunctive without **ut,** but the infinitive is the commoner construction, especially with **licet ; necesse est** admits either construction.

2. **Cōnstituō,** when denoting another act of the same subject, more commonly takes an infinitive than an **ut**-clause.

3. **Prohibeō** is much more commonly construed with an infinitive than with a Substantive Clause introduced by **nē, quō minus,** or **quīn,** *e.g.* **sī quīs tē introīre prohibuerit,** *if any one should prevent your entering.* In Cicero and Caesar **prohibeō** never occurs followed by a **quīn**-clause, though it may take **quō minus.**

4. **Impediō quīn** does not occur in Cicero's speeches or philosophical works, though **impediō quō minus** is frequent.

5. In general, after negative expressions of *hindering,* **quō minus** is often used in preference to **quīn.**

VOCABULARY.

advise, **moneō, ēre, uī, itus.**

behooves, it behooves, **oportet, ēre, uit.**

bring about, **efficiō, ere, fēcī, fectus.**

exhort, **cohortor, 1.**

necessary, it is necessary, **necesse est.**

perish, **intereō, īre, iī, itūrus.**

prevent, **impediō, īre, īvī, ītus.**

put to death, **interficiō, ere, fēcī, fectus.**

reveal, **indicō, 1.**

see to it, **prōvideō, ēre, vīdī, vīsus.**

understand, **intellegō, ere, lēxī, lēctus.**

wish, **volō, velle, voluī.**

EXERCISE.

1. See to it, O Senators, that you do not neglect your duty!   2. I hear the voices of those who fear that I will not defend the state.   3. Lentulus advised Catiline to use the assistance of the slaves.   4. The Senate decreed that the conspirators should be put to death.   5. I exhort you to reveal all things without fear.   6. We beg that the immortal gods may preserve this city and the lives[1] of our wives and children.   7. It is much more to be feared that we shall forget our friends. 8. Cicero brought it about that no good man perished. 9. I wish[2] my father were living.   10. We wish[2] that he had not received these letters.   11. We will make[3] him understand.   12. It behooves you to obey my commands.   13. It is necessary that you leave this city. 14. You prevented me from seeing these places.

Suggestions on the Exercise.

1. *lives:* the Latin regularly uses the singular here.
2. See Examples 13–15.
3. *will make:* translate ; *will bring it about that.*

LESSON XXIII.

QUOD CLAUSES. — INDIRECT QUESTIONS.

GRAMMATICAL REFERENCES.

QUOD CLAUSES.

1. Substantive Clauses introduced by *quod*. 299. 1, 2; A. & G 572 and *a*; H. 588. 3.

INDIRECT QUESTIONS.

2. Simple Questions. 300. 1–3; A. & G. 574, 575. *b*, 576. *a*; H. 649. II.

3. Double Questions. 300. 4; *cf.* A. & G. 334, 335. *d*; H. 650. 1, 2.

4. *Haud sciō an, nesciō an.* 300. 5; A. & G. 575. *d*; H. 650. 4.

EXAMPLES.

1. quid quod tū ipse in cūstōdiam dedistī, *what of the fact that you gave yourself into custody?* (**1**)

2. cūr molestē ferāmus quod accessit exercitus, *why should we resent the fact that an army has approached?* (**1**)

3. quā celeritāte haec gesta sint, vidētis, *you see with what rapidity these things have been achieved.* (**2**)

4. quaerunt ā mē ubi sit pecūnia, *they inquire of me where the money is.* (**2**)

5. exquīre num quid scrīpserit, *ask whether he has written anything.* (**2**)

6. nesciō cūr hoc putēs, *I do not know why you think this.* (**2**)

7. rogāvī pervēnissentne Agrigentum, *I asked whether they had come to Agrigentum.* (**2**)

8 quaerō ā tē nōnne putēs, *I ask of you whether you do not think.* (**2**)

9. **nesciō quō mē vertam,** *I do not know whither to turn* (direct:
quō vertam, *whither am I to turn?*) **(2)**

10. **quaerō utrum vērum an falsum sit,**

11. **quaerō vērumne an falsum sit,** ⎱ *I ask whether it is true*

12. **quaerō vērum an falsum sit,** ⎰ *or false.* **(3)**

13. **quaerō vērum falsumne sit,**

14. **dī utrum sint necne quaeritur,** *it is asked whether there are
gods or not.* **(3)**

15. **haud sciō an mālim,** *I am inclined to think I prefer.* **(4)**

Remarks.

1. To denote future time in indirect questions, periphrastic
forms are used where ambiguity would otherwise result; as, **nōn
quaerō quid dictūrus sīs,** *I do not ask what you will say.*

2. **Nōnne** in indirect questions is used only after **quaerō**; see
the 8th example above.

3. In indirect double questions **necne** is commonly used to express *or not;* **annōn** is much less frequent.

VOCABULARY.

call together, **convocō**, 1.

gain possession, **potior, īrī, ītus.**

initiate, **ineō, īre, iī, itus.**

order, **mandātum, ī,** *n.*

route, **iter, itineris,** *n.*

think, have an opinion, **sentiō
īre, sēnsī, sēnsus.**

where? **ubi.**

whether . . . or, **utrum . . . an**

EXERCISE.

1. He inquired of the Gauls why they had ever come
to his home.   **2.** What of the fact,[1] that, as you approached, the other senators withdrew?   **3.** Cicero
showed where Catiline had been, what plans he had
initiated, whom he had called together.   **4.** I know who
has gained possession of Etruria; who is in charge of
the camp at Faesulae.   **5.** We asked him what he
thought concerning these letters.   **6.** You understand

what I ordered to be done. 7. You already know what I think of him. 8. We did not at that time know whether he had been in Sicily or not. 9. Let us ask whether he will remain here or will go to Rome. 10. I am inclined[2] to think that greater labors must be undertaken by us. 11. Do you know by what route he set out? 12. I do not know whether he set out or remained in the city.

Suggestions on the Exercise.

1. *what of the fact:* see Example 1.
2. *inclined to think:* see Example 15.

The Defense of Roscius (*continued*).

Although all feared Chrysognus, as the friend of Sulla, yet Cicero boldly undertook the defense of Roscius. In the very beginning of his oration he openly accused Chrysogonus. He spoke thus: " Chrysogonus, O judges, has gained possession of the fortune of another man,[1] and since that man lives, he asks you to condemn him and so deliver him himself from fear, for while Roscius is alive,[2] he fears that he himself will not retain this excellent inheritance[3]."

Suggestions on the Exercise.

1. *of another man:* use **aliēnus, a, um,** in agreement with **fortūnīs.**
2. *while Roscius is alive:* express by the Ablative Absolute.
3. *inheritance:* **hērēditās, ātis, f.**

LESSON XXIV.

CONDITIONAL SENTENCES.

GRAMMATICAL REFERENCES.

1. First Type. Nothing Implied. 302. 1–4; A. & G. 515 and *a*; 518. *a, b*; 516. *a*; H. 574 and 2, 580. 1.

2. Second Type. *Should . . . would* **Type.** 303· A. & G. 516. *b*; H. 576.

3. Third Type. Contrary to Fact. 304 entire; A. & G. 517 and *a, c, d*; H. 579 and 1, 582, 583.

EXAMPLES.

1. sī hōc dīcis, errās, *if you say this, you are mistaken.* **(1)**
2. sī hōc dīcēbās, errābās, *if you were saying this, you were mistaken.* **(1)**
3. sī hōc dīcēs, errābis, *if you say* (i.e. *shall say*) *this, you will be mistaken.* **(1)**
4. sī hōc dīxistī, errāvistī, *if you said this, you were mistaken.* **(1)**
5. memoria minuitur, nisi eam exerceās, *memory grows weak unless you exercise it.* **(1)**
6. sī quicquam caelātī aspexerat, manūs abstinēre nōn poterat, *if ever he had seen any embossed silverware, he could not keep his hands off of it.* **(1)**
7. in exsilium, sī hanc vōcem exspectās, proficīscere, *go forth into exile, if you are waiting for this command!* **(1)**
8. sī hōc dīcās, errēs,   ⎫ *If you should say this, you would*
9. sī hōc dīxerīs, errāverīs, ⎬   *be mistaken.* **(2)**
10. sī hōc dīcerēs, errārēs, *if you were saying this, you would be mistaken.* **(3)**

11. **sī hōc dīxissēs, errāvissēs,** *if you had said this, you would have been mistaken.* (**3**)

12. **nisi eum cursum vītae tenuissem, cōnsul esse potuī,** *I might have been consul, unless I had pursued that course of life.* (**3**)

13. **eum patris locō colere dēbēbās, sī ūlla in tē pietās esset,** *you ought to revere him as a father, if you had in you any sense of devotion.* (**3**)

14. **sī occīsus esset, fuistisne ad arma itūrī,** *if he had been slain, would you have proceeded to arms?* (**3**)

VOCABULARY.

deserve, **mereō, ēre, uī, itus.**

escape, **ēvādō, ere, vāsī, vāsū-rus.**

exile, **exsilium, ī, n.**

forthwith, **statim.**

judge, **jūdicō, 1.**

ought, **dēbeō, ēre, uī, itus.**

remove, **tollō, ere, sustulī, sublā-tus.**

risk, **perīculum, ī, n.**

EXERCISE.

1. If Cicero had judged (it) best, he would have removed Catiline at the risk of his own life.   2. If you go [1] by the Appian Way, you will overtake your friends before night.   3. If they remain in this city, they will suffer the punishment which they deserve.   4. If I order you to be arrested and put to death, what should I fear?   5. If you should go into exile forthwith, I should scarcely bear the storm of hatred.   6. If your mother and father hated you, what would you do?   7. Unless he had been guarded, he might have escaped.[2]   8. If you had not forgotten your duty, you ought to be defending [3] the state.   9. If we love our country, let us obey her decrees.   10. If you ask [4] him why he remains here, he will make no answer.[5]   11. If he had had friends, they would have come.   12. Do not withdraw,[6] unless you wish.

Suggestions on the Exercise.

1. *if you go:* in this and other sentences where the present has the future force, the Latin future must be used in translating into Latin.

2. *might have escaped:* see Example 12.

3. *ought to be defending:* see Example 13. Translate *to be defending* the same as *to defend.*

4. *if you ask him:* this is meant to be the indefinite *you;* see Example 5.

5. *will make no answer:* translate: *will answer nothing.*

6. *do not withdraw:* see Lesson XVII, Example 12.

LESSON XXV.

USE OF *nisi, sī nōn, sin.* — CONDITIONAL CLAUSES OF COM-
PARISON. — SUBORDINATE ADVERSATIVE CLAUSES IN-
TRODUCED BY *quamvīs, quamquam, etc.* — PROVISOS.

GRAMMATICAL REFERENCES.

1. *Nisi, sī nōn, sīn.* 306 entire; *cf.* A. & G. 525. *a.* 1, 2, *d* ;
H. 575. 2, 4, 5, 7.

2. Conditional Clauses of Comparison. 307. 1, 2 ; A. & G.
524 and N. 2 ; H. 584 and 1, 2.

3. Subordinate Adversative Clauses. 309. 1–5 ; A. & G. 527
and *a–e* ; H. 585, 586, I, II.

4. Provisos. 310. II ; A. & G. 528 ; H. 587.

EXAMPLES.

1. hōc enim nōn facerem, nisi necesse esset, *for I should not be
doing this unless it were necessary.* **(1)**

2. etiam sī vir bonus nōn esset, *even if he were* NOT *a good
man.* **(1)**

3. dolōrem sī nōn potuerō frangere, tamen occultābō, *if I cannot
subdue my grief, yet I will hide it.* **(1)**

4. sī futūrum est, fīet ; sī nōn futūrum est, nōn fīet, *if it is
destined to be, it will be ; if it is not destined, it will not
be.* **(1)**

5. hunc mihi timōrem ēripe ; sī est vērus, nē opprimar ; sīn
falsus, ut timēre dēsinam. *take away this terror from me ;
if it is real, in order that I may not be crushed ; but if
unfounded, in order that I may cease to fear.* **(1)**

6. ēdūc tēcum omnīs tuōs ; sī minus, quam plūrimōs, *lead out
with you all your followers ; if not (all), as many as
possible.* **(1)**

7. **nōmen petis quasi incertum sit,** *you ask for the name as if it were uncertain.* (**2**)

8. **hōc locō sedēbat, quasi reus ipse esset,** *he sat in this place as if he were himself under accusation.* (**2**)

9. **ita loquor quasi ego illud fēcerim,** *I speak as though I had done that.* (**2**)

10. **quamvīs mihi rēs nōn placeat, tamen pugnāre nōn poterō,** *though the matter should not please me, I shall not be able to contend.* (**3**)

11. **quamvīs amplum sit, parum est,** *however extensive it be, it is too little.* (**3**)

12. **quamquam premuntur aere aliēnō, dominātiōnem tamen exspectant,** *though they are overwhelmed with debt, yet they expect power.* (**3**)

13. **etsī omnēs probābant,** *though all approved.* (**3**)

14. **Sōcratēs cum facile posset ēdūcī ē cūstōdiā, nōluit,** *though Socrates might have been led out of jail, yet he refused.* (**3**)

15. **magnō mē metū līberābis, dum modo inter mē atque tē mūrus intersit,** *you will relieve me of a great fear, provided only a wall intervenes between me and you.* (**3**)

Remark.

1. Etsī, *although,* is carefully to be distinguished from **etsī,** *even if;* the latter is a conditional particle and takes any of the constructions admissible for **sī ;** see Lesson XXIV.

VOCABULARY.

approve, **probō, 1**
as if, **quasi.**
at first, **prīmō.**
condemn, **condemnō, 1.**
conquer, **vincō, ere, vīcī, victus.**
contend, **dīmicō, 1.**
diligence, **dīligentia, ae, *f*.**

severity, **sevēritās, ātis, *f*.**
show, **ostendō, ere, endī, entus.**
undergo, **subeō, īre, iī, itus.**
unpopularity, **invidia, ae, *f*.**
ward off, **dēpellō, ere, dēpulī pulsus.**

EXERCISE.

1. Provided only these dangers be warded off from my fellow-citizens, I shall gladly undergo this storm of un popularity. **2.** Though at first he had answered ar rogantly, yet finally he denied nothing. **3** If you exercise severity, that will be better; if not, we do not know what will happen. **4.** It is not necessary for us to fear,[1] provided he does not come[2] nearer. **5.** You ask me what I shall do, as if I had not already shown[3] you my plans. **6.** Though nothing be found in the letters, yet over-diligence[4] is not to be feared by us. **7.** If Catiline goes forth, the city will be delivered from the greatest peril; if he does not go forth, we shall have to contend[5] with him always. **8.** Although many of those who have remained at Rome are citizens, I warn them again not[6] to attempt anything against the republic. **9.** You defend this man, as if all his acts were[3] good **10.** The soldiers returned home, as if they had conquered **11.** If we do not return, nevertheless be of good courage. **12.** If this man is condemned, all will approve; but if he is acquitted, they will blame us. **13.** Even **if he** enters the senate house, no one will salute him.

Suggestions on the Exercise.

1. *for us to fear:* see Lesson XXII, Example 7.

2. *come:* use **accēdō, ere, cessī, cessūrus.**

3. *had not shown,* etc. : observe the principle for sequence of tenses in Clauses of Conditional Comparison.

4. *over-diligence:* **nimia dīligentia.**

5. *have to contend:* translate: *it will have to be contended by us.*

6. *not to attempt:* the negative in such clauses is **nē.**

Defense of Roscius (*continued*).

Cicero then set forth how Roscius, the father, had been killed through hatred, how the assassins[1] had persuaded Chrysogonus to add Roscius' name to the list of the proscribed, how they had finally accused the son of the murder. Cicero did not blame Sulla himself, but excused[2] (him) on the ground that[3] he was ignorant of the deeds of his freedman. Roscius was acquitted by the votes[4] of the judges, yet Cicero soon after withdrew from Rome and betook himself to Athens and Asia Minor.[5]

Suggestions on the Exercise.

1. *assassin:* sīcārius, ī, m.

2. *excuse:* excūsō, 1.

3. *on the ground that:* quod (with the subjv.).

4. *vote:* sententia, ae, f.

5. *Asia Minor:* Asia, ae, f. The preposition must be used here.

LESSON XXVI.

INDIRECT DISCOURSE.

GRAMMATICAL REFERENCES.

Moods.

1. Declarative Sentences. 314. 1, 3; 331. I; A. & G. 580; H. 642, 643. 3, 4.

2. Interrogative Sentences. 315. 1-3; A. & G. 586, 587; H. 642 and 2, 3.

3. Imperative Sentences. 316 and *a*; A. & G. 588 and *a*; H. 642.

Tenses.

1. Of the Infinitive. 317 and *a*; A. & G. 584 and *a*; H. 644, 617.

2. Of the Subjunctive. 318 and *a*; A. & G. 585 and *a*; H. 644.

EXAMPLES.

1. crēdō vōs mīrārī quid hōc sit, *I suppose you wonder what this is.* **(1)**

2. negō quemquam vestrum esse quīn hōc saepe audierit, *I deny that there is any one of you who has not often heard this.* **(1)**

3. tū, ā quō sciam esse praemissōs quī tibi praestōlārentur, *you, by whom I know men have been sent on ahead to wait for you.* **(1)**

4. intellegō nēminem tam stultum fore quī nōn videat conjūrātiōnem esse factam, *I appreciate that no one will be so foolish as not to see that a conspiracy has been made.* **(1)**

5. nostrā, quī remānsissēmus, caede tē contentum esse, dīcēbās *you said you were content with the massacre of us who had remained.* **(1)**

6. **hanc contrōversiam fuisse dīxērunt, quod Lentulō Sāturnā-libus caedem fierī placēret,** *they said that there had been this dispute, that Lentulus wished to have the massacre take place on the Saturnalia.* (1)

7. **dīxērunt sē factūrōs quod imperātum esset,** *they said they would do what had been commanded.* (1)

8. **crēdidit eum quī ōrātiōnem bonōrum imitārētur, facta quoque imitātūrum,** *he supposed that a man who imitated the language of the good would also imitate their acts.* (1)

9. **sciō tē haec ēgisse,** {
    I know you were doing this. (Direct: **agēbās.**)
    I know you did this. (Direct: **ēgistī.**)
    I know you had done this. (Direct: **ēgerās.**)
    (1)
}

10. **videor ostendisse quālēs deī essent,** *I seem to have shown of what nature the gods are.* (Direct: **ostendī.**) (1)

Remarks.

1. Note that a dependent perfect infinitive is treated as an historical tense whenever, if resolved into an equivalent indicative, it would be historical. See the last example above.

2. Note that for the sake of vividness a present tense of the direct discourse is not infrequently retained in the indirect after an historical tense. This is called **repraesentātiō,** 'a bringing back to the present.'

VOCABULARY.

anxious, **sollicitus, a, um.**
dangerous, **perīculōsus, a, um.**
drive, cast out, **ēiciō, ere, ējēcī, ējectus.**

indulgence, **lēnitās, ātis,** *f.*
move, affect, **moveō, ere, mōvī, mōtus.**

EXERCISE.

1. There were some who said that Cicero had driven Catiline into exile. 2. You saw that the senators were anxious concerning his danger. 3. Cethegus wrote that he would do all those things which he had promised to the envoys of the Allobroges. 4. Why do you hope

that my indulgence will be permanent ?   5. They perceive that I know what they are plotting against the republic, and yet [1] they are not moved.   6. How many men do you think there are who believe all these things which I have reported? [2]   7. Cicero saw that Catiline would be the leader of a dangerous war, if he should allow him to go out from the city.   8. I say that you sold all these things for a very high [3] price.   9. Cicero said that he who was an enemy of the republic was in no way [4] a citizen.   10. I wrote you that when the senators saw Catiline, they left the benches empty.   11. He does not know that I found the letters which he had sent.   12. I believe you said nothing concerning this matter before he had arrived.

Suggestions on the Exercise.

1. *and yet . . . not:* **neque tamen.**
2. *report:* **dēferō, ferre, tulī, lātus.**
3. *very high:* translate : *very great.*
4. *in no way:* **nūllā ratiōne.**

LESSON XXVII.

INDIRECT DISCOURSE (*continued*)

GRAMMATICAL REFERENCES.

Conditional Sentences in Indirect Discourse. 319 *322* entire
B. & G. 589 entire; H. 646, 647.

EXAMPLES.

NOTE. — The direct form is given first in parenthesis.

(sī hōc crēdis, errās, *if you believe this, you are wrong.*)

1. dīcō tē, sī hōc crēdās, errāre, *I say that, if you believe this, you are wrong.*

2. dīxī tē, sī hōc crēderēs, errāre, *I said that, if you believed this, you were wrong.*

   (sī hōc crēdēs, errābis, *if you believe* (i.e. *shall believe*) *this, you will be wrong.*)

3. dīcō tē, sī hōc crēdās, errātūrum esse, *I say that if you believe* (i.e. *shall believe*) *this, you will be wrong.*

4. dīxī tē, sī hōc crēderēs, errātūrum esse, *I said that if you should believe this, you would be wrong.*

   (sī hōc crēdideris, errābis, *if you shall have believed this, you will be wrong.*)

5. dīcō tē, sī hōc crēdideris, errātūrum esse, *I say that if you shall have believed this, you will be wrong.*

6. dīxī tē, sī hōc crēdidissēs, errātūrum esse, *I said that, if you should have believed this, you would be wrong.*

   (sī hōc crēdās, errēs, *if you should believe this, you would be wrong.*)

7. dīcō tē, sī hōc crēdās, errātūrum esse, *I say that if you should believe this, you would be wrong.*

8. dīxī tē, sī hōc crēderēs, errātūrum esse, *I said that, if you should believe this, you would be wrong.*

(sī hōc crēderēs errārēs, *if you were believing this, you would be in error.*)

9. dīcō (dīxī) tē, sī hōc crēderēs, errātūrum esse, *I say (said) that, if you were believing this, you would be wrong.*

(sī hōc crēdidissēs, errāvissēs, *if you had believed this, you would have been wrong.*)

10. dīcō (dīxī) tē, sī hōc crēdidissēs, errātūrum fuisse, *I say (said) that, if you had believed this, you would have been wrong.*

(sī hōc dīxissēs, pūnītus essēs, *if you had said this, you would have been punished.*)

11. dīcō (dīxī) sī hōc dīxissēs, futūrum fuisse ut pūnīrēris, *I say (said) that, if you had said this, you would have been punished,* lit. *it would have happened that you were punished.*

12. nōn dubitō quīn, sī hōc dīxissēs, errātūrus fuerīs, *I do not doubt that if you had said this, you would have been wrong.*

13. quaerō, num, sī hōc dīxissēs, errātūrus fuerīs, *I ask whether you would have made a mistake, if you had said this.*

EXERCISE.

1. We know that if Cicero had judged it best, he would have removed Catiline at the risk of his own life.   2. I said that if you went by the Appian Way you would overtake your friends before night.   3. I believe that if they remain in the city, they will suffer the punishment which they deserve.   4. You knew that if I should order you to be arrested and put to death, nothing would have to be feared[1] by me.   5. I saw that if you should go into exile forthwith, I should scarcely bear the storm of unpopularity.   6. I said, let him not withdraw,[2] unless he wished.   7. You know that if he has friends they will come to his aid.   8. It is evident[3] that if Catiline goes forth, the city will be delivered from the greatest peril; that if he does not go forth, we shall have to contend

with him always.   9. I believe that if he enters the
senate house, no one will salute him.   10. You see that
if you ask why he remains here, he will make no answer
11. I say that if you had not forgotten your duty, you
would have defended the state.   12. I do not know what
you would have done, if you had heard this.

Suggestions on the Exercise.

1. *would have to be feared:* use the Second Periphrastic Con
jugation.

2. *let him not withdraw:* an imperative clause in indirect dis
course.

3. *it is evident:* cōnstat.

4. *shall have to contend:* use the Second Periphrastic Conjuga
tion.

Reasons for Cicero's Temporary Retirement.

In another work Cicero tells us he withdrew from Rome
At that time he says that his body was weak and that
his friends feared that he was not able to endure the
labors of the forum.   Both friends and physicians[1] therefore advised him to abandon[2] his profession.   But Cicero
says that he preferred to undergo all risks rather than to
abandon the profession which he had chosen.   He thought
that if he should change his style,[3] and should cultivate
a less impassioned[4] oratory,[5] he would avoid all risks.
Hence he decided to go away from Rome.

Suggestions on the Exercise.

1. *physician:* medicus, ī, m.

2. *abandon:* dēpōnō, ere, posuī, positus.

3. *style:* genus dīcendī, lit. *kind of speaking* (genus, eris, n.;

4. *less impassioned:* remissior, us, lit. *more relaxed.*

5. *oratory:* ōrātiō, ōnis, f.

LESSON XXVIII.

THE INFINITIVE.

GRAMMATICAL REFERENCES.

1. Infinitive without Subject Accusative, used as Subject. 327. 1, 2 and *a*; A. & G. 452. N. 2, 455. *a*; H. 615, 612. 3.

2. Infinitive without Subject Accusative, used as Object. 328. 1, 2; A. & G. 456; H. 607 and 1, 2, 608. 4, 612 and 1.

3. Infinitive with Subject Accusative, used as Subject. 330; A. & G. 455. 2; H. 615.

4. Infinitive with Subject Accusative, used as Object. 331 entire; A. & G. 459; H. 613. 1–3.

5. Passive Construction of Verbs which in the Active are followed by the Infinitive with Subject Accusative. 332 entire; H. 611. 1, 2 and Notes 1, 3.

EXAMPLES.

1. difficile est ōrātiōnis exitum invenīre, *it is difficult to find an end of my speech.* (**1**)

2. eīs frūmentum accipere licet, *it is permitted to them to receive grain.* (**1**)

3. Caecīnae placuit experīrī, *it pleased Caecina to make the trial.* (**1**)

4. Rōscium dēfendere nōn audent, *they do not dare to defend Roscius.* (**2**)

5. avī mōrēs dēbēbās imitārī, *you ought to have imitated the character of your grandfather.* (**2**)

6. nōs omnīs vītā prīvāre cōnātī sunt, *they tried to deprive us all of life.* (**2**)

7. ēvādere nōn potuērunt, *they could not escape.* (**2**)

8. tibi frūmentum dare parātus sum, *I am prepared to give you grain.* (**2**)

9. rēs nēminī dubia esse potest, *the matter can be doubtful to no one.* (**2**)

10. quō animō mē esse oportet, *of what feeling ought I to be ?* (**3**)

11. turpe est mē mortem timuisse, *it is disgraceful for me to have feared death.* (**3**)

12. cōnsul lūdōs fierī vetuit, *the consul forbade the games to be held.* (**4**)

13. sinite mē praeterīre nostram calamitātem, *permit me to pass over our misfortune.* (**4**)

14. nōn molestē ferēbant sē libīdinum vinculīs laxātōs esse, *they did not regret* (lit. *bear it ill*) *that they had been freed from the fetters of passion.* (**4**)

15. īre in exsilium jussus est, *he was ordered to go into exile.* (**5**)

16. vidēbātur magnam glōriam cōnsecūtus,[1] *he seemed to have attained great glory.* (**5**)

Note on the Examples.

1. Observe that the participle in the compound tenses of the infinitive agrees with the subject of the main verb in constructions of this type. The auxiliary esse is also freely omitted.

Remarks.

1. Note that where the English says 'ought to have done,' 'might have done,' the Latin uses dēbuī, oportuit, potuī, with the present infinitive, as, dēbuit venīre, *he ought to have come;* potuit venīre, *he might* (*could*) *have come.*

2. Note that verbs which have no participial stem express the future infinitive active and passive by fore ut or futūrum esse ut, with the subjunctive, as spērō fore ut hostēs arceantur, *I hope the enemy will be kept off*, lit. *I hope it will happen that the enemy will be kept off.*

VOCABULARY.

arise, **orior, īrī, ortus.**

beautiful, **pulcher, chra, chrum.**

desire, **cupiō, ere, īvī,** *or* **iī, ītus.**

easy, **facilis, e.**

follow up, **persequor, ī, secūtus.**

keep from, **prohibeō, ēre, uī, itus.**

permitted, it is permitted. **licet, ēre, uit,** *impersonal.*

seem, **videor, ērī, vīsus.**

word, **verbum, ī,** *n.*

EXERCISE.

1. No crime seems capable of being undertaken[1] which does not arise from you.   2. For a long time you have been desiring[2] to lay waste this most beautiful city with fire and sword.   3. I saw that I should not be able to follow up[3] his accomplices.   4. As soon as he was ordered to leave this city, he departed.   5. He will be said by many to have been visited with excessive punishment.   6. This letter was said to have been written by Lentulus.   7. This seal ought to have kept you from so great a crime.   8. No harm can be done me[4] by these men.   9. I remember that you said[5] this as soon as you arrived.   10. It is easy to believe that he could not come.   11. You seem to have been moved by my words.   12. It was permitted us to return these letters to you.

Suggestions on the Exercise.

1. *capable of being undertaken:* translated : *seems to be able to be undertaken.*

2. See Lesson XVII, Example 1.

3. *that I should not be able to follow up:* translate: *saw that it would be that I should not be able to follow up;* see Remark 2.

4. *no harm can be done me:* the Latin idiom is: *it cannot be harmed (to) me,* the impersonal use.

5. *I remember that you said:* **meminī,** when used of personal experience and referring to the past, regularly takes the present infinitive.

LESSON XXIX.

PARTICIPLES.

GRAMMATICAL REFERENCES.

1. Tenses of the Participle. 336. 1–5; A. & G. 489 and 491. H. 640 and 1.

2. Use of Participles. 337. 1–3, 5, 8, *a*, *b*. 1), 2); A. & G 494; 496, 497 and *d*; 500 and 1, 2, 4; H. 638, 1–3, 639, 613. 5

EXAMPLES.

1. **audiō tē loquentem,** *I hear you as you speak.* **(1)**

2. **audivī tē loquentem,** *I heard you as you were speaking.* **(1)**

3. **audiam tē loquentem,** *I shall hear you as you speak,* i.e. *as you shall be speaking.* **(1)**

4. **locūtus tacet,** *he has spoken and is silent,* lit. *having spoken, he is silent.* **(1)**

5. **locūtus tacuit,** *he had spoken and was silent.* **(1)**

6. **locūtus tacēbit,** *he will speak and then be silent.* **(1)**

7. **Catōnem vīdī in bibliothēcā sedentem,** *I saw Cato sitting in his library.* **(2)**

8. **hōc mihi prīmum post hanc urbem conditam togātō contigit,** *I am the first man in civil life to whom this has happened since the foundation of the city.* **(2)**

9. **huic generī hominum parcendum est,** *this class of men must be spared.* **(2)**

10. **lēgem scrībendam cūrāvit,** *he saw to the engrossing of the law.* **(2)**

11. **eum jugulandum vōbīs trādidērunt,** *they handed him over to you to be put to death.* **(2)**

193

Remarks.

1. Note that the perfect passive participle is often equivalent to a coördinate clause in English, as, **C. Servīlius Ahāla Sp. Maelium ɔccupātum interēmit,** *Gaius Servilius Ahala surprised and slew Spurius Maelius,* lit. *slew him having been surprised.*

2. Observe that the present active participle is used much less freely in Latin than in English. We employ it somewhat loosely ᴗo denote an act prior to that of the verb with which it is connected ; as, ' Finding no means of escape, he surrendered.' Here the *finding* is anterior to the *surrender*. In such cases the Latin would employ some other form of expression ; in that language the present participle is strictly limited to the expression of acts *contemporary with* the action of the main verb.

VOCABULARY.

burn, **combūrō, ere, ussī, ūstus.**	just as, **sīcut.**
contract for, **locō,** 1.	rout, **fugō,** 1.
endure, **perferō, ferre, tulī, lātus.**	see to (doing something), **cūrō, 1.**
erect, **collocō,** 1.	summon, **vocō,** 1.
escort, **prōsequor, ī, secūtus.**	worship, **veneror, 1.**
impair, **imminuō, ere, uī, ūtus.**	

EXERCISE.

1. Will you see to the writing and sending of these letters ?   **2.** The arrest of the conspirators affected all the Romans with the greatest joy   **3.** We see the Roman people to-day thinking one and the same thing. **4.** Having worshipped the gods, return to your homes and defend them, just as last night.   **5.** The consuls ɔontracted for the erection of this statue.   **6.** When you leave[1] this city, all the citizens will most gladly ᴣscort you to the gates.   **7.** We left our temples and dwellings to be plundered and burned.   **8.** Cethegus, suspecting nothing, was immediately summoned by me.

9. Having attacked the army of Catiline, the consul soon routed (it). **10.** Let us not endure the impairing of the freedom [2] of Roman citizens. **11.** Within three days we saw him withdrawing from the city. **12.** This temple, plundered by Verres, lost all its most beautiful statues.

Suggestions on the Exercise.

1. *when you leave, will escort :* translate : *will escort you leaving.*

2. *the impairing of the freedom :* translate : *the freedom impaired.*

Cicero's Studies at Athens and in Asia.

When Cicero had come to Athens, he was six months with Antiochus,[1] a very eminent philosopher, and renewed the pursuit of philosophy [2] which had been cultivated by him from his earliest youth. At the same time he heard Demetrius,[3] a famous master [4] of oratory.[5] In several towns of Asia he also enjoyed the learning [6] and discipline of the most distinguished teachers. Finally he came to Rhodes,[7] where he heard the same Molo whom he previously knew at Rome, a most judicious [8] man and a most excellent teacher.

Suggestions on the Exercise.

1. *Antiochus :* Antiochus ī, m.

2. *philosophy :* philosophia, ae, f.

3. *Demetrius :* Dēmētrius, ī, m.

4. *master :* magister, trī, m.

5. *of oratory :* dīcendī, lit. *of speaking.*

6. *learning :* doctrīna, ae, f.

7. *Rhodes :* Rhodus, ī, f.

8. *judicious :* sapiēns, entis.

LESSON XXX.

THE GERUND; THE GERUNDIVE CONSTRUCTION; THE SUPINE.

GRAMMATICAL REFERENCES.

1. **The Gerund.** 338. 1–5. A. & G. 502; 504 and *b*; 505 and
   506 and N. 2; 507; H. 624, 626, 627, 628 and footnote 2,
   529.

2. **The Gerundive Construction.** 339. 1–5; A. & G. 503 ; 504
   and *b*, 505, 506, 507; H. 621, 623 and 1, 628.

3. **The Supine.** 340 entire; A. & G. 509, 510 and N. 2;
   H. 632 and 1, 633, 635 and 1, 2, 4.

EXAMPLES.

1. cupidus tē audiendī, *desirous of hearing you.* **(1)**

2. glōriandi causā, *for the sake of boasting.* **(1)**

3. rem quaeris praeclāram ad discendum, *you seek an excellent subject for learning.* **(1)**

4. hominibus salūtem dandō, *by giving safety to men.* **(1)**

5. cōnsilium urbis dēlendae et cīvium trucīdandōrum, *the plan of destroying the city and massacring the citizens.* **(2)**

6. Brūtus in līberandā patriā interfectus est, *Brutus was slain in freeing his country.* **(2)**

7. cui ad sollicitandōs pāstōrēs Āpūlia attribūta est, *to whom Apulia has been assigned for the purpose of tampering with the shepherds.* **(2)**

8. ad agrum fruendum [1] nōs allectat senectūs, *old age invites us to enjoy the farm.* **(2)**

9. suī cōnservandī [2] causā, *for the sake of saving themselves.* **(2)**

10. exclūsī eōs quōs tū ad mē salūtātum mīserās, *I kept out those whom you had sent to greet me.* **(3)**

11. sī hōc optimum factū jūdicārem, *if I thought this best to do.* **(3)**

196

Notes on the Examples.

1. Note that **fruor**, like the other deponents governing the ablative, admits the gerundive construction.

2. **Cōnservandī** agrees merely in form with **suī** and **vestrī**; in sense it is plural.

Remark.

1. The dative of the gerund and of the gerundive are both rare in Ciceronian Latin; consequently the construction, though common later, is hardly to be imitated by the beginner in Latin writing.

VOCABULARY.

aid, **auxilium, ī, n.**

appease, **plācō, 1.**

assign, **attribuō, ere, uī, ūtus.**

disturbance, **tumultus, ūs, m.**

omit, **omittō, ere, mīsī, missus.**

Sicilians, **Siculī, ōrum, m.**

stir up, **excitō, 1.**

suspicion, **suspīciō, ōnis, f.**

tend, **pertineō, ēre, uī.**

EXERCISE.

1. Envoys of the Allobroges had been sent to Rome for the purpose of[1] stirring up a Gallic disturbance. 2 Nothing was omitted which tended[2] to appease the gods.[3] 3. I see that all these have assembled for the sake of defending the republic. 4. What shall we say concerning the choice of a leader[4] for[5] this war? 5. For the sake of avoiding suspicion, he made no reply. 6. You prepared men for killing the consuls and praetors. 7. We were most desirous of coming. 8. It is easy to understand why he is absent. 9. The Sicilians sent messengers to Cicero at Rome[6] to seek aid. 10. They came to complain of[7] the wrongs of Verres. 11. It is difficult to say when they will arrive 12. He assigned us to Cethegus to be put to death.

Suggestions on the Exercise.

1. *for the purpose of :* ad, with the Gerundive Construction.

2. *which tended :* a Clause of Characteristic.

8. *to appease the gods :* translate: *to the gods to be appeased.*

4. *the choice of a leader :* translate: *concerning a leader to be chosen.*

5. *for :* ad.

6. *to Cicero at Rome :* translate: *to Rome to Cicero.*

7. *of :* dē.

REVIEW.

1. I will never desire, fellow citizens, that you may hear that Lucius Catiline is leading an army against you. 2. The conspirators feared that Cicero and the Senate would exercise severity towards them. 3. Let him lay aside the plan of war and go immediately into exile! 4 If you will listen to me, I do not see why you cannot do this. 5. We have arrested men who remained at Rome for receiving Catiline. 6. When he hesitated,[1] I asked him why he had not already set out. 7. Those who sailed on this sea feared that their fortunes would not be safe. 8. While they were conferring concerning terms, another ambassador arrived. 9. We waited two days for your friends to bring the letters. 10. It is difficult to understand how Catiline found so many accomplices. 11. I do not know whether you remember my words or not. 12. I do not believe that death was ordained[2] by the gods for the sake of punishment.

Suggestions on the Exercise.

1. *hesitate :* haesitō, 1.

2. *ordain :* cōnstituō, ere, uī, ūtus.

SUPPLEMENTARY EXERCISES IN CONTINUED DISCOURSE.

13.

Cicero Elected Quaestor.

One year after Cicero returned [1] to Italy, he was elected quaestor, an office which he held [2] in the consulship of Cotta and Octavius. In accordance with [3] a law of the Dictator Sulla, each [4] quaestor after he left office [5] became senator for life.[6] But before he began to perform the duties of a senator, Cicero by lot secured [7] Sicily (as) his province and betook himself to Lilybaeum.[8] At that time there were two quaestors in Sicily, one of whom resided [9] at Lilybaeum, the other at Syracuse.

Suggestions on the Exercise.

1. *returned:* for the mood and tense, see Lesson XX, Example 9.

2. *an office which he held:* translate: *which office he held.* For *office*, use **magistrātus, ūs, m.**; for *hold,* use **gerō, ere, gessi, gestus.**

3. *in accordance with :* **ex**, prep. with abl.

4. *each :* **omnis.**

5. *leave office :* translate : *go away from office.*

6. *for life :* **perpetuus, a, um.**

7. *secure by lot* **sortior, īrī, ītus.**

8. *Lilybaeum.* **Lilybaeum I, n.**

9. *reside* **habitō, 1.**

14.

Conditions at Rome at this Time.

At the age of thirty-two years Cicero returned **again to Rome** from Sicily. At that time the optimates or nobles were in control[1] in the republic. These nobles had inherited the splendid[2] traditions[3] of their ancestors, who had made Rome great and powerful at the time of the Punic and Macedonian wars.[4] All were nobles who could reckon curule[5] magistrates among their ancestors, and he was noblest in whose hall[6] was the greatest number of family portraits[7] of consuls, censors, and dictators

Suggestions on the Exercise.

1. *to be in control:* dominor, 1.

2. *splendid:* ēgregius, a, um.

3. *traditions:* mōrēs, um, m., lit. *customs.*

4. *at the time . . . of wars:* translate: *in the . . . wars,* using prep. For *Punic* and *Macedonian,* use **Pūnicus, a, um,** and **Macedonicus, a, um.**

5. *curule:* curūlis, e.

6. *hall:* ātrium, ī, n.

7. *family portrait:* imāgō, inis, f.

15.

Conditions at Rome at this Time (*continued*).

At this time also the nobles had already for many years won[1] all the offices.[2] No one unless born of noble family could be elected a magistrate. This had not been laid down[3] by law, but was the custom. It was entirely according to[4] law for a Roman knight or even for any citizen whatever[5] to be elected consul, but, never theless, the Romans did not favor "new men," as they called those whose fathers had not been curule magistrates

Suggestions on the Exercise.

1. *win :* **adipīscor, ī, adeptus.**
2. *office :* **honor, ōris, m.,** lit. *honor.*
3. *lay down, enact :* **sanciō, īre, sānxī, sānctus.**
4. *according to :* **secundum,** prep. with acc.
5. *any whatever :* **quīvīs, quaevīs, quodvīs.**

16.

Conditions at Rome at this Time (*continued*).

Formerly this nobility had possessed all the best virtues: bravery, steadfastness, endurance,[1] prudence, wisdom; and the Roman people gladly followed its leaders and used its counsels. But during the last fifty years before Cicero's birth,[2] its power had been gradually broken, so that it no longer enjoyed, as previously, the confidence of the people; and although later its prestige had again increased,[3] yet the Roman equestrian order[4] was now particularly hostile to it.

Suggestions on the Exercise.

1. *endurance :* **patientia, ae, f.**

2. *before Cicero's birth :* translate : *before Cicero born;* see Lesson XXIX, Example 8.

3. *increase :* **crēscō, ere, crēvī.**

4. *order :* in this sense : **ōrdō, inis, m.**

17.

The Accusation of Gaius Verres.

During a hundred years only one "new man" had been able to win the consulship, the highest honor of the re

public. This was Gaius Marius, another citizen of Arpi
num.[1] Cicero determined to try to do the same. But
before he could attain the consulship, it was necessary
first to hold lower offices, the aedileship[2] and praetorship.[3] Meanwhile he gained great reputation by accus-
ing Gaius Verres, one of the nobles, who for three years
had been praetor in Sicily, where he plundered the provincials in every way.

Suggestions on the Exercise.

1. *citizen of Arpinum :* translate by one word : **Arpīnās, ātis, m.**
2. *aedileship :* **aedīlitās, ātis, f.**
3. *praetorship :* **praetūra, ae, f.**

18.

The Career of Verres.

In Sicily no class had been exempt from Verres' avarice,[1] cruelty, or insults.[2] The rich he plundered of money
or works of art;[3] others he compelled to pay heavier
taxes;[4] he visited all with as heavy burdens[5] as possible.[6] In three years he desolated[7] the island more than
either the two servile[8] wars or the long war between
Rome and Carthage. So diligently[9] did he use his op-
portunities[10] that he boasted that he had secured enough
for[11] a life of ease,[12] even if he should be compelled to
relinquish[13] more than half[14] of his plunder.

Suggestions on the Exercise.

1. *avarice :* **avāritia, ae, f.**
2. *insult :* **contumēlia, ae, f.**
3. *work of art :* **artificium, ī, n.**
4. *tax :* **vectīgal, ālis, n.**

5. *burden :* onus, eris, n.
6. *heavy as possible :* use **quam** with the superlative.
7. *desolate :* vāstō, 1.
8. *servile :* servīlis, e.
9. *diligently :* dīligenter.
10. *opportunity :* opportūnitās, ātis, f.
11. *for :* **ad,** prep. with acc.
12. *of ease :* ōtiōsus, a, um.
13. *relinquish :* reddō, ere, didī, ditus, lit. *give back.*
14. *half :* dīmidia pars, dīmidiae partis, f.

19.

The Indictment of Verres.

As soon as Verres departed from Sicily, the Sicilians determined to call him to[1] trial, and persuaded Cicero, who had been quaestor at Lilybaeum five years before, to undertake the case. Verres was defended by Hortensius and was relying upon the assistance of all the nobility. At first his friends tried to prevent[2] the prosecution[3] by bribes[4] and threats; when they discovered that this could not be done, they attempted to substitute another prosecutor[5] in place of[6] Cicero.

Suggestions on the Exercise.

1. *to :* translate : *into.*
2. *prevent :* use tollō, ere, sustulī, sublātus, lit. *do away with*
3. *prosecution :* āctiō, ōnis, f.
4. *bribe :* largītiō, ōnis, f.
5. *prosecutor :* āctor, ōris, m.
6. *in place of :* prō, prep. with abl.

20.

The Trial of Verres.

The prosecutor whom Verres' friends tried to substitute in place of Cicero, was Quintus Caecilius Niger, who had been quaestor to[1] the defendant,[2] had had a controversy with him, and on that account, as was said, seemed to be the better able to convict Verres of wrongdoing. But the Sicilians rejected this Caecilius, not only as not a match for[3] Hortensius, but as not devoted to their cause. By[4] a process of law[5] which the Romans called *divinatio*,[6] the judges determined who should be chosen prosecutor.

Suggestions on the Exercise.

1. *to :* translate : *of*.
2. *defendant :* reus, ī, m.
3. *a match for :* translate : *equal to*.
4. *by :* per, prep. with acc.
5. *process of law :* āctiō, ōnis, f.
6. dīvīnātiō, ōnis, f.

21.

The Trial of Verres (*continued*).

In this *divinatio* Cicero delivered a speech by which he persuaded the judges to choose him to defend the Sicilians.[1] This speech is called the "Divinatio in Quintum Caecilium." But hope did not yet abandon Verres and his friends. The judges ordered the evidence to be collected in Sicily itself and allotted[2] Cicero one hundred and ten days for this purpose.[3] Meanwhile Verres tried again to substitute another prosecutor, who should accuse him on account of his former crimes committed in Achaia.

Suggestions on the Exercise.

1. *to defend the Sicilians:* use the Gerundive Construction with **ad.**

2. *allot:* **trībuō, ere, uī, ūtus.**

3. *purpose:* **rēs.**

4. *Achaia:* **Achāia, ae, f.**

22.

The Trial of Verres (*continued*).

But tnis new prosecutor never went out of Italy to make investigation.[1] Cicero, assisted by[2] his cousin[3] Lucius, completed his labors in fifty days, and returned equipped with a mass[4] of evidence and accompanied by a crowd of witnesses[5] gathered from all parts of the island. Hortensius now grasped[6] at the one remaining hope of an acquittal, which seemed a not unlikely[7] (one). He knew that if the matter could be postponed[8] a year, Verres would be safe, since he himself would then be[9] consul and Metellus would be praetor.

Suggestions on the Exercise.

1. *to make investigation:* translate · *for the sake of investigating* (**inquīrō, ere, quīsīvī, quīsītus**).

2. *assisted by his cousin:* translate: *his cousin Lucius assisting.*

3. *cousin:* **cōnsobrīnus, ī, m.**

4. *mass:* **cōpia, ae, f.**

5. *crowd of witnesses:* **testēs frequentēs,** lit. *witnesses in crowds.*

6. *grasp at.* **captō, 1.**

7. *not unlikely:* **nōn dubius, a, um.**

8. *postpone:* **differō, ferre, distulī, dīlātus.**

9. *would be:* use the periphrastic conjugation.

23.

The Trial of Verres (*continued*).

Hortensius knew that the new praetor, Metellus, would substitute corrupt judges for those whom the praetor Manius Acilius Glabrio[1] had chosen, but Cicero thwarted this plan, and in his first speech, which is called " Actio Prima," set forth the evidence which he had collected. Hortensius, who had been relying on delay,[2] was not prepared to answer, and, after the first day, abandoned the case. Before the evidence was all heard, Verres withdrew from Rome and was condemned in his absence.[3]

Suggestions on the Exercise.

1. Mānius Acīlius Glabriō (-ōnis).
2. *delay :* dīlātiō, ōnis, f.
3. *in his absence :* translate : (*was condemned*) *absent.*

24.

The Verrine Orations.

Of the seven Verrine[1] orations, only two, the " Divinatio in Q. Caecilium" and the " Actio Prima," were delivered, and the remaining five were written out[2] by Cicero after Verres was condemned, and had gone into exile at Marseilles.[3] In the first oration[4] Cicero treated of[5] Verres' city praetorship[6]; in the remaining four, of those things which he had done in Sicily : his dispensation of justice,[7] the tithes[8] on grain,[9] his thefts of statues,[10] and his unjust punishments of citizens.

Suggestions on the Exercise.

1. *Verrine :* Verrīnus, a, um.
2. *write out :* cōnscrībō, ere, scrīpsī, scrīptus.

3. *into exile at Marseilles :* translate : *to Marseilles into exile.*

4. *in the first oration :* use the simple abl.

5. *treat of :* **trāctō, 1,** trans.

6. *city praetorship :* **praetūra urbāna, ae,** f.

7. *dispensation of justice :* **jūris dictiō, ōnis,** f., lit. *pronouncing of law.*

8. *tithe :* **decuma, ae,** f.

9. *on grain :* use the adj. **frūmentārius, a, um.**

10. *statue :* **signum, ī,** n.

25.

Verres' Dispensation of Justice.

Whenever a man had died and had left property,[1] Verres used to drag[2] the heir into court and to terrify him so that he either gave a bribe or allowed himself to be deprived of his inheritance.[3] Before he left Rome, Verres had heard that a large fortune had been bequeathed[4] to a certain Dio,[5] on this condition,[6] that he should set up[7] certain statues in the forum. For it was a custom among the Sicilians, that men in wills bade[8] their heirs to beautify[9] their (native) city.

Suggestions on the Exercise.

1. *property :* **bona, ōrum,** n.

2. *drag :* **trahō, ere, trāxī, trāctus.**

3. *inheritance :* **hērēditās, ātis,** f.

4. *bequeathe :* **lēgō, 1.**

5. **Diō, ōnis,** m.

6. *on this condition :* **eā condiciōne.**

7. *that he should set up :* a Substantive Clause Developed from the Volitive.

8. *bid :* **jubeō, ēre, jussī, jussus.** Use the Subjunctive.

9. *beautify :* **exōrnō, 1.**

26.

Verres' Dispensation of Justice (*continued*).

Whenever an heir neglected to set up a statue as ordered (to) by the will, he was compelled to pay a fine [1] to Venus Erycina,[2] the goddess[3] who was worshipped in a temple on Mount Eryx.[4] Now this Dio had set up the statues according to[5] the will. Nevertheless Verres in the name[6] of Venus accused Dio, who by false testimony[7] was finally condemned. But the fine which he was compelled to pay, he was ordered to pay not to Venus, but to Verres. This is merely one of many[8] examples[9] of Verres' dispensation of justice.

Suggestions on the Exercise.

1. *fine :* multa, ae, f.
2. *Venus Erycina :* Venus (eris) Erycīna, f.
3. *goddess :* dea, ae, f.
4. *Mount Eryx :* Mōns Eryx, Montis Erycis, m.
5. *according to :* ex.
6. *in the name :* use the simple abl.
7. *testimony :* testimōnium, ī, n.; use the plu.
8. *of many :* express by ex with abl.
9. *example :* exemplum, ī, n.

27.

Verres' Collection of Grain Taxes.

There were in Sicily three kinds of taxes[1] on grain.[2] Of these the first was the tithe, — the tenth part, as the name signifies,[3] of the crop,[4] — which the farmers paid to the state. The second was the *emptum,* which was so called because it was grain bought from[5] the farmers by the state. It was a tax because the law compelled the farmers to sell at a lower price [6] than the grain was worth.[7] The third tax was the *aestimatum*, which was so called because the farmers were compelled to furnish the praetor either grain for [8] his own [9] use, or an equal amount [10] of money.

Suggestions on the Exercise.

1. *tax :* **vectīgal, ālis,** n.

2. *on grain :* see Selection 24, Suggestion 9.

3. *signify :* **significō,** 1.

4. *crop :* **messis, is,** f.

5. *from :* **ex.**

6. *at a lower price :* see Lesson XII, Example 15.

7. *than the grain was worth :* **quam quantī frūmentum erat,** lit. *than (as much) as the grain was of.*

8. *for :* **ad.**

9. *own :* **ipsīus.**

10. *amount :* **summa, ae,** f.

28.

Verres' Collection of the Grain Tax (*continued*).

These taxes were heavy and unjust, as [1] they were, but Verres made (them) much heavier by the way in which they were collected.[2] First of all [3] he established [4] new laws, having rejected [5] the entire law of Hiero,[6] which had previously been in force.[7] He issued [8] this edict [9] : "Whatever the collector [10] declares the farmer ought to pay, so much he shall be compelled to pay to the collector." Thus the wretched [11] farmers could be deprived (*spoliō*) of all their grain by [12] the wickedness of the collectors.

Suggestions on the Exercise.

1. *as* . sīcut.
2. *collect :* cōgō, ere, coēgī, coāctus.
3. *of all :* use the plu.
4. *establish :* cōnstituō, ere, uī, ūtus.
5. *reject :* reiciō, ere, jēcī, jectus.
6. Hierō, ōnis, m.
7. *be in force :* valeō, ēre, uī, itūrus.
8. *issue :* prōpōnō, ere, posuī, positus.
9. *edict :* ēdictum, ī, n.
10. *collector :* decumānus, ī, m.
11. *wretched :* miser, a, um.
12. *by :* use per.

29.

Verres' Thefts of Statues.

There was a certain Gaius Heius, a rich citizen of Messana,[1] with whose home Verres was greatly delighted.[2] This Heius had a chapel[3] in which were kept[4] four very beautiful statues, which had been wrought[5] by the most famous Greek artists,[6] Praxiteles,[7] Myron, and Polycletus. These were so wonderful that all who visited Messana came to behold them; but Verres took them away and pretended[8] that he had bought them from Heius for a small (sum), although Heius had been compelled by force to sell them.

Suggestions on the Exercise.

1. *citizen of Messana :* Māmertīnus, ī, m.
2. *delight :* dēlectō, 1.
3. *chapel :* sacrārium, ī, n.
4. *keep :* servō, 1.
5. *wrought :* use faciō.

6. *artist :* **artifex, icis, m.**

7. **Prāxitelēs, is ; Myrōn, ōnis ; Polyclētus, ı.**

8 *pretend* : **simulō, 1.**

30.

Verres' Thefts of Statues (*continued*).

Whenever a Roman praetor withdrew from Sicily and returned to Rome, the Sicilians were wont[1] to send envoys to declare to the Senate how well and kindly[2] the praetor had administered[3] the province. Accordingly when Verres returned to Rome, deputations[4] were sent, and among the envoys was this Gaius Heius. Heius did not wish[5] to say how Verres had gained possession of his statues, but when Cicero urged him to tell the truth,[6] he revealed[7] all.

Suggestions on the Exercise.

1. *am wont :* **soleō, ēre, solitus.**

2. *kindly* **benignē.**

3. *administer:* **administrō, 1.**

4. *deputation :* **lēgātiō, ōnis, f.**

5. *did not wish :* translate : *was unwilling.*

6. *tell the truth :* translate : *tell true (things)*

7. *reveal :* **patefaciō, ere, fēcī, factus.**

31.

Verres' Thefts of Statues (*continued*).

Cicero says that Heius was a man of the highest rank in his own city ; that he had come to Rome to praise Verres because he had been compelled to do this by his (fellow)-citizens ; he had never had these statues for sale[1] in his house, and unless he had been forced, no one would ever have persuaded him to sell the sacred statues which his ancestors had left him (as) the ornaments[2] of his chapel; nevertheless he had come to praise Verres, and would not[3] have spoken against him, if he had been permitted[4] to remain silent.[5]

Suggestions on the Exercise.

1. *for sale:* vēnālis, e.
2. *ornament:* ōrnāmentum, ī, n.
3. *and . . . not:* neque.
4. *if he had been permitted:* translate: *if it had been permitted to him.*
5. *to remain silent:* taceō, ēre, uī.

32.

Verres' Thefts of Statues (*continued*).

Finally in this speech[1] "On Statues," Cicero enumerates[2] the many thefts which Verres has committed in Syracuse, and he compares[3] two Romans well-known[4] to the Syracusans[5]: Marcellus,[6] who had besieged it as an enemy and taken it; and Verres, who had been sent to administer it in peace. Marcellus had saved the lives of the Syracusans; Verres had made the Forum run[7] with their blood. The city itself, most beautiful of all the cities of Sicily, Marcellus had spared; Verres had stripped[8] it of all its public[9] ornaments.[10]

Suggestions on the Exercise.

1. *in this speech:* see Selection 24, Suggestion 4.
2. *enumerates:* ēnumerō, 1.
3. *compare:* comparō, 1.
4. *well-known:* nōtus, a, um.
5. *Syracusans:* Syrācūsānī, ōrum.
6. **Mārcellus, ī,** m.

7. *had made the Forum run :* translate : *had made that the F. ran.* For *run,* use **redundō, 1.**

8. *strip :* **spoliō, 1.**

9. *public :* **pūblicus, a, um**

10. *ornament :* see previous exercise.

33.

Verres' Unjust Punishments.

In the final[1] speech, "On Punishments," Cicero tells how Verres took vengeance on those who had resisted him, and what cruelty he exercised towards them. A certain Gavius[2] had escaped from a prison[3] in Syracuse[4] and betaken himself to Messana, where he openly[5] boasted that he would soon be far[6] from Verres and his cruelties. It so happened that Verres was in Messana at that time, and when he had heard from certain friends what Gavius was boasting, at once ordered him to be publicly[7] flogged.[8]

Suggestions on the Exercise.

1. *final :* **postrēmus, a, um.**

2. **Gāvius, ī.**

3. *prison :* **carcer, is, m.**

4. *in Syracuse :* use the adj., **Syrācūsānus, a, um.**

5. *openly :* **palam.**

6. *be far (from) :* **absum, esse, āfuī, āfutūrus.**

7. *publicly :* **palam.**

8. *flog :* **verberō, 1.**

34.

Verres' Unjust Punishments (*continued*).

While Gavius was being flogged, he exclaimed,[1] "I am a Roman citizen." Verres pretended that he did not believe this, and said that he was a runaway slave

When the wretched man again exclaimed that he was a
Roman citizen, Verres did not hesitate to set up a cross[s]
on the shore and to crucify[3] the man, in sight of Italy,
(the land) where he had boasted he soon would be.   Verres
thus violated[4] the name of "Roman citizen," which
hitherto had always been held sacred.

Suggestions on the Exercise.

1. *exclaim:* exclāmō, 1.

2. *cross:* crux, crucis, f.

3. *crucify:* in crucem tollō (ere, sustulī, sublātus).   Here write
in eam (the cross) tollere.

4. *violate:* violō, 1.

35.

Results of Verres' Trial.

After his condemnation,[1] Verres withdrew into exile
at[2] Marseilles, where he remained many years.   Finally
he returned to Rome, where he was living when, after
the murder of Julius Caesar, the Civil War broke out.
The story goes that he was put to death by Antonius,
because he was unwilling to give up[3] a certain statue
which he had stolen[4] many years before from the Syracusans.   Cicero was elected aedile[5] in the very year in
which Verres was condemned, and a few years later won
first the praetorship,[6] then the consulship.

Suggestions on the Exercise.

1. *after his condemnation:* translate : *having been condemned.*

2. *at:* translate : *to.*

3. *give up :* trādō, ere, trādidī, trāditus.

4. *steal:* adimō, ere, ēmī, ēmptus, with the dat.

5. *aedile:* aedīlis, is, m.

6. *praetorship :* praetūra, ae, f.

PART THREE.

SENIOR REVIEW.

SENIOR REVIEW.

1.

The Philippics of Cicero.

When Julius Caesar was slain on the Ides of March in the seven hundred and tenth year of the City, Marcus Antonius was his colleague in the consulship. He,[1] fearing[2] that the conspirators would kill him also (a thing which[3] they are said to have intended[4] to do), concealed[5] himself on that day and fortified his house. But when he perceived[6] that nothing was attempted against him, he ventured to show himself in public[7] on the following day. Lepidus was near Rome with an army, ready to depart for Spain, which province had been assigned to him with a part of Gaul. In the night after Caesar's assassination, he occupied the Forum with his troops, and even intended to make himself master[8] of the City; but Antonius persuaded him not to do this, and won him over to himself, by giving his daughter[9] in marriage[10] to Lepidus' son. He also made Lepidus Pontifex Maximus,[11] which priestly office[12] had been made vacant[13] by Caesar's death.

Suggestions on the Exercise.

1. *he* ille
2. *fearing :* veritus.
3. *a thing which* id quod.
4. *intend :* cōgitō, 1
5. *conceal :* abdō, ere, didī, ditus.

217

6. *perceive:* sentiō, īre, sēnsī, sēnsus.

7. *in public:* in pūblicō.

8. *master:* dominus, ī, m.

9. *by giving him his daughter:* translate: *his daughter having been given to him.*

10. *in:* translate: *into.*

11. *Pontifex Maximus:* Pontifex (-icis) Maximus, ī, m.

12. *priestly office:* sacerdōtium, ī, n.

13. *make vacant·* vacuēfaciō, ere, fēcī, factus.

2.

The Philippics of Cicero (*continued*).

Antonius at first pretended to be friendly to the con spirators, sent his son to them as a hostage, and so deceived them that Brutus dined[1] with Lepidus and Cassius with Antonius Thus he persuaded them to approve a decree which he made, by which all of Caesar's acts[2] were ratified. Finally at Caesar's funeral[3] he so inflamed the minds of the people against the conspirators that Brutus and Cassius with difficulty defended their houses and lives,[4] and a little afterwards departed from the City with all the other conspirators Cicero also, who greatly disapproved[5] the vacillation[6] of the con spirators, left the City. On the first of June,[7] Antonius assembled the Senate to deliberate[8] concerning the safety of the republic; but before it met, he had visited all parts of Italy, in order to discover of what temper men were towards the conspirators

Suggestions on the Exercise.

1. *dine* cēnō, 1.

2. *acts* ācta, ōrum, n.

3 *funeral* fūnus, eris, n.

4. *lives :* remember that the Latin regularly uses the singular in this expression.

5. *disapprove :* improbō, 1.

6. *vacillation :* incōnstantia, ae, f.

7. *(June),* of June : Jūnius, a, um.

8. *to deliberate :* express by a Clause of Purpose

3.

The Philippics of Cicero (*continued*).

Meanwhile the young Octavius,[1] who had been left by his uncle,[2] Caesar, the heir of his name and estate,[3] returned from Macedonia[4] to Italy, as soon as he heard of his uncle's death, and arrived at[5] Naples on the eighteenth of April. Hirtius and Pansa brought him to Cicero, whose advice Octavius promised he would obey. At this time, he was eighteen years old.[6] When he returned to Rome, he first gave[7] shows[8] and games in honor[9] of Caesar's victories. Meanwhile Antonius, as he went through Italy, was using the decree, by which Caesar's acts had been ratified. He even invented,[10] and added to these, many things which were not in[11] (them). Among other things, having been bribed[12] by money, he restored to King Deiotarus the kingdom of which Caesar had deprived him, because he had borne aid to Pompey in the Civil War. He also took the public money which Caesar had deposited[13] in a temple at Rome, and used it for bribing Dolabella,[14] who had seized the consulship, and the greater part of the army.

Suggestions on the Exercise.

1. *young Octavius :* Octāvius adulēscēns, lit. *Octavius, the young man.*

2. *uncle :* avunculus, I, m.

3. *estate* bona, ōrum, n.
4. Macedonia, ae, f.
5. *at :* translate : *to.*
6. *eighteen years old :* translate : *was of eighteen years.*
7. *give :* ēdō, ere, ēdidī, ēditus, lit. *exhibit.*
8. *show :* spectāculum, ī, n.
9. *in honor :* translate : *into honor.*
10. *invent :* fingō, ere, fīnxī, fīctus.
11. *be in :* īnsum, inesse, īnfui, īnfuturus.
12. *bribe :* corrumpō, ere, rūpī, ruptus, lit. *spoil.*
13. *deposit :* condō, ere, condidī, ditus.
14. Dolābella, ae, m.

4.

The Philippics of Cicero (*continued*).

On the 22d of May Cicero decided to return to Rome, in order to be present, when the Senate should meet on the 1st of June. But since many friends urged him not to enter the City, he determined to go away again [1] and to travel in Greece. That he might do this the more willingly Dolabella named him (as) one of his lieutenants. Antonius also, in order to remove Brutus and Cassius from the City, commissioned [3] them to buy [4] grain in Asia and Sicily for the use of the Republic. Meanwhile Sextus Pompeius, son of Pompey the Great, who was in charge of a large army in Spain, sent letters to the consuls in which he proposed terms of peace and friendship. When the Senate had accepted these, he left Spain and came to Marseilles. Cicero, who had set out for Greece, was forced by contrary [5] winds to return to Italy On the 17th of August he arrived at Velia,[6] where he had a conference with Brutus, who soon after departed for his province, Macedonia.

Suggestions on the Exercise.

1. *again :* rūrsus.
2. *travel :* peregrīnor, 1.
3. *commission :* lēgō, 1.
4. Use a Relative Clause of Purpose.
5. *contrary :* adversus, a, um.
6. Velia, ae, î.

5.

The Philippics of Cicero (*continued*).

After this conference, Cicero returned to Rome, where he arrived on the 31st of August. On the following day the Senate met, and Cicero was expressly [1] summoned by Antonius, but he excused [2] himself, on the ground that [3] he had not yet sufficiently recovered [4] from the labor of the journey. His absence greatly displeased [5] Antonius, who in his speech [6] threatened openly that he would order Cicero's house to be torn down. The reason on account of which Cicero was unwilling to be present was that Antonius desired to decree certain new honors to Caesar. Cicero was unwilling to agree to [7] these, although he knew that it was useless [8] to resist them. The following day also the Senate met, and Antonius was absent; but Cicero was present and delivered a speech, the first of [9] fourteen [10] which he delivered against Antony. All these are called Philippics, [11] because they were similar to the orations which Demosthenes delivered against Philip, [12] king of Macedonia.

Suggestions on the Exercise.

1. *expressly* nōminātim.
2 *excuse ·* excūsō, 1.
8. *on the ground that ·* quod, with the subjunctive.

4. *recover :* **sē reficere (reficiō, ere, fēcī, fectus).**

5. *displease, it displeases :* **displicet, ēre, uit ; with dat.**

6. *in his speech :* express by the simple abl.

7. *agree to :* **assentior, īrī, sēnsus ; with dat.**

8. *useless :* **inūtilis, e.**

9. *of :* **ex.**

10. *fourteen :* **quattuordecim.**

11. *Philippics :* **Philippicae, ārum, f.**

12. *Philip :* **Philippus, ī, m.**

6.

The First Philippic.

In the First Philippic Cicero discussed [1] certain acts of Antonius, who pretended that the decrees which he had issued [2] had been found by him in the papers [3] left by Caesar.   Nevertheless Antonius had not observed the laws which had been enacted [4] by Caesar   One of these forbade any one to hold a praetorian [5] province more than a year, or a consular (province) more than two years. Although Antonius had done away with [6] this law, he kept saying [7] that the "acts of Caesar" must be observed, and kept bringing forth [8] things which Caesar had entered in [9] notebooks [10] (or at least [11] which Antonius said he had entered in notebooks), as "Caesar's acts."   "I wish that Antonius himself were present," [12]   exclaimed [13] Cicero; "then [14] he would tell us in what way he would defend the acts of Caesar."   This speech is short, but it is full of dignity and boldness.   Antonius, when he learned what Cicero had said, was so angry that he summoned [15] the Senate and ordered Cicero to be present.

Suggestions on the Exercise.

1. *discuss :* **disputō,** 1 ; with **dē.**
2. *issued :* translate · *made.*
3. *papers :* **libellī, ōrum, m.**
4. *enact :* **ferō, ferre, tulī, lātus.**
5. *praetorian :* **praetōrius, a, um.**
6. *do away with :* **tollō, ere, sustulī, sublātus.**
7. *keep saying :* **dictitō,** 1.
8. *bring forth :* **prōferō, ferre, tulī, lātus.**
9. *enter in :* **referō, ferre, rettulī, relātus ;** with **in** and **acc.**
10. *notebooks :* **libellī, ōrum, m.**
11. *at least :* **saltem.**
12. *I wish . . . were present :* see Lesson XXII, Example 14.
13. *exclaim :* **exclāmō,** 1.
14. *then :* **tum.**
15. *summon :* **convocō,** 1.

7.

Antonius' Reply to Cicero.

When Antonius had read Cicero's first speech, he seems to have understood that it was necessary either to vanquish Cicero or to be vanquished by him. The Senate had met on the 2d of September. Then Antonius went to the country, where he wrote a speech in which to reply · to Cicero. The Senate then met in the Temple of Concord, but Cicero's friends, who feared the violence [2] of Antonius, had persuaded him not to be present. Antonius spoke with the greatest vehemence [3] against Cicero, and declared that he had been the author [4] of Caesar's assassination, hoping thus to rouse [5] against him the soldiers, whom he had stationed near the temple, where they could hear his voice. Soon after, Cicero went to his villa[6] near Naples, where he wrote the Second Philippic. This he did not publish[7] immediately, but first sent it to Brutus and Cassius, whom it greatly pleased.

Suggestions on the Exercise.

1. *in which to reply :* use a Relative Clause of Purpose.
2. *violence :* **vīs, (vis), f.**
3 *with the greatest vehemence :* use superlative of **vehementer**
4. *author :* **auctor, ōris, m.**
5. *to rouse :* **excitō, 1 ;** use fut. inf. with subj. acc.
6. *villa :* **vīlla, ae, f.**
7 *publish :* **ēdō, ere, ēdidī, itus.**

8.

Cicero's Second Philippic.

Let no one[1] think that Cicero ever intended to deliver this Second Philippic. Nor is it at all certain that he wished it to be read by Antonius, or that Antonius ever saw it. There are some who believe that this speech was the cause of Antonius' anger against Cicero, and, finally, of the latter's death. Cicero, when he had heard what Antonius had said against him in the Senate, wrote in this speech those things which he himself felt,[2] not those things which he wished to publish. The oration is full of abuse,[3] and many have accused Cicero of cowardice, because he did not dare to deliver it openly[4] in the Senate, as it seems to be delivered. For he who reads it, finds again and again,[5] "Patres Conscripti" and similar words, (just) as if the orator had been present in the Senate. He even asks why Antony is not present.

Suggestions on the Exercise.

1. *no one :* **nē** quis.

2. *feel :* **sentiō, īre, sēnsī, sēnsus.**

3. *abuse :* **contumēlia, ae, f.**

4. *openly :* **palam.**

5 *again and again :* **identidem.**

9.

The Second Philippic (*continued*).

Cicero first asks why it has happened that for twenty years the Republic has had no enemy who has not also been his enemy. "And you, Antonius, whom I have never injured[1] by a word, why have you attacked me with your insults? You say that Caesar was killed by my advice? I fear, O senators, that I may seem to have secured some false witness, to bestow[2] upon me praises which are not mine. Who has ever heard me named[3] in that glorious affair? Of those who were authors of the deed, whose name has been hidden?[4] Many, indeed,[5] have boasted that they were there,[6] although they were absent; so greatly have they desired to be considered participants in[8] the deed. But no one who was present has ever tried to conceal his name. If I had been present, I should neither have wished nor have been able to conceal mine."

Suggestions on the Exercise.

1. *injure :* **laedō, ere, laesī, laesus.**

2. *bestow upon :* **impertiō, īre, īvī, ītus ;** with the dat. of indir. obj.

3. (*heard me*) *named :* use the inf.

4. *hide :* **occultō, 1.**

5. *indeed* **quidem.**

6. *be there :* **adsum, esse, adfuī, futūrus.**

7. *participant :* particeps, ipis, m.

8. *in :* express by the genitive.

10.

The Second Philippic (*continued*).

"I will omit the crimes of your private life. There are things which I cannot mention here: but let us review your public acts. I will lay bare a few of the most shameful[1] things you have done. When you had been elected quaestor, you betook yourself at once to Caesar, whom you knew to be the sole refuge[2] for[3] wickedness and vice. When you had enriched[4] yourself by his favors, you won the tribunate,[5] in which office you furnished Caesar the excuse[6] for attacking[7] his country. For he declared that in you the tribunate had been violated, and so pretended that he must come to the assistance[8] of the republic. I will say nothing against Caesar, although there is nothing on account of which it is permitted a man to attack his country. But concerning you, Antonius, it must be confessed that you were the cause of the wretched civil war which then broke out."

Suggestions on the Exercise.

1. *shameful :* foedus, a, um.

2. *refuge :* perfugium, ī, n.

3. *for :* express by the gen.

4. *enrich :* locuplētō, 1.

5. *tribunate :* tribūnātus, ūs, m.

6. *excuse :* causa, ae, f.

7. *for attacking :* use the gen. of the Gerundive Construction.

8. *that he must come to the assistance :* translate : *that it must be come by him to the assistance of* (succurrō, ere, currī, cursum, with dat.).

11.

The Second Philippic (*continued*).

" If praise, Antonius, cannot induce you to act rightly, cannot fear turn you away[1] from the most shameful[1] deeds ?   Remember what end has always fallen to the lot[3] of tyrants !   You are not afraid[4] even of the courts ; if because you are innocent, I praise you ; but if because you trust your own power and believe you can overthrow them, (then) again I ask whether you understand what that man has to fear[5] who despises the courts.   If you do not stand in awe[4] of brave men and illustrious citizens, because they are prevented from attacking you by your armed followers, still believe me (that) these very followers will not long endure you !   You compare yourself to Caesar.   I confess that you are like him in your desire for regal power, but in other things I cannot see that you deserve to be compared[6] with him."

Suggestions on the Exercise.

1. *turn away :* āvertō, ere, vertī, versus.
2. *shameful :* see Selection 10, Suggestion 1.
3. *fall to the lot of :* accidō, ere, accidī ; with dat.
4. *be afraid of, stand in awe of,* **vereor, ērī, veritus.**
5. *has to fear :* translate   *ought to fear.*
6. *deserve to be compared with* · use the Second Periphrastic Conjugation.

12.

Antonius and Octavian.

After Cicero had written the Second Philippic, Octavian, the adopted[1] son and heir of Julius Caesar, thinking that there was reason why[2] he should fear Antonius, tried to assassinate him by means[3] of certain slaves, but this plot was discovered. Meanwhile Antonius showed himself more (and more) hostile to the conspirators. In the Forum he erected a statue to Caesar with the inscription:[4] "To the most worthy Defender of his country." Octavianus at the same time was trying to win over to himself the soldiers of Caesar and vying[5] with Antonius in the promises which he made to them, so that soon he gathered a large and powerful army of veterans. But as he had no magistracy, he courted[6] the Senate, in order that it might more readily[7] sanction[8] his acts.

Suggestions on the Exercise.

1. *adopt :* adoptō, 1.
2. *why ·* quam ob rem.
3. *by means of :* per.
4. *inscription :* titulus, ī, m.
5. *vie with :* certō, 1.
6. *court :* colō, ere, coluī, cultus.
7. *more readily :* libentius
8. *sanction :* cōnfīrmō, 1.

13.

Antonius and Octavian (*continued*).

Octavian especially urged Cicero to return to Rome and assist him. But Cicero for a long time hesitated to come, partly because he distrusted the capacity[1] of the young man, partly because he disapproved his friendship with the murderers of his uncle, Caesar. At last, however, he returned, on this condition, that Octavian should use all his forces for defending Brutus and his accomplices. Antonius left Rome on the twenty-eighth of September, in order to hire[2] four legions of Caesar which were returning from Macedonia. But when these arrived at Brundisium, three of them refused[3] to follow him; thereupon[4] he ordered all their centurions to the number of three hundred to be put to death before the eyes of himself and Fulvia, his wife; then he returned to Rome with one legion, which he had induced to accompany him. Meanwhile the three other legions remained neutral.[5]

Suggestions on the Exercise.

1. *capacity :* **ingenium, ī, n.**
2. *hire :* **condūcō, ere, dūxī, ductus.**
3. *refused :* translate : *were unwilling.*
4. *thereupon :* **tum.**
5. *remain neutral :* **quiēscō, ere, ēvī, ētus.**

14.

Antonius and Octavian (*continued*).

Antonius, when he had come to Rome, issued[1] many very strict edicts, and summoned the Senate for the 28th of October. Two days before it met, he heard that two out of the three legions which were at Brundisium had followed Octavian and were at Alba.[2] He was so much alarmed by this news that he abandoned the plan of proscribing Octavian, and having distributed several provinces among his friends, left the City, to take possession of cis-alpine Gaul,[3] which had been assigned to him by a pretended law of the people, against the will of the Senate.[4] On the departure of Antonius, Cicero returned to Rome, where he arrived on the ninth of December. He immediately conferred with Pansa,[5] one of the con-

suls elect,[6] (as to) what was best to do. Octavian, in
order to show his good will[7] toward the Republic, allowed
Casca,[8] who had stabbed[9] the Dictator first, to become
tribune of the people on the 10th of December.

Suggestions on the Exercise.

1. *issue :* prōpōnō, ere, posuī, positus, lit. *post, set up.*
2 Alba, ae, f.
3 *cis-alpine :* citerior, us, lit. *hither, on this side.*
4. *against the will of the Senate :* translate : *the Senate being
unwilling.*
5. Pānsa, ae, m.
6. *elect :* dēsignātus, a, um.
7. *good will :* voluntās, ātis, f.
8. Casca, ae, m.
9. *stab :* percutiō, ere, cussī, cussus.

15.

The Third Philippic.

The tribunes summoned the Senate for the nineteenth
of December. Cicero had intended to be absent on that
day, but, one day before, he had received the edict of
Decimus Brutus, to whom Caesar a little before his death
had assigned Hither Gaul as a province, and whom
Antonius now ordered to withdraw. In this edict Brutus
boldly declared that he would not hand the province over
to Antonius, but would defend it against him by force,
if it was necessary. He accordingly forbade Antonius to
enter the province. When the Senate had assembled in
great numbers, Cicero delivered the Third Philippic, in
which he praises Octavian and tells how he (had) de-
tached[1] two legions from Antonius. He then abuses

Antonius, and compares him to Tarquinius Superbus,[3] the last king, whose name was most hateful to the Romans   Finally he urges that the Senate send support to Decimus Brutus.

Suggestions on the Exercise.

1. *detach :* abstrahō, ere, trāxī, trāctus.
2. *abuse :* vituperō, 1
3. Tarquinius Superbus, ī, m.

16.

The Fourth Philippic.

After he had delivered his speech in the Senate, Cicero then descended into the Forum, where he delivered before[1] the people the speech which is called the Fourth Philippic   In this he tells the people what had been said and done in the Senate.   He again praises Octavian and the loyalty of the two legions which had followed him rather[2] than Antonius; he again abuses Antonius. He congratulates the Romans and bids them rejoice that they have a man such as Decimus Brutus, to protect their liberty.[3]   His words, which were few, seem to have stirred the people deeply,[4] so that they shouted to him that he had on that day saved the Republic a second time.   No one can say that either on this day or after this day Cicero hid his anger or was silent from fear When we consider[5] his age,[6] and the dangers which he incurred,[7] we cannot sufficiently admire the spirit[8] which he exhibited in these last months of his life.

Suggestions on the Exercise.

1. *before :* ad.
2. *rather :* potius.

3. *to protect their liberty :* express by the Gerundive Construction.

4. *stir deeply :* concitō, 1.

5. *consider :* reputō, 1.

6. *age :* aetās, ātis, f.

7. *incu₁* subeō, īre, iī, itus.

8. *spirit :* animus, ī, m.

17.

Antonius and the Senate.

The consuls, Hirtius and Pansa, were very friendly to Cicero, consulted him often, and highly [1] valued his opinion. But they had also been friends of Caesar and Antonius. Accordingly they were unwilling to use severe [2] measures [3] against the latter. As soon as they had entered upon their magistracy, they summoned the Senate, that it might determine what was best to be done for the Republic. Both spoke with great firmness, [4] promised that they would defend the liberty of the state, and exhorted the Senate to do the same. Then they asked that a certain Fufius, who had been consul four years before and was Pansa's father-in-law, [5] deliver [6] his opinion first. Cicero wished to declare Antonius an enemy [7] of the republic at once, but this Fufius, who was a friend of Antonius, proposed [8] that before they did this, they should send envoys to him to warn him not to enter Hither Gaul.

Suggestions on the Exercise.

1. *highly :* Lesson VIII, Example 12.

2. *severe :* sevērus, a, um.

3. *measure :* ratiō, ōnis, f.

4. *firmness :* cōnstantia, ae, f.

5. *father-in-law:* socer, ī, m.

6. *deliver:* dīcō, ere, dīxī, dictus.

7. *declare an enemy:* the regular Latin expression is **hostem jūdicāre.**

8. *propose, move:* cēnseō, ēre, uī, cēnsus; with **ut-clause.**

18.

The Fifth Philippic.

Other senators also agreed with[1] this opinion of Fufius, on the ground that[2] it was cruel and unjust to condemn a man, unless they should first hear whether he was able to defend his acts Against this opinion Cicero delivered in the Senate his Fifth Philippic, in which he moved that the Senate declare Antonius an enemy and offer pardon to those soldiers who should return to their duty before the first of February; also that it extend thanks to Brutus for[3] those things which he had done in Gaul; decree a statue to Marcus Lepidus; and extend thanks to Octavian and make him a senator Cicero declared that if these things should be decreed without delay, the Senate would do all things which the occasion[4] demanded; but that there was need of promptness;[5] (and) that if they had used this[6] already, they would have had no war.

Suggestions on the Exercise.

1. *agree with:* assentior, īrī, sēnsus; with dat.

2. *on the ground that* express by **quod** with the proper mood.

3. *for:* prō.

4. *occasion* tempus, oris, n.

5. *promptness:* celeritās, ātis, f.

6. *that if they had used this:* translate: *which if they had used*

19.

The Sixth Philippic.

To Octavian the Fathers decreed not only the honors which Cicero had proposed, but even greater (ones). But they did not agree[1] concerning the sending of ambassadors[2] to Antonius. For three days they deliberated, and finally would have done all the things which Cicero ordered, had not[3] a tribune of the people[4] vetoed (them).[5] The ambassadors therefore set out for Antonius, but they were charged[6] only to order him to withdraw from Mutina,[7] where he was besieging Brutus, and to do no injury[8] to the province of Gaul; likewise (they were charged) to go to Brutus himself in Mutina,[9] and extend to him and his army the thanks of the Roman people. Since the Senate deliberated so long, the people desired to know what had been done. Accordingly they asked Cicero to come forth[10] from the senate-house and address them.[11]

Suggestions on the Exercise.

1. *agree:* cōnsentiō, īre, sēnsī, sēnsum.

2. *concerning the sending of ambassadors:* express by Gerundive Construction.

3. *had not:* i.e. *unless.*

4. *tribune of the people:* tribūnus plēbis.

5. *veto:* intercēdō, ere, cessī, cessūrus.

6. *they were charged:* translate: *it had been charged to them* (praescrībō, ere, scrīpsī, scrīptus).

7. **Mutina, ae, f.**

8. *and to do no injury:* translate: *nor* (**neque**) *to injure anything;* Lesson VI, Remark 1.

9. *to Brutus in Mutina :* translate : *to Mutina to Brutus.*

10. *come forth :* ēgredior, ī, gressus.

11. *address them :* translate : *make words before* (**ad**) *them.*

20.

The Sixth Philippic (*continued*).

I think, Quirites, that you have already heard what has been done by the Senate. For the matter has been discussed[1] since the 1st of January. I know that the opinion of the Senate is disapproved by you. For to whom are we sending ambassadors ? To a man, who, having committed many nefarious crimes hitherto, is now attacking a commander of the Roman people and besieging your most loyal and gallant colony. And yet it is not an embassy, but a declaration[2] of war, unless he obeys. For men have been sent to order[3] him not to attack[4] the consul elect, not to besiege Mutina, not to lay waste the province, not to enroll troops, but to submit[5] himself to the Senate and Roman people. But I will now say again what I have just said in the Senate. I will predict[6] that Antonius will do none[7] of these things, but will besiege Mutina and enlist troops, where ever he can.

Suggestions on the Exercise.

1. *discuss :* **agitō**, 1.

2. *declaration :* **dēnūntiātiō**, ōnis, f.

3. *order :* use **imperō**, 1.

4. *not to attack :* use **nē** with the subjunctive.

5. *submit :* **dēdō, ere, dēdidī, itus,** lit. *give up.*

6. *predict :* **praēdīcō, ere, dīxī, dictus.**

7. *none :* translate : *nothing*

21.

The Seventh Philippic.

After the ambassadors had set out for the camp of Antonius, his friends at Rome, under the leadership of Fufius,[1] were trying to win over the rest of the citizens. They sent and received letters from Antonius and gave out[2] those letters of his which seemed likely to please[3] the Senate and people. Cicero, however, felt that the dangers which threatened the state had not yet been warded off, and delivered in the Senate his seventh speech against Antonius Although it was still uncertain what replies Antonius would make to the embassy which the Senate had sent to him, Cicero urged that they should not accept any conditions which Antonius might propose; (saying) that all ranks[4] of the Roman people were in agreement;[5] that armies and generals were ready; that nothing was to be feared, provided only they should exhibit the courage and steadfastness which became' Romans.

Suggestions on the Exercise.

1. *under the leadership of Fufius :* translate : *Fufius being leader.*
2. *give out :* ēdō, ere, ēdidī, itus.
3. *likely to please :* express by the future active participle.
4. *ranks :* ōrdinēs, um, m.
5. *be in agreement :* cōnsentiō, īre, sēnsī, sēnsum.
6. *become, befit :* decet, ēre, decuit.

22.

Antonius' Reply to the Ambassadors.

After the embassy left Rome, the consuls prepared for war, in case Antonius should reject the demands of the

ambassadors. On February 6th the ambassadors brought
back word that Antonius would obey none of the demands
of the Senate, nor allow the ambassadors to go to Decimus Brutus. They even brought with them demands
from [1] Antonius, of which the principal [2] were these
that the Senate should reward his troops; that all his
acts should be ratified; that no account [3] of the money
which Caesar had left and which he himself had taken
should be rendered, [4] and that he should be put in charge
of Further Gaul with an army of six legions. Pansa
summoned the Senate to hear the words of the ambassadors, when Cicero delivered a vigorous [5] speech, in which [6]
he urged that the Senate exercise the greatest severity [7]
towards Antonius.

Suggestions on the Exercise.

1. *from :* translate : *of.*
2. *principal :* **praecipuus, a, um.**
3. *account :* **ratiō, ōnis, f.**
4. *render :* **reddō, ere, didī, ditus.**
5. *vigorous :* **vehemēns, entis.**
3. *in which :* see Selection 5, Suggestion **6.**
1 *severity :* **sevēritās, ātis, f**

23.

The Eighth Philippic.

When the Senate had received the answer of Antonius
and had heard the demands which the ambassadors
brought, some wished to send another embassy, but
Cicero prevented this from being done. On the following day, when the Senate had met again, in order to
draw up in form [1] the resolution [2] which they had

passed[3] the day before,[4] Cicero delivered his eighth
speech against Antonius. " Some," said he, " say that
there is a tumult,[5] but I say there is war. Has not
Hirtius called it war, (he) who has written in a letter:
'I have taken the town. Their cavalry has been put to
flight. Many have been slain.' Do you call this
peace ? " Then he mentions other civil wars, and compares them with this, in which all men who are worthy
the name of Romans, have one and the same sentiment.[6]

Suggestions on the Exercise.

1. *draw up in form :* **perscrībō, ere, scrīpsī, scrīptus.**
2. *resolution :* **senātūs cōnsultum, ī, n.**
3. *pass :* translate : *made.*
4. *day before :* **priōre diē.**
5. *tumult :* **tumultus, ūs, m.**
6. *have one and the same sentiment :* translate : *think one and
the same (thing).*

24.

The Ninth Philippic.

Servius Sulpicius, one of the three ambassadors who
had gone to Antonius, had died near Mutina, and on the
day after Cicero delivered his Eighth Philippic, Pansa
again called the Senate together, to deliberate (on) what
honors they should pay[1] to his memory. The consul
himself proposed a public funeral[2] and a statue. Others
said that a statue ought to be set up[3] only to those who
had been slain by violence in defending the republic;
but Cicero, who from youth had been a friend of Sulpicius and who admired him (as) especially versed in
the law, urged the Senate in a speech which is called
the Ninth Philippic, to adopt the view[4] of Pansa. In

this he said that if chance had brought death to Sul
picius, he should not have considered him worthy of a
monument, but now no one could doubt that it was the
embassy itself which had been the cause of his death,[6]
and the highest honors ought to be paid[1] him.

Suggestions on the Exercise.

1. *pay:* **tribuō, ere, uī, ūtus.**

2. *funeral:* **fūnus, ēris, n.**

3. *set up:* **pōnō, ere, posuī, positus.**

4. *adopt the view:* **sententiam sequī.**

5. *chance:* **cāsus, ūs, m.**

6. *that it was the embassy which had been the cause:* **translate :** *that the embassy itself had been the cause.*

25.

The Tenth Philippic.

A little after the Ninth Philippic had been delivered,
news was brought to the consuls that Marcus Brutus had
gained possession of Macedonia, from which he had
driven out Gaius Antonius, brother of Marcus, and
had gained many other successes.[1] As soon as Pansa
received this news, he summoned the Senate to hear
them. He himself praised Brutus and moved that
thanks be extended to him. But Fufius, who followed
him, declared that since Brutus had acted[2] without the
authority of the Senate, he ought to give up[3] his army at
once. Cicero then arose and delivered another speech,
which is called the Tenth Philippic, in which he praises
the courage and patience of Brutus, and urges the
Romans to rush together[4] from all sides to quench[5] the
flames[6] of civil war which Antonius has lighted,[7] (say

ing) that he[8] alone was the cause of bloodshed, and that they would have peace, if they should only crush him.

Suggestions on the Exercise.

1. *had gained many other successes :* translate : *had managed* (gerere) *many other things successfully* (fēlīciter).

2. *act :* agō, ere, ēgī, āctus.

3. *give up :* trādō, ere, didī, ditus.

4. *rush together :* concurrō, ere, currī, cursum.

5. *quench :* exstinguō, ere, tīnxī, tīnctus.

6. *flame :* flamma, ae, f.

7. *light :* incendō, ere, cendī, cēnsus.

8. *he :* iste.

26.

Dolabella in Asia.

While these things were being done[1] in Macedonia Dolabella,[2] who had been the colleague of Antonius in the consulship, arrived in Asia and killed Trebonius,[3] who had been put in charge of that province by the Senate. Having been informed of these things, the consuls summoned the Senate, which at once declared that Dolabella was an enemy of the Republic and confiscated[4] his property.[5] Then the question was discussed,[6] whom they should put in charge of the war against Dolabella. Some wished to send Publius Servilius,[7] others the two consuls Hirtius and Pansa, and to assign to them the two provinces (of) Asia and Syria.[8] Pansa himself wished this, as did also his friends and (those) of Antonius, who saw that in this way they would prevent the consuls from coming to the assistance[9] of Decimus Brutus, who was still besieged in Mutina.

Suggestions on the Exercise.

1. *do :* use agō, ere, ēgī, āctus.

2. Dolābella, ae, m.

3. Trebōnius, ī, m.

4. *confiscate :* pūblīco, 1.

5. *property :* bona, ōrum, n.

6. *the question was discussed :* translate : **it was discussed,** impers. (agitō, 1).

7. Servīlius, ī, m.

8. Syria, ae, f.

9. *come to the assistance of :* translate : **to Brutus** (dat.) *for assistance.*

27.

The Eleventh Philippic.

Cicero, since he thought it was unjust to send another to the province where Cassius already was, strove to bring it about[1] that a resolution of the Senate should be passed[2] by which the command of this province should be entrusted to him, although many of Cassius' friends advised him not to oppose[3] Pansa. He persevered,[4] however, and delivered a speech, the Eleventh Philippic, in support of[5] this opinion; (saying) that since Dolabella had been adjudged an enemy, he ought to be followed up by war; that he had a legion, runaway slaves, a wicked band of impious men: therefore a commander[6] ought to be chosen at once against him. But meanwhile Cassius had already defeated Dolabella, who killed himself in order not to come into the hands of the victor.

Suggestions on the Exercise.

1. *bring it about :* efficiō, ere, fēcī, fectus.

2. *pass :* translate : *make*

3. *oppose :* **resistō, ere, titī.**

4. *persevere :* **persevērō, 1.**

5. *in support of :* **prō.**

6. *commander :* **imperātor, ōris, m.**

28.

The Twelfth Philippic.

Decimus Brutus was so hard pressed[1] in Mutina that his friends feared that he would be captured and visited with the most dreadful[2] punishment, as Trebonius (had been) in Asia. Accordingly, since the friends of Anto-nius said that he was now ready to make peace with the Senate, many advised that a second embassy be sent to him. Even Cicero at first approved this and allowed himself to be named with Servilius and three other sena-tors of consular rank.[3] But soon he persuaded himself that Antonius was merely trying to secure delay till Ventidius should bring three other legions to him. Ac-cordingly Cicero delivered another speech in the Senate, in which he repudiated[4] this plan and spoke so vehe-mently,[5] that it was abandoned,[6] and Pansa soon after-wards set out to join Hirtius[7] and Octavian against Antonius.

Suggestions on the Exercise.

1. *be hard pressed :* use passive of **premō, ere, pressī, pressus.**

2. *dreadful :* **atrōx, ōcis.**

3. *of consular rank :* **cōnsulāris, e.**

4. *repudiate :* **repudiō, 1.**

5. *vehemently :* **vehementer.**

6. *abandon :* **abiciō, ere, jēcī, jectus.**

7. *to join Hirtius :* translate : *to join himself with Hirtius.* For *join,* use **conjungō, ere, jūnxī, jūnctus.**

29.

The Thirteenth Philippic.

When Antonius had written a letter to Hirtius and Octavian, in order to persuade them that they were damaging both themselves and their reputation, in that [1] they had joined themselves with those who had slain Julius Caesar, they did not reply, but sent the letter to Cicero. At the same time Lepidus sent a public letter to the Senate, in which he urged it to make peace with Antonius. This greatly displeased the Senate. And so, while they extended thanks to Lepidus on account of his love of peace, they asked that he should leave that to them; (saying) that there could be no peace with Antonius, until he laid down his arms. Encouraged by Lepidus' letter, the friends of Antonius again urged that the Senate make a treaty with him. Cicero then delivered the Thirteenth Philippic, in which he shows how useless it would be to make peace with Antonius.

Suggestions on the Exercise.

1. *in that :* quod, with the subjv.

30.

The Fourteenth Philippic.

When Pansa with four new legions had set out for Hirtius' camp near Mutina, Antonius tried to attack him before he should arrive. A fierce battle ensued,[1] in which Hirtius came to the assistance of Pansa, and Antonius was defeated with great loss. When this news was brought to Rome, the people assembled in great numbers before the house of Cicero and bore him to the Capitol. On the following day, when Marcus Cornūtus, the praetor, had called the Senate together, in order that it might deliberate concerning the letters which he had received from the consuls and Octavian, Servilius advised that the citizens should lay aside the sagum,[2] which they had assumed[3] several days before. Cicero, who was unwilling to permit this, arose and delivered the Fourteenth Philippic, in which he urged that they retain the sagum, and blamed Servilius because he had not called Antonius an enemy.

This was the last Philippic. The two consuls fell at Mutina. Then Octavian, Antonius, and Lepidus were appointed triumvirs.[4] At their order, Cicero was proscribed,[5] and soon after, on the 7th of December, was put to death.

Suggestions on the Exercise.

1. *a fierce battle ensued :* translate : *it was fought fiercely.*

2. The *sagum* (**sagum, ī, n.**) was a military dress often worn by citizens in time of war.

3. *assume :* **sūmō, ere, sūmpsī, sūmptus.**

4. *triumvirs :* **triumvirī, ōrum, m.**

5. *proscribe :* **prōscrībō, ere, scrīpsī, scrīptus.**

PART FOUR.

ORAL COMPOSITION.

ORAL COMPOSITION.

PART ONE.

LESSON I. *(Page 3.)*

1. These horsemen are brothers. **2.** Marcus and Quintus, leaders of the horsemen. **3.** Come, brother; draw up our troops! **4.** The barbarians are leading out the foot-soldiers. **5.** These leaders of the barbarians seem (*video*) very brave.

LESSON II. *(Page 6.)*

1. Neither the ship nor the rowers were seen. **2.** We praise the pilots of the ships of war. **3.** The chieftain and his wife were sent into this camp. **4.** The great influence and prudence of this consul. **5.** The forces of this chieftain have been surrounded. **6.** Either I or my son will come.

LESSON III. *(Page 9.)*

1. Before your arrival we promised aid. **2.** The multitude which surrendered itself, was very great. **3.** We will praise our ancestors, who guarded freedom. **4.** The remaining barbarians whom you saw. **5.** We did not set their camp on fire.

LESSON IV. *(Page 12.)*

1. I chose Marcus as my friend. **2.** You were called a friend of the consul. **3.** These foot-soldiers were of very little avail. **4.** Caesar crossed this river. **5.** You have been chosen leader of these forces. **6.** No one surpasses us in prudence.

LESSON V. *(Page 15.)*

1. We have delayed ten days here.   2. He has asked me my opinion.   3. I have been asked this.   4. My brother came to Geneva.   5. This camp extends five miles.   6. These troops will be transported across the Rhone.

LESSON VI. *(Page 18.)*

1. Who was in charge of this bridge?   2. Caesar placed troops around the camp.   3. I am spared; you are spared; he is spared.   4. I persuaded you and your brother.   5. He will place us in charge of the bridge.

LESSON VII. *(Page 21.)*

1. We have lands and forests.   2. This bridge must be guarded by them.   3. Horsemen must be quickly sent by you.   4. We shall send these troops as a protection to you.   5. These forests are not suitable for a camp.

LESSON VIII. *(Page 24.)*

1. You have no prudence.   2. We have come for the sake of peace.   3. He sent five thousand horsemen. 4. The Gauls were of great fickleness.   5. One of Ariovistus's wives was captured.   6. Induced by hatred of us.

LESSON IX. *(Page 27.)*

1. I remember the opinion of your father.   2. We are not eager for controversies and dissensions.   3. My comrades accused me of fickleness.   4. I do not repent of my prudence.   5. This does not concern us.

LESSON X. *(Page 30.)*

1. No one is dearer to me than my father.   2. We have more than two thousand foot-soldiers.   3. These

two men are descended from an ancient family.   4. We withdrew from these woods.   5. We were freed from these dangers by you.   6. These things were accomplished by the prudence of the general.

LESSON XI.   (*Page 33.*)

1. We shall secure possession of the smaller camp. 2. I have always used your help.   3. The barbarians had filled the woods with their troops.   4. For fear of the runaway slaves, we withdrew from this place. 5. They were always boasting of their bravery.

LESSON XII.   (*Page 36.*)

1. I have seen no one of greater prudence and bravery. 2. They advanced towards the mountain with incredible speed.   3. We shall tarry here three days longer. 4. He came with two cohorts ; he came with all his forces.   5. According to our custom the common people enjoy all advantages.

LESSON XIII.   (*Page 39.*)

1. He surpasses all his friends in prudence.   2. The Roman army was defeated in the consulship of Titus Veturius and Spurius Postumius.   3. We saw a thousand Gauls in these woods.   4. I found you in no place.   5. When these tribes had been conquered, Caesar returned from Gaul.   6. He set out from Geneva.

LESSON XIV.   (*Page 42.*)

1. You will find my brother either at Tolosa or at Narbo.   2. We returned home last night.   3. Within four months you will see me at Rome.   4. I was in camp

March 10th.   5. May 4th; June 17th; October
10th.   6. I shall be at home at midnight.

LESSON XV. (*Page 44.*)

1. The bad always envy the good.   2. I will gladly
say a few things.   3. We were the last to ask aid of
you.   4. These tribes were very powerful.   5. We
moved our camp at the end of summer.

LESSON XVI. (*Page 48.*)

1. He found his father; I found his father.   2. We
shall gladly defend ourselves and our (property).
3. The former things seem easy, the latter difficult.
4. These tribes had contended with each other for many
years.   5. You yourself were in the same camp.

LESSON XVII. (*Page 51.*)

1. I will withdraw at once, if any one wishes.   2. We
have some knowledge of a certain man.   3. Some protect us; others abandon us.   4. The one hostage we
spared; the other we have killed.   5. Both arrived on
the same day.   6. We summoned the remainder to us.

LESSON XVIII. (*Page 55.*)

1. We are wont to defend our own (possessions).
2. They are familiar with the plans of the enemy.
3. Our men kept attacking the fortifications of the
enemy.   4. The remaining horsemen were withdrawing
from the river.   5. Those men whom I knew were
wont to do this.

LESSON XIX. (*Page 57.*)

1. Caesar sent me to visit this island.   2. I have
come in order to inform you concerning these things.

3. In order the more easily to defend ourselves, we have asked help of you.   4. In order that no one might see us, we remained at home.   5. This man is worthy to be placed in charge of the camp.

LESSON XX. *(Page 60.)*

1. There is no one who does not see these things. 2. You are the only one who spared the enemy. 3. There were some who remained gladly.   4. The Gauls were so terrified that they did not withstand the attack of our men.   5. The Germans were of such bravery that fear seized our army.

LESSON XXI. *(Page 62.)*

1. Because I know you, I have said this.   2. He accused his men, because they feared the Germans. 3. After they had filled the trenches of the enemy, they easily captured the town.   4. As soon as you arrived, we got possession of the camp.   5. When the envoys heard that, they withdrew.

LESSON XXII. *(Page 65.)*

1. When we had heard this, fear seized us all.   2. We waited two days for troops to arrive.   3. We did not land our troops until ('before') all the ships arrived. 4. While the Romans were hastening to camp, the Gauls attacked them.   5. As long as you were here, the soldiers were of good courage.

LESSON XXIII. *(Page 67.)*

1. He entreated that we would send help to him. 2. You do not doubt that all these things are true. 3. No one shall prevent me from saying this.   4. I warned him to avoid the dangers of a conference.

5. I exhort you all to take arms and fight.   6. You have permitted us to assemble in a suitable place.

LESSON XXIV.   (*Page 70.*)

1. I fear that our troops will not return home.
2. You feared that we would not send the cavalry to you.
3. It happened that the messengers remained three days.
4. It is our custom to be of good courage.   5. Another fact was that the cavalry were inexperienced in battle of this kind.

LESSON XXV.   (*Page 72.*)

1. I ask whether the horsemen came.   **2.** I inquired of the general whether the grain had been brought or not.   3. Who knows whether the envoys will remain in Geneva?   4. He has shown us what they wish.   5. The scouts have informed me by what route the cavalry withdrew.

LESSON XXVI.   (*Page 75.*)

1. Unless we send ambassadors, we shall never make peace.   2. If the Germans had fought before the full moon (*lūna*), they would not have conquered.   3. We should escape dangers, if we should go by the more difficult route.   4. You acted (*ago*) in the conference as if peace had already been declared.   5. What would you do, if I should say this?

LESSON XXVII.   (*Page 78.*)

1. I said that I had come to you for the sake of peace.
2. He answered that he would send envoys to us.   **3.** I know that we have enough grain.   4. We knew that the enemy _had more grain.   **5.** Do you believe that

Gaul will be subdued ? 6. We think the cavalry will follow us.

LESSON XXVIII. (*Page 81.*)

1. We were ordered to lay waste your lands. 2. It is not permitted to march through our territories. 3. We shall dare to do all things. 4. It will be our duty to avoid all these dangers. 5. We shall try to execute ('do') all your commands.

LESSON XXIX. (*Page 84.*)

1. We saw the enemy setting out from their camp. 2. Alarmed by fear of treachery, we ordered the envoys to depart. 3. I had these ambassadors called to me. 4. These bridges need to be repaired. 5. Who will have this legion led into winter quarters?

LESSON XXX. (*Page 87.*)

1. I was desirous of gaining possession of the bridge. 2. No time was given for drawing up a line of battle. 3. He conferred with us concerning the sending of ambassadors. 4. We shall never be skilled in talking. 5. He has come to accuse us.

PART TWO.

LESSON I. (*Page 109.*)

1. Our homes and temples must be protected. 2. Protect your authority and dignity, O consuls! 3. Labor and virtue must not be despised. 4. The fruit of our peace and harmony has been reaped. 5. My son and daughter have been praised.

LESSON II. *(Page 111.)*

1. The consul whom you saw has sent me ahead.
2. You, O Roman citizens, who perceived these plots, deserved to be praised. 3. They will easily plunder the temples which you saw. 4. We, who are present, will prevent the conflagration of our homes. 5. Those who reported our plans, are now awaited.

LESSON III. *(Page 113.)*

1. Will you not bring these conspirators into the Senate? 2. Have you ever found a severer punishment? 3. We did not retain the money, did we? 4. Do you prefer the punishment of the conspirators or not? 5. Where ('whither') have these ambassadors been brought? 6. Did he return these lands or retain them?

LESSON IV. *(Page 115.)*

1. Do they call you our leader? 2. These consuls were reckoned energetic. 3. We regard these conspirators as most cruel. 4. Will you not reply briefly? 5. Have you and your son passed (*praetereō, īre, iī, itus*) by these old temples? 6. He called us most painstaking.

LESSON V. *(Page 118.)*

1. Your father taught me all the things which I know. 2. Did you not ask us this? 3. We shall not allow you to betake yourself to Faesulae. 4. Cicero delivered this oration (when) fifty-five years old. 5. This temple is ten miles distant from the city. 6. For three years we were most fortunate.

LESSON VI. (*Page 121.*)

1. Who persuaded your father (of) this? 2. I was not persuaded (of) this. 3. We shall thwart those who harm the city. 4. I am harmed; you are harmed; they are harmed. 5. I always placed harmony before all things. 6. No one will lay hands upon us.

LESSON VII. (*Page 124.*)

1. These pirates were hostile to all men. 2. We shall defend the lands and houses which we have. 3. This man has the name Lucius. 4. You have not been equal to all these labors. 5. Our lands and houses must be defended by our friends.

LESSON VIII. (*Page 127.*)

1. We see more labor than dignity in these plans. 2. This consul has less authority. 3. The honor of the consulship was always highly valued. 4. The plans of these conspirators ought to be despised by you. 5. These men are of the highest dignity and honor.

LESSON IX. (*Page 130.*)

1. We have always been mindful of the zeal of these witnesses. 2. You do not forget, do you, the cruelty of these wars? 3. He has accused us of these plots. 4. Are you not ashamed of these men? 5. I pity all men who have been accused of crime.

LESSON X (*Page 133.*)

1. Julius Caesar was born of most noble parents. 2. I, the consul, have delivered you all from slavery. 3. I shall keep these conspirators away from the senate-house. 4. These men lack dignity and honor. 5. Who has been more painstaking than Cicero, the consul?

LESSON XI. *(Page 136.)*

1. I shall use the help of all who favor our plans.
2. We shall always enjoy the fruit of all these labors.
3. We need harmony and loyalty.   4. Relying on your wisdom and patience, I did all these things.   5. By this answer you outraged our patience.

LESSON XII. *(Page 139.)*

1. He did these things with the greatest patience and wisdom.   2. Set out for the vicinity of Faesulae with your friends!   3. We sold this house for the lowest price.   4. We bought another house for a lower price. 5. These men are of the greatest cruelty.   6. Three years afterwards he was elected consul.

LESSON ΧIII. *(Page 142.)*

1. Those are worthy of honor, who surpass in wisdom. 2. When strong guards had been stationed by us, the city was safe (*tutus*).   3. These things were done in the consulship of Gnaeus Pompey and Marcus Crassus. 4. This camp will be established at Faesulae.   5. We came from Faesulae to Rome.   6. I handed over these letters to you in Gaul.

LESSON XIV. *(Page 145.)*

1. Two Roman consuls were slain at Mutina.   2. We came to Rome March 15th.   3. December 15th; January 2d; February 5th.   4. We shall be at home again within four months.   5. At this time there was (only) one consul.   6. He died at Brundisium.

LESSON XV. *(Page 148.)*

1. I remember all things which you said.   2. The ancients are most worthy of honor.   3. You did many

things unwillingly.   4. This punishment is too severe.
5. Cicero was the first who saw the dangers of this conspiracy.   6. At the end of my oration I said this.

LESSON XVI. (*Page 153.*)

1. He who envies us is unworthy of honor.   2. I
handed over the same letter that you gave me.
3. I shall be glad, if any one will free us from these
dangers.   4. Some accuse the conspirators; others defend them.   5. One of these men is worthy of honor,
the other of blame.   6. Both died on this very day.

LESSON XVII. (*Page 156.*)

1. Of all the men whom I know this (one) is most
loyal.   2. We are wont to neglect advantages.   3. For
a long time we have known this.   4. Let us not neglect
the advantage of the republic.   5. Are we to fear
dangers? Are we not to defend our country?   6. Let
virtue and bravery prevail over plots and wickedness.

LESSON XVIII. (*Page 159.*)

1. May the immortal gods protect this city !   2. Would
that we had stationed stronger guards in this place.
3. I should think this man worthier of honor.   4. We
have done this in order that we might the more easily
protect your homes.   5. Catiline sent ahead men to
await him.   6. There was no one suitable for us to
follow.

LESSON XIX. (*Page 162.*)

1. There is no one who is not acquainted with your
wickedness.   2. Who is there who does not praise loyal
friends ?   3. These deeds were so foolish that all men
thought them worthy of blame.   4. No one, so far as I

have heard, threatens your prestige.   5. There are many who think slavery worse than death.

LESSON XX. *(Page 165.)*

1. Cicero accused Lentulus because he had written this letter.   2. He has left the city because I ordered him to depart.   3. After Cicero had delivered his fourth oration, the conspirators were condemned to death.   4. Three years after he had been praetor, he was elected consul.   5. As soon as Catiline had heard these words of Cicero, he set out for Marseilles, as he said.

LESSON XXI. *(Page 168.)*

1. While these things were being done in the senate-house, a great multitude had gathered.   2. We waited till this statue should be set up in the Forum.   3. As long as Catiline remained in the city, there was the greatest danger.   4. When Cicero said these things, the conspirators were greatly alarmed.   5. Many wished Catiline to be arrested before he should leave the city.   6. The conspiracy was not crushed until ('before') Catiline withdrew from the city.

LESSON XXII. *(Page 171.)*

1. I unwillingly brought about the arrest of this man. 2. Many demanded that Catiline should be killed at once.   3. Nothing shall prevent me from reading these letters aloud.   4. I exhort you to understand the plans of these men.   5. We were afraid that you would not return home.   6. It behooves us to put these men to death.

LESSON XXIII. *(Page 174.)*

1. This is worthy of praise, that all citizens are most

loyal. 2. Do you know what words had been written in this letter? 3. Cicero in the temple of Concord asked Lentulus whether he recognized the seal of this letter. 4. I am inclined to think that no one is worthier of praise than the consul. 5. I asked whether the consul has called the Senate together or not.

LESSON XXIV. *(Page 177.)*

1. If I were to arrest and kill Catiline, I should accomplish nothing. 2. If I had arrested and killed Catiline, I should have accomplished nothing. 3. If you wish to depart at once, no one will hinder you. 4. If all entertain the same sentiments ('think the same things') concerning the republic, we shall be in no dangers. 5. If you think these conspirators worthy of death, let us order them to be killed.

LESSON XXV. *(Page 180.)*

1. Provided only you leave the city, I shall rejoice. 2. If we are not relieved of this fear, I shall fear for the republic. 3. Although no one else should remain loyal, I shall always trust the Roman knights. 4. Lentulus replied as though he had not written this letter. 5. If you depart, the city will be safe; if not, we shall be in the greatest dangers.

LESSON XXVI. *(Page 184.)*

1. I know that Lentulus wrote this letter. 2. You know, Catiline, that you will not go to Marseilles. 3. Who says that the Roman knights are not most loyal? 4. Who said that the Roman knights were not most loyal? 5. I said that these plots were most dangerous to the republic.

LESSON XXVII. *(Page 187.)*

1. Do you think that Cicero would have crushed the conspiracy, if he had put Catiline to death? 2. Did you promise that you would come, if I should write this letter? 3. Who denies that we injure the republic, if we favor bad citizens? 4. I say that you will not be loyal, if you defend these conspirators. 5. I do not doubt that Catiline would have plundered the city, if he had been able.

LESSON XXVIII. *(Page 190.)*

1. We were ordered to follow up these men. 2. Who will forbid us to visit the wicked with the severest punishments? 3. We shall try to be most loyal. 4. It pleased us to order this statue to be set up in the Forum. 5. Were you unwilling for us to be defended by our friends? 6. It was not permitted me to remain here longer than three days.

LESSON XXIX. *(Page 193.)*

1. We saw Cicero in the temple of Jupiter delivering this oration. 2. Having worshipped the immortal gods, Quirites, return to your homes! 3. We saw to the setting up of this statue in the Forum. 4. We handed over these conspirators to be visited with the severest penalties. 5. Thinking his life to be of small (account), the consul boldly underwent all dangers.

LESSON XXX. *(Page 196.)*

1. Desirous of defending the republic, we did not fear the wickedness of abandoned men. 2. Have I ever consulted for my own safety for the sake of avoiding dangers? 3. My friends came in great numbers to congratulate me. 4. All these things tend to stir up a disturbance. 5. Are these things not easy to do?

GENERAL VOCABULARY.

NOTE. — Words enclosed in parenthesis are not themselves defined,
but are inserted to assist in the definition of other words. Regular
verbs of the first conjugation are indicated by the numeral 1 following
the present indicative.

abandon, dēserō, ere, uī, sertus.

able, be able, possum, posse,
potuī.

abode, domicilium, ī, n.

about, concerning, dē, prep.
with abl.
with numerals, ferē.

absence, absentia, ae, f.

absent, absēns, entis.
absent, be absent, absum,
esse, āfuī, āfutūrus.

accept, accipiō, ere, cēpī, ceptus.

accompanied by, comitātus, a,
um, w. simple abl.

accompany, comitor, 1.

accomplice, socius, ī, m.

accomplish, efficiō, ere, fēcī,
fectus ; perficiō, ere, fēcī,
fectus ; cōnficiō, ere, fēcī,
fectus.

accord, (of one's) accord,
sponte, abl. sing. fem.

accordingly, itaque.

(account), on account of, prop-
ter, prep. with acc.; **on
that account**, proptereā.

accuse, īnsimulō, 1 ; accūsō, 1.

accustomed, am accustomed,
perfect tenses of cōnsuēscō,
ere, suēvī, suētus.

achieve, gerō, ere, gessī, gestus.

acquainted, be acquainted with,
perfect tenses of cognōscō,
ere, nōvī, nitus.

acquit, absolvō, ere, solvī, solūtus.

acquittal, absolūtiō, ōnis, f.

across, trāns, prep. with acc.

act (noun), factum, ī, n.

act (verb), agō, ere, ēgī, āctus.

add, addō, ere, didī, ditus ;
be added, accēdō, ere,
cessī, cessūrus ; literally,
approach; **it is added**,
accēdit, ere, accessit.

adjudge, jūdicō, 1.

administer, administrō, 1.

admire, admīror, 1.

Aduatuca, Aduatuca, ae, f.

Aduatuci, Aduatucī, ōrum, m.

advance, prōgredior, ī, gressus
sum.

advantage, ūtilitās, ātis, f. ;
commodum, ī, n. ; ūsus,
ūs, m.

advice, cōnsilium, ī, n.

advise, moneō, ēre, uī, itus.

affair, rēs, reī, f.

affect, afficiō, ere, fēcī, fectus.

afraid, be afraid, timeō, ēre, uī.

after, conj., postquam.

1

after, *prep.*, post, *with acc.*

afterwards, posteā.

again, a second time, iterum.

against, in, *prep. with acc.*

against, contrary to, contrā, *prep. with acc.*

(age), at the age of, nātus, construed *with the acc. of the age.*

ago, ante, *adv.*

agriculture, agricultūra, ae, *f.*

aid, subsidium, ī, *n.*; auxilium, ī, *n.*

air, spīritus, ūs, *m.*

Aisne, Axona, ae, *m.*

alarm, commoveō, ēre, mōvī, mōtus.

Alesia, Alesia, ae, *f.*

alive, vīvus, a, um.

all, omnis, e.

all the best, noblest, etc., quisque, *with superl.*

allies, sociī, ōrum, *m.*

Allobroges, Allobrogēs, um, *m.*

allow, sinō, ere, sīvī, situs; patior, ī, passus.

almost, paene.

alone, ūnus, a, um.

along, ūnā ; along with, ūnā cum.

Alps, Alpēs, ium, *f.*

already, jam.

already for a long time, jam diū.

also, etiam ; quoque, *post-positive.*

although, though, quamquam ; etsī ; quamvīs ; cum.

always, semper.

ambassador, lēgātus, ī, *m.*

ambush, īnsidiae, ārum, *f.*

among, apud, *prep. with acc.*

among, between, in the midst of, inter, *prep. with acc.*

among, in, in, *prep. with abl. or acc.*

ancestors, majōrēs, um, *m.*

ancient, antīquus, a, um ; prīstinus, a, um.

and, et ; -que (*enclitic*) ; atque.

and not, nēve, neu ; neque.

and yet, quamquam ; atquī.

anger, īra, ae, *f.*

angry, īrātus, a, um.

animal, animal, ālis, *n.*

announce, nūntiō, 1.

annually, quotannīs.

another, alius, a, ud.

answer (*noun*), respōnsum ī, *n.*

answer (*verb*), respondeō, ēre, spondī, spōnsum.

Antonius, Antōnius, ī, *m.*

anxious, sollicitus, a, um.

any, ūllus, a, um.

anybody, any one, anything, quisquam, quaequam, quicquam ; quis, quid.

appearance, speciēs, ēī, *f.*

appease, plācō, 1.

Appian Way, Appia Via, ae, *f.*

Appius, Appius, ī, *m.*

appoint, cōnstituō, ere, uī ūtus.

appoint, elect, creō, 1 ; appoint (*a dictator*), dīcō, ere, dīxī, dictus.

approach, adventus, ūs, *m.*

approach somebody or something, adeō, īre, iī, itus
(*trans.*); approach (*intrans.*) appropinquō, 1;
accēdó, ere, cessī, cessūrus, *followed by* ad *with
acc.*

approve, probō, 1.

(April), cf April, Aprīlis, e.

Aquileia, Aquileia, ae, *f.*

Aquitania, Aquītānia, ae, *f.*

archer, sagittārius, ī, *m.*

Ariovistus, Ariovistus, ī, *m.*

arise, spring up, coorior, īrī,
coortus; orior, īrī, ortus.

arise, stand up, surgō, ere,
surrēxī, surrēctum.

arm, armō, 1.

armed, armātus, a, um.

arms, weapons, arma, ōrum, *n.*

army, exercitus, ūs, *m.*

army (*on the march*), agmen,
inis, *n.*

Arpinum, Arpīnum, ī, *n.*

arrest (*noun*), comprehēnsiō,
ōnis, *f.*

arrest, comprehendō, ere,
hendī, hēnsus.

arrival, adventus, ūs, *m.*

arrive, adveniō, īre, vēnī,
ventum; perveniō, īre,
vēnī, ventum.

arrogantly, īnsolenter.

Arverni, Arvernī, ōrum, *m.*

as, ut.

as, when, cum; ut; ubi.

as, *correlative with previous
so or as,* quam.

as = *so,* tam.

as if, as though, velut sī;
quasi.

as long as, dum.

as not to, *after so, such, etc.;
in a negative clause,* quīn.

as soon as, simul atque (ac).

as to the fact that, quod.

ashamed, it shames, pudet,
ēre, uit, *impersonal.*

Asia, Asia, ae, *f.*

ask (*a question*), rogō; inter-
rogō, 1.

ask, inquire of, quaerō, ere,
quaesīvī, quaesītus.

ask, request, petō, ere,
petīvī, petītus; ōrō, 1;
rogō, 1.

assassinate, occīdō, ere, cīdī,
cīsus.

assassination, caedēs, is, *f.*

assault (*noun*), oppugnātiō,
ōnis, *f.*

assault (*verb*), oppugnō, 1.

assemble (*intrans.*), conveniō,
īre, vēnī, ventum; *trans.*
convocō, 1.

assign, attribuō, ere, uī, ūtus.

assist, adjuvō, āre, jūvī, jūtus.

assistance, auxilium, ī, *n.*

at, ad, *prep. with acc.; also* in,
prep. with abl.

(at hand), be at hand, adsum, esse, adfuī, adfu-
tūrus.

at all, omnīnō.

at first, prīmō.

at last, postrēmō.

at least, saltem.

at once, statim.

Atrebates, Atrebātēs, um, *m*

attack (*noun*), impetus, ūs, *m.*
attack (*verb*), adorior, īrī, ortus sum.
attack, assault (*a town, troops, or camp*) oppugnō, 1
attack, assail (*an individual*), petō, ere, īvī, ītus.
attain, assequor, ī, secūtus.
attempt (*noun*), cōnātus, ūs, *m.*
attempt (*verb*), cōnor, 1; temptō, 1.
attend, accompany, comitor, 1.
auspices, auspicia, ōrum, *n.*
author, auctor, ōris, *m.*
authority, auctōritās, ātis, *f.*
auxiliaries, auxilia, ōrum, *n.*
avail, valeō, ēre, uī, itūrus.
avarice, avāritia, ae, *f.*
avenge, ulcīscor, ī, ultus.
avoid, vītō, 1.
await, exspectō, 1.
away, be away, be distant, absum, esse, āfuī, āfutūrus.

B

Baculus, Baculus, ī, *m.*
bad, malus, a, um.
baggage, impedīmenta, ōrum, *n.*
band, manus, ūs, *f.*
bank, rīpa, ae, *f.*
bar, obstruō, ere, strūxī, strūctus.
barbarians, barbarī, ōrum, *m.*
battle, proelium, ī, *n.*; pugna, ae, *f.*
be, sum, esse, fuī, futūrus.
  be without, careō, ēre, uī, itūrus.

bear, ferō, ferre, tulī, lātus.
  bear in mind, meminī, isse, *with acc. or gen.*
beast of burden, jūmentum, ī, *n.*
beautiful, pulcher, chra, chrum.
because, quod; quia; cum.
become, fīō, fierī, factus sum.
before, in the presence of, apud, ad, *preps. with acc.;* in front of, prō, *prep. with obl.*
before (*adv.*), ante; anteā.
before (*conj.*), antequam, priusquam.
beg, ōrō, 1.
begin, coepī, coepisse; *when governing a pass. inf. the perf. ind. is regularly* coeptus est.
begin (*a thing*), īnstituō, ere, uī, ūtus; begin battle, proelium committō, ere, mīsī, missus.
beginning, initium, ī, *n.*
(behalf) in behalf of, prō, *prep. with abl.*
behold, spectō, 1.
behoove, it behooves, oportet, ēre, uit, *impersonal.*
Belgians, Belgae, ārum, *m.*
believe, crēdō, ere, crēdidī, crēditus, *with dat.*
Bellovaci, Bellovacī, ōrum, *m.*
bench, subsellium, ī, *n.*
besides (*adv.*), praetereā.
besiege, obsideō, ēre, sēdī, sessus.
best, *superl. of* bonus.

bestow upon, impertiō, īre, iī, ītus.

betake one's self, recipiō, ere, cēpī, ceptus, *with a reflexive.*

better, *adj.*, melior; *adv.*, melius.

between, inter, *prep. with acc.*

Bibracte, Bibracte, is, *n.*

Bibrax, Bibrax, actis, *f.*

Bibulus, Bibulus, ī, *m.*

bid, jubeō, ēre, jussī, jussus.

Bituriges, Biturīgēs, um, *m.*

blame (*verb*), culpō, 1.

blameless, innocēns, entis.

block, obstruct, interclūdō, ere, clūsī, clūsus : obstruō, ere, strūxī, strūctus.

blood, sanguis, inis, *m.*

bloodshed, caedēs, is, *f.*

boast, make a boast, glōrior, 1.

boat, nāvis, is, *f.*; nāvigium, ī, *n.*

body, corpus, oris, *n.*

bold, audāx, ācis.

boldly, audācter.

boldness, audācia, ae, *f*

borders, fīnēs, ium, *m.*

born, be born, nāscor, ī, nātus. born, nātus, a, um.

both . . . and, et . . . et.

both, each, uterque, utraque, utrumque.

boundless, īnfīnītus, a, um.

boy, puer, erī, *m.*

Bratuspantium, Brātuspantium, ī, *n.*

brave, fortis, e.

bravely, fortiter.

bravery, fortitūdō, inis, *f.*

break (*of camp*), moveō, ēre, mōvī, mōtus ; break, impair, imminuō, ere, uī ūtus.

break down, rescindō, ere, scidī, scissus.

break out, arise, coorior, īrī. coortus sum.

bribe, largītiō, ōnis, *f.*

bridge, pōns, pontis, *m.*

briefly, breviter.

bring (*of things*), afferō, ferre. attulī, allātus : (*of persons*), addūcō, ere, dūxī, ductus.

bring about. efficiō, ere, fēcī. fectus.

be brought about, fīō, fierī, factus sum.

bring back, redūcō, ere, dūxī, ductus.

bring back word, referō, ferre, rettulī, relātus.

bring out, efferō, ferre, extulī, ēlātus.

bring in, into, intrōdūcō, ere dūxī, ductus, *followed by* in *and acc.*

bring on or upon, īnferō, ferre, intulī, illātus ; *with dat. of indir. obj.*

Britain, Britannia, ae, *f.*

Britons, Britannī, ōrum, *m.*

broad, lātus, a, um.

brother, frāter, tris, *m.*

Brundisium, Brundisium, ī, *n.*

build (*a bridge*), faciō, ere, fēcī, factus.

building, aedificium, ī, *n.*

burn (*tr.*) (*of things*), comburō, ere, ussī, ūstus ; (*of persons*), cremō, 1.

business, negōtium, ī, *n.*

but (*if strongly adversative*), sed.

but (*denoting transition*), autem, *post-positive.*

but if, sīn.

buy, emō, ere, ēmī, ēmptus.

by (*of personal agent*), ā, ab, *prep. with abl.*

C

Caecilius, Caecilius, ī, *m.*

Caesar, Caesar, is, *m.*

call, name, appellō, 1.

call, summon, vocō, 1.

call together, convocō, 1.

camp, castra, ōrum, *n.*

can, be able, possum, posse, potuī.

Capital, Capitōlium, ī, *n.*

captive, captīvus, ī, *m.*

capture, capiō, ere, cēpī, captus.

carry, portō, 1.

case, causa, ae, *f.*

Cassius, Cassius, ī, *m.*

Casticus, Casticus, ī, *m.*

Catiline, Catilīna, ae, *m.*

Cato, Catō, ōnis, *m.*

Catulus, Catulus, ī, *m.*

cause, causa, ae, *f.*

cavalry, equitātus, ūs, *m.* ; equitēs, um, *m. pl.; as adj.*, equester, tris, tre.

Cenabum, Cenabum, ī, *n.*

centurion, centuriō, ōnis, *m.*

certain, certain one, quīdam,

quaedam, quiddam or quoddam ; **certain, sure,** certus, a, um.

Cethegus, Cethēgus, ī, *m.*

change (*noun*), commūtātiō, ōnis, *f.*

change (*verb*), mūtō, 1.

changeable, mōbilis, e.

chapel, sacrārium, ī, *n.*

character, nature, nātūra, ae, *f.*

charge (*noun*), crīmen, inis, *n.*

charge, be in charge, praesum, esse, fuī, *construed with dat.*

charge, put in charge, praeficiō, ere, fēcī, fectus, *construed with dat.*

chariot, war chariot, essedum, ī, *n.*

charioteer, aurīga, ae, *m.*

chief, prīnceps, ipis, *m.*

chieftain, prīnceps, ipis, *m.*

children, līberī, ōrum, *m.* ; puerī, ōrum, *m.*

choose, dēligō, ere, lēgī, lēctus.

Cicero, Cicerō, ōnis, *m.*

Cimbrians, Cimbrī, ōrum, *m.*

circumstance, rēs, reī, *f.*

citadel, arx, arcis, *f.*

citizen, fellow-citizen, cīvis, is, *m.*

city, urbs, urbis, *f.*

civil, cīvīlis, e.

class, genus, eris, *n.*

Claudius, Claudius, ī, *m.*

clemency, clēmentia, ae, *f.*

cohort, cohors, ortis, *f.*

colleague, collēga, ae, *m.*

collect, colligō, ere, lēgī, lēctus.

colony, colōnia, ae, *f.*

come, veniō, īre, vēnī, ventum.
come out, come forth, prō-
deō, īre, iī, itūrus.
come together, conveniō,
ēre, vēnī, ventum.

command (*noun*), instruction,
mandātum, ī, *n.*; com-
mand, control, imperium,
ī, *n.*

command (*verb*), imperō, 1;
be in command, praesum,
esse, fuī, *with dat.*

commander, dux, ducis, *m.*;
imperātor, ōris, *m.*

commit, committō, ere, mīsī,
missus.

common, commūnis, e.

common people, plēbs, is, *f.*

compare, comparō, 1.

compel, cōgō, ere, coēgī, coāctus.

complain, queror, ī, questus
sum.

complete, perficiō, ere, fēcī,
fectus.

comrade, commīlitō, ōnis, *m.*

conceal, cēlō, 1; occultō, 1.

concern, it concerns, interest,
esse, fuit; rēfert, ferre,
rëtulit, *impersonal. Both
verbs govern the gen.*

concerning, dē, *prep. with abl.*

concord, concordia, ae, *f.*

condemn, condemnō, 1.

condition, condiciō, ōnis, *f.*

conduct, escort, dēdūcō, ere,
dūxī, ductus.

confer (*with*), colloquor, ī,
locūtus.

conference, colloquium, ī, *n.*

confess, cōnfiteor, ērī, fessus

confidence, fīdūcia, ae, *f.*;
trustworthiness, fidēs, eī,
f.

confine, contineō, ēre, uī, tentus.

conflagration, incendium, ī, *n*

congratulate, grātulor, ārī
ātus sum, *with the dat.*

conquer, vincō, ere, vīcī, victus.

consider, regard, putō, 1; exīstimō, 1.

considerate, mītis, e.

consideration, ratiō, ōnis, *f.*

conspiracy, conjūrātiō, ōnis, *f.*

conspirators, conjūrātī, ōrum
m.

conspire, conjūrō, 1.

constantly, semper.

construct, aedificō, 1.

consul, cōnsul, is, *m.*

consular, cōnsulāris, e.

consulship, cōnsulātus, ūs, *m.*

consult, cōnsulō, ere, uī, sultus.

contemplate, cōgitō. 1.

contempt, contemptiō, ōnis, *f.*

contend, contendō, ere, endī
entum; dīmicō, 1.

contract, contract for, locō, 1.

contrary to, contrā, *prep. with
acc.*

controversy, contrōversia, ae, *f.*

convey, perferō, ferre, tuli,
lātus.

convict, condemnō, 1.

corrupt, improbus, a, um.

Cotta, Cotta, ae, *m.*

council, concilium, ī, *n.*

counsel, cōnsilium, ī, *n.*

country, native country, patria, ae, *f.*

country (*as opposed to the city*), rūs, rūris, *n.*

courage, animus, ī, *m.* ; fortitūdō, inis, *f.*

courageous, fortis, e.

courageously, fortiter.

court, jūdicium, ī, *n.*

cowardice, ignāvia, ae, *f.*

Crassus, Crassus, ī, *m.*

crime, scelus, eris, *n.*

cross, trānseō, īre, iī, itūrus.

crowd, multitūdō, inis, *f.*

in crowds, frequēns, entis.

crowded, crowded together, cōnfertus, a, um.

cruel, crūdēlis, e.

cruelly, crūdēliter.

cruelty, crūdēlitās, ātis, *f.*

crush, opprimō, ere, pressī, pressus.

cultivate, colō, ere, coluī, cultus.

custom, cōnsuētūdō, inis ; mōs, mōris, *m.*

cut off, interclūdō, ere, clūsī, clūsus.

cut to pieces, concīdō, ere, cīdī, cīsus.

D

dagger, sīca, ae, *f.*

daily, cottīdiē.

damage, laedō, ere, laesī, laesus.

danger, perīculum, ī, *n.*

dangerous, perīculōsus, a, um.

dare, audeō, ēre, ausus.

daughter, fīlia, ae, *f.*

day, diēs, ēī, *m.*

dear, cārus, a, um.

death, mors, mortis, *f.*

(December), of December, December bris, bre.

deceive, fallō, ere, fefellī, falsus.

decide, cōnstituō, ere, uī, ūtus.

declare, dēclārō, 1.

decree (*noun*), dēcrētum, ī, *n.*

decree (*verb*), dēcernō, ere, crēvī, crētus.

deed, factum, ī, *n.*

deep, altus, a, um.

defeat, superō, 1.

defence, dēfēnsiō, ōnis, *f.*

defend, dēfendō, ere, fendī, fēnsus.

defender, dēfēnsor, ōris, *m.*

Deiotarus, Deiotarus, ī, *m.*

delay (*verb*), moror, 1.

delay (*noun*), mora, ae, *f.*

deliberate, dēlīberō, 1.

deliver (*a speech*), habeō, ēre, uī, itus.

deliver from, līberō, 1.

demand (*verb*), postulō, 1 ; flāgitō, 1 ; poscō, ere, poposcī.

demand (*noun*), postulātum, ī, *n.*

democratic, populāris, e.

Demosthenes, Dēmosthenēs, is, *m.*

dense, dēnsus, a, um.

deny, negō, 1.

depart, dēcēdō, ere, cessī, cessūrus.

departure, profectiō, ōnis, *f.* ;
  discessus, ūs, *m.*
depend, nītor, ī, nīsus *or* nīxus
  sum.
deprive, prīvō, 1.
descend, dēscendō, ere, endī.
desert, dēserō, ere, uī, sertus.
deserve, mereō, ēre, uī, itus.
design, cōnsilium, ī, *n.*
desire, wish, cupiō, ere, cupīvī,
  or iī, ītus.
desire, eagerness, cupiditās,
  ātis, *f.* ; libīdō, inis, *f.*
desirous, cupidus, a, um ;
  avidus, a, um.
desist, dēsistō, ere, dēstitī.
despise, contemnō, ere, tempsī, temptus.
destroy, break down, re-
  scindō, ere, scidī, scissus.
detain, retineō, ēre, uī, tentus.
determine, cōnstituō, ere, uī,
  ūtus.
develop, alō, ere, aluī, altus *or*
  alitus.
devote, devote one's self to
  something, dēdō, ere, dēdidī, dēditus, *with a reflexive pronoun.*
devoted, dēditus, a, um.
dictator, dictātor, ōris, *m.*
die, morior, morī, mortuus sum.
difficult, difficilis, e.
difficulty, difficultās, ātis, *f.* ;
  with difficulty, vix.
dignity, dignitās, ātis, *f.*
diligence, dīligentia, ae, *f.*
direction, pars, partis, *f.*
disapprove, improbō, 1.
discipline, disciplīna, ae, *f.*

discover, comperiō, īre, comperī, compertus.
dismiss, dīmittō, ere, mīsī,
  missus.
dismount, dēsiliō, īre, iī *or* uī,
  sultum.
displease, displiceō, ēre, uī.
disposition, animus, ī, *m.*
dissension, dissēnsiō, ōnis, *f.*
distant, be distant, absum,
  esse, āfuī, āfutūrus,
distinguished, clārus, a, um.
distress, dolor, ōris, *m.*
distribute, distribuō, ere, uī,
  ūtus.
district, regiō, ōnis, *f.*
distrust, diffīdō, ere, fīsus
  with dat.
disturbance, tumultus, ūs, *m.*
ditch, fossa, ae, *f.*
Divitiacus, Dīvitiācus, ī, *m.*
divide, dīvidō, ere, vīsī, vīsus.
do, faciō, ere, fēcī, factus.
Domitius, Domitius, ī, *m.*
door, jānua, ae, *f.*
doubt, dubitō, 1.
drag, drag along, trahō, ere,
  trāxī, trāctus.
draw near, appropinquō, 1 ;
  construed with dat.
draw up, īnstruō, ere, strūxī,
  strūctus.
drive away, drive back, repellō,
  ere, reppulī, repulsus.
drive, drive out, drive from,
  expellō, ere, pulī, pulsus.
Dumnorix, Dumnorīx, īgis, *m.*
duty, officium, ī, *n.* ; it is a
  duty, oportet, ēre, oportuit. *impers.*

dwell, incolō, ere, coluī, cultus; *figuratively*, īnsum, inesse, īnfuī, *construed with in and the abl.*

dwelling, tēctum, ī, *n.*, *lit.* roof.

E

each, quisque, quaeque, quicque.

each (of two), uterque, utraque, utrumque.

each other, *for the first and second persons, use the plural of* ego *and* tū; *for the third person use* suī.

eager, alacer, cris, cre.

eager for, cupidus, a, um, *with the gen.*

earliest, prīmus, a, um.

easily, facile.

easy, facilis, e.

edict, ēdictum, ī, *n.*

efforts, opera, ae, *f.*

eight, octō, *indecl.*

eighteen, duodēvīgintī.

eighth, octāvus, a, um.

eight hundred, octingentī, ae, a.

either . . . or, aut . . . aut, *if the two alternatives exclude each other; otherwise*, vel . . . vel.

either, either one (of two), utervīs, utravīs, utrumvīs.

elect (*adj.*), dēsignātus, a, um.

eiect, creō, 1.

election, comitia, ōrum, *n.*

eleventh, ūndecimus, a, um.

else, alius, a, ud.

embankment, agger, eris, *m.*

embassy, lēgātiō, ōnis, *f.*

eminent, praestāns, antis.

empire, imperium, ī, *n.*

empty, inānis, e.

enact, statuō, ere, uī, ūtus.

encourage, cohortor, 1; cōn-fīrmō, 1.

end, fīnis, is, *m.*; end, fate, exītus, ūs, *m.*

(end), at the end of, extrēmus, a, um, *with a substantive.*

endure, perferō, ferre, tulī, lātus.

enemy (*in military sense*), hostis, is, *c.*; (*collectively*), hostēs, ium, *m.*

personal enemy, inimīcus, ī, *m.*

energetic, vehemēns, entis.

energy, virtūs, ūtis, *f.*

enjoy, fruor, ī, frūctūrus.

enlist, cōnscrībō, ere, scrīpsī, scrīptus.

enormous, immānis, e.

enough, satis.

enroll, cōnscrībō, ere, scrīpsī, scrīptus.

enter, ingredior, ī, gressus sum.

enter into, enter upon, ineō, īre, iī, itus, *trans.*

entire, tōtus, a, um.

entirely, omnīnō.

entreat, obsecrō, 1.

entrust, committō, ere, mīsī, missus.

envoy, lēgātus, ī, *m.*

envy, invideō, ēre, vīdī, vīsum, *with dat.*

equal(*verb*), adaequō, 1 ; *trans.*
equal (*adj.*), pār, paris.
equestrian, equester, tris, tre.
equip, īnstruō, ere, strūxī, strūctus.
erect, collocō, 1.
escape, get away (*intrans.*), ēvādō, ere, vāsī, vāsum.
escort, prōsequor, ī, secūtus.
especially, maximē ; praecipuē.
establish, collocō, 1.
Etruria, Etrūria, ae, *f.*
even, etiam.
  not even, nē . . . quidem, *with the emphatic word or phrase between.*
ever, at any time, unquam.
  ever, always, semper.
every, omnis, e.
evidence, argūmenta, ōrum, *n.*
excel, praestō, āre, stitī.
excellent, ēgregius, a, um.
except, praeter, *prep. with acc. ; with negs.*, nisi, *conj.*
excessive, nimius, a, um.
excuse (*noun*), excūsātiō, ōnis, *f.*
excuse (*verb*), pūrgō, 1 ; excūsō, 1.
exempt, līber, a, um.
exercise, ūtor, ī, ūsus.
exhaust, cōnficiō, ere, fēcī, fectus.
exhibit, praestō, āre, stitī, stitus.
exhort, cohortor, 1.
exile, exsilium, ī, *n.*
(expected, supposed,—sooner, larger) than expected, or

supposed, opīniōne, *abl. of* opīniō, ōnis.
extend (*thanks*), agō, ere, ēgī, āctus.
extend, stretch, pateō, ēre, uī.
extensive, amplus, a, um.
extent, magnitūdō, inis, *f.*
extinguish, exstinguō, ere, īnxī, īnctus.
eye, oculus, ī, *m.*

F

Fabius, Fabius, ī, *m.*
fact, rēs, reī, *f.* ; **as to the fact that**, quod.
Faesulae, Faesulae, ārum, *f.*
fail, dēficiō, ere, fēcī, fectus.
faithful, fidēlis, e.
fall, cadō, ere, cecidī, cāsūrus.
fall in with, incidō, ere, incidī, *construed with* in *and acc.*
false, falsus, a, um.
familiar, am familiar with, *perf. of* cognōscō, ere, nōvī, nitus, *trans.*
family, stock, genus, eris, *n.*
famous, clārus, a, um.
far, by far, longē, *adv.*
farmer, agricola, ae, *m.*
farther, ulterior, us.
father, pater, patris, *m.*
fault, culpa, ae, *f.*
favor(*noun*), beneficium, ī, *n.*
favor (*verb*), faveō, ēre, fāvī, fautūrus, *with dat.*
fear (*noun*), timor, ōris, *m.* ; metus, ūs, *m.*
fear (*verb*), metuō, ere, uī ; vereor, ērī, itus.

(February), of February, Februārius, a, um.
feel, sentiō, īre, sēnsī, sēnsus.
fertile, ferāx, ācis.
few, paucī, ae, a.
very few, perpaucī, ae, a.
fickle, mōbilis, e.
fickleness, levitās, ātis, *f.*
field, ager, agrī, *m.*
fiercely, ācriter.
fifteen, quīndecim.
fifth, quīntus, a, um.
fifty, quīnquāgintā.
fight, pugnō, ɪ.
fill, fill up, compleō, ēre, ēvī, ētus.
finally, postrēmō ; dēnique.
find (*by searching*), reperiō, īre, repperī, repertus.
find, come upon, inveniō, īre, vēnī, ventus.
find out something (*by investigation*), comperiō, īre, perī, pertus.
find (*good, bad, etc.*), ūtor, ī, ūsus, *with pred. abl.*
fire, īgnis, is, *m.*
first, prīmus, a, um.
first (*adv.*), prīmum ; at first, prīmō.
five, quīnque.
five hundred, quīngentī, ae, a.
flee, fugiō, ere, fūgī, fugitūrus.
fleet, classis, is, *f.*
flight, fuga, ae, *f.*
flourishing, flōrēns, entis.
follow, sequor, ī, secūtus ; follow up, persequor, ī, secūtus.
follower, comes, itis, *m.*

following, next, posterus, a, um.
fond of, studiōsus, a, um.
foolish, stultus, a, um.
foot, pēs, pedis, *m.*
foot of, base of, īnfimus *or* īmus, a, um.
foot-soldier, pedes, itis, *m.*
for, *denoting purpose*, ad, *prep. with acc.; denoting motion*, in, *with acc.;* for, in behalf of, in place of, prō, *prep. with abl.*
for (*conj.*), nam; *or* enim, *post-positive.*
forage, procure forage, pābulor, 1.
forbid, vetō, āre, uī, itus.
force, compel, cōgō, ere, coēgī, coāctus.
force, vīs, vis, *f.*
(military) force, forces, cōpiae, ārum, *f.*
ford, vadum, ī, *n.*
foresight, prūdentia, ae, *f.*
forest, silva, ae, *f.*
forget, oblīvīscor, ī, oblītus sum.
form, make, faciō, ere, fēcī, factus.
former . . . (latter), ille, a, ud.
former, *with reference to the present*, superior, us.
formerly, ōlim.
forthwith, statim.
fortification, mūnītiō, ōnis, *f.*
fortify, mūniō, īre, īvī, ītus.
fortunate, fēlīx, īcis.
fortune, fortūna, ae, *f.*
fortune (*in sense of property*), fortūnae, ārum, *f.*

forty, quadrāgintā.

Forum, Forum, ī, *n.*

found, condō, ere, didī, ditus.

fountain, fōns, fontis, *m.*

four, quattuor.

four years, quadriennium, ī, *n.*

fourteenth, quārtus decimus.

fourth, quārtus, a, um.

free (*adj.*), līber, a, um ; free from, clear of, vacuus, a, um.

free (*verb*), līberō, 1.

freedman, lībertus, ī, *m.*

freedom, lībertās, ātis, *f.*

frequent, crēber, bra, brum.

fresh (*of water*), dulcis, e.

friend, amīcus, ī, *m.* ; amīca, ae, *f.*

friendly, amīcus, a, um.

friendship, amīcitia, ae, *f.*

frighten, terreō, ēre, uī, itus.

from, ā, ab ; from, out of, ē, ex ; down from, dē ; *prepositions with abl.*

    from the vicinity of, ā, ab, *with abl.*

    from (*after verbs of hindering, etc.*), quō minus, nē, quīn.

front, frōns, frontis, *f.*

fruit, frūctus, ūs, *m.*

Fufius, Fūfius, ī, *m.*

Fulvia, Fulvia, ae, *f.*

full, plēnus, a, um.

furnish, praebeō, ēre, uī, itus.

fury, furor, ōris, *m.*

G

Gabinius, Gabīnius, ī, *m.*

gain, pariō, ere, peperī, par-tus, *originally*, bring forth, produce.

gain possession of, potior, īrī, ītus.

Gaius, Gāius, ī, *m.* ; *abbreviated* C.

Galba, Galba, ae, *m.*

gallant, fortis, e.

Gallic, Gallicus, a, um

game, lūdus, ī, *m.*

gate, porta, ae, *f.*

gather (*trans.*), cōgō, ere, coēgī, coāctus.

gather (*intrans.*), conveniō, īre, vēnī, ventum.

Gaul, a Gaul, Gallus, ī, *m.*

Gaul, the country, Gallia, ae, *f.*

general, dux, ducis, *m.*

Geneva, Genava, ae, *f.*

Gergovia, Gergovia, ae, *f.*

German, Germānus, a, um ; *as noun*, Germānī, ōrum, *m.*

Germany, Germānia, ae, *f.*

get ready (*trans.*), comparō, 1.

give, dō, dare, dedī, datus.

glad, laetus, a, um.

glorious, clārus, a, um.

glory, glōria, ae, *f.*

Gnaeus, Gnaeus, ī, *m.* ; *abbreviated* Cn.

go, eō, īre, īvī, itum.

    go around, circumeō, īre, iī, itus.

    go away, abeō, īre, iī, itūrus.

    go back, redeō, īre, iī, itūrus.

    go out, forth, exeō, īre, iī, itum.

god, deus, ī, *m.*

good, bonus, a, um; good fortune, fortūna, ae, *f.*

Gracchus, Gracchus, ī, *m.*

gradually, paulātim.

grain, frūmentum, ī, *n.*; grain supply, rēs frūmentāria, reī frūmentāriae, *f.*

grant, concēdō, ere, cessī, cessus.

great, magnus, a, um.

greatest (*of qualities*), summus, a, um.

greatly, magnopere.

Greece, Graecia, ae, *f.*

greed, avāritia, ae, *f.*

guard, a guard, cūstōs, ōdis, *m.*

guard (*verb*), servō, 1; cūstōdiō, īre, īvī, ītus; be on one's guard (against), caveō, ēre, cāvī, cautūrus.

H

Haeduan (*adj.*), Haeduus, a, um; *as noun*, Haeduus, *m.*; Haedui, Haeduī, ōrum.

hand, manus, ūs, *f.*

hand, be at hand, adsum, esse, adfuī, adfutūrus.

hand, be on hand, suppetō, ere, īvī *or* iī.

hand over, trādō, ere, didī, ditus.

happen, be done, fīō, fierī, factus; accidō, ere, ī.

harangue, cōntiō, ōnis, *f.*

harbor, portus, ūs, *m.*

harm (*noun*), dētrīmentum, ī, *n.*

harm, do harm, noceō, ēre, uī, itūrus, *with dat. of indirect obj.*

harmony, concordia, ae, *f.*

hasten, press on, contendō, ere, endī, entum.

hate, ōdī, ōdisse.

hateful, odiōsus, a, um.

hatred, odium, ī, *n.*

have, habeō, ēre, uī, itus; have something done, cūrō, 1, *with gerundive.*

he who, is quī.

heap, acervus, ī, *m.*

headship, prīncipātus, ūs, *m.*

hear, hear of, audiō, īre, īvī, ītus.

heavy, gravis, e.

height, altitūdō, inis, *f.*

heir, hērēs, ēdis, *m.*

help (*noun*), auxilium, ī, *n.*

Helvetii, Helvetians, Helvētiī, ōrum, *m.*

hence, hinc.

her, suus, a, um, *reflexive.*

here, hīc.

hesitate, dubitō, 1.

hide, cēlō, 1; occultō, 1.

high, altus, a, um.

high (*of price*), magnus, a, um.

higher, at a higher price (*with verbs of* valuing, buying, *and* selling), plūris.

highest (*of qualities*), summus, a, um.

hill, collis, is, *m.*

himself, herself, suī, sibi, sē.

hinder, impediō, īre, īvī, ītus.

his, suus, a, um, *reflexive.*

hither, citerior, us.

hitherto, anteā.

hold, teneō, ēre, uī ; *of office,*
gerō, ere, gessī, gestus.

hold, regard, habeō, ēre, uī,
itus.

home, domus, ūs, *f.* ; at home,
domī ; from home, domō.

home, to one's (their) home,
domum ; domōs.

honor (*noun*), honor, ōris, *m.* ;
honestās, ātis, *f.*

hope, spēs, eī, *f.*

hope, hope for, spērō, 1, *trans.*

horse, equus, ī, *m.*

horseman, eques, itis, *m.*

Hortensius, Hortēnsius, ī, *m.*

hostage, obses, idis, *m.*

hostile, inimīcus, a, um.

hour, hōra, ae, *f.*

house, domus, ūs, *f.* ; in one's
house, domī.

how, *if used to introduce the
sentence as a whole,* quī
or quō modō *in direct
questions,* quō modō *or* ut
in indirect; quam, *if used
to modify an adjective or
adverb in the sentence.*

how great, how high, quantus,
a, um.

how many, quot, *indecl.*

how much, quantum ; *often
followed by gen. of the
whole.*

however, autem, *post-positive.*

hundred, centum.

hurdle, crātēs, is, *f.*

hurl, coniciō, ere, conjēcī, con-
iectus.

I

I, ego, meī.

Ides, Īdūs, uum, *f.*

if, sī, *conj.*

if not, nisi ; sī nōn ; sī minus,
when the verb is omitted.

ignorant, ignārus, a, um.

illustrious, illūstris, e.

immediately, statim.

immortal, immortālis, e.

impair, imminuō, ere, uī, ūtus.

impel, indūcō, ere, dūxī, ductus.

impious, impius, a, um.

in, in, *prep. with abl.*

inasmuch as, quoniam.

increase, augeō, ēre, auxī, auc-
tus.

incredible, incrēdibilis, e.

induce, indūcō, ere, dūxī, ductus.

indulge, indulgeō, ēre, dulsī,
dultūrus.

indulgence, lēnitās, ātis, *f.*

Indutiomarus, Indutiomārus, ī,
m.

inexperienced, imperītus, a,
um.

infantry, peditātus, ūs, *m.* ; as
adj.; pedester, tris, tre.

inflame, incendō, ere, cendī,
cēnsus.

inflict on, īnferō, ferre, intulī,
illātus ; *with dat.;* inflict punishment, suppli-
cium sūmere dē.

influence, auctōritās, ātis, *f.*

inform, certiōrem faciō, ere,
fēcī, factus.

be informed, certior fīō,
fierī, factus.

inhabit, incolō, ere, uī, cultus.
inherit, receive, accipiō, ere, cēpī, ceptus.
initiate, ineō, īre, iī, itus.
injure, noceō, ēre, uī, itūrus, *with the dat., used of persons;* laedō, ere, laesī, laesus, *used of both persons and things.*
injury, injūria, ae, *f.*
innocent, innocēns, entis.
inquire, quaerō, ere, quaesīvī, ītus.
institution, īnstitūtum, ī, *n.*
insult, contumēlia, ae, *f.*
intact, integer, gra, grum.
intend, cōgitō, 1.
intervene, intersum, esse, fuī, futūrus.
into, in, *prep. with acc.*
invite, invītō, 1.
island, īnsula, ae, *f.*
Italy, Italia, ae, *f.*
it, is, ea, id.
its, ejus; suus, a, um.

J

(January), of January, Jānuārius, a, um.
javelin, jaculum, ī, *n.*; pīlum, ī, *n.*
join (*battle*), committō, ere, mīsī, missus.
join (*oneself*), conjungō, ere, jūnxī, jūnctus.
journey, iter, itineris, *n.*
joy, gaudium, ī, *n.*
judge (*noun*), jūdex, icis, *m.*
judge (*verb*), jūdicō, 1.

Julius Caesar, Jūlius Caesar, Jūlī Caesaris, *m.*
(June), of June, Jūnius, a, um.
Jupiter, Juppiter, Jovis, *m.*
just, jūstus, a, um.
just, just now, modo.
just as, sīcut.

K

Kalends, Kalendae, ārum, *f.*
keep, keep in, confine, teneō, ēre, uī.
keep apart, distineō, ēre, uī, tentus.
keep away, ward off, arceō, ēre, uī.
keep from, keep away from (*tr.*), prohibeō, ēre, uī, itus.
kill, occīdō, ere, cīdī, cīsus.
kind, genus, eris, *n.*; modus, ī, *m.*
kindness, beneficium, ī, *n.*
king, rēx, rēgis, *m.*
knight, eques, itis, *m.*
know, understand, sciō, īre, īvī, ītus.
know, be familiar with, *perfect tenses of* cognōscō, ere, nōvī, nitus.
not know, nesciō, īre, iī.
knowledge, scientia, ae, *f.*

L

Labienus, Labiēnus, ī, *m.*
labor, labor, ōris, *m.*
lack (*verb*), careō, ēre, uī, itūrus; be lacking, dēsum, dēesse, dēfuī, dēfutūrus.

land (*noun*), ager, agrī, *m.*
land, *as opposed to the water*, terra, ae, *f.*
land (*verb*) *trans.*, expōnō, ere, posuī, positus.
language, lingua, ae, *f.*
large, magnus, a, um.
in large part, magnam partem ; bonam partem.
so large, tantus, a, um.
last, final, ultimus, a, um.
last, previous, proximus, a, um.
later, post, posteā.
latter, *the latter of two already mentioned*, hīc, haec, hōc.
law, the law, jūs, jūris, *n,*
law, statute, lēx, lēgis, *f.*
law-court, basilica, ae, *f.*
lay aside, lay down, dēpōnō, ere, posuī, itus.
lay bare, patefaciō, ere, fēcī, factus.
lay upon, īnferō, ferre, tulī, illātus.
lay waste, vāstō, 1.
lead, lead on, dūcō, ere, dūxī, ductus.
lead across, trādūcō, ere, dūxī, ductus.
lead back, redūcō, ere, dūxī, ductus.
lead forth, lead out, ēdūcō, ere, dūxī, ductus.
lead on, indūcō, ere, dūxī, ductus.
leader, dux, ducis, *m.*
leading man, prīnceps, ipis, *m.*

learn (*by study*), discō, ere, didicī.
learn, find out, comperiō, īre, perī, pertus.
leave, relinquō, ere, līquī, līctus.
left, remaining, reliquus, a, um.
left (hand), sinister, tra, trum.
legion, legiō, ōnis, *f.*
lend (*help*), ferō, ferre, tulī, lātus ; be lent, be added, accēdō, ere, cessī, cessūrus.
Lentulus, Lentulus, ī, *m.*
less, *adj.*, minor ; *adv.*, minus.
lest, nē.
let go, ēmittō, ere, mīsī, missus.
letter, *of the alphabet*, littera, ae, *f.* ; letter, epistle, litterae, ārum, *f.; or* epistula, ae, *f.*
liberty, lībertās, ātis, *f.*
lieutenant, lēgātus, ī, *m.*
life, vīta, ae, *f.*
like, similis, e.
likewise, item ; *also expressed by* īdem, *in agreement with subject.*
Lilybaeum, Lilybaeum, ī, *n.*
line, line of battle, aciēs, ēī, *f.*
Liscus, Liscus, ī, *m.*
listen, listen to, audiō, īre, īvī, ītus, *with acc.*
Litaviccus, Litaviccus, ī, *m.*
little, a little, paulum.
very little, minimum ; paullulum, *with gen.*
little while before or ago, paulō ante.

live, vīvō, ere, vīxī, vīctūrus.
live, dwell, habitō, 1.
long, longus, a, um.
long, long time, diū, *adv.;*
  already for a long time,
  jam diū; no longer, jam
  nōn.
lose, āmittō, ere, mīsī, missus,
  the general word; perdō,
  ere, perdidī, itus, *where
  the responsibility of the
  subject is implied.*
loss, damnum, ī, *n.*
love, amor, ōris, *m.*
love, amō, 1.
low (*of price*), parvus, a, um.
lower, īnferior, us.
loyal, fidēlis, e.
loyalty, fidēs, eī, *f.*
Lucius, Lūcius, ī, *m.*, abbreviated L.
Lucullus, Lūcullus, ī, *m.*

M

Macedonia, Macedonia, ae, *f.*
magistracy, magistrate, magistrātus, ūs, *m.*
magnitude, magnitūdō, inis, *f.*
maintain, retineō, ēre, uī, tentus.
make, faciō, ere, fēcī, factus.
make answer, respondeō
  ēre, spondī, spōnsus.
make (*somebody or some-
  thing safe, bold, clear,*
  etc.), reddō, ere, reddidī,
  redditus ; faciō *may also be
  used.*
man, homō, inis, *m.*, *the general term:* man as opposed

to woman, or as a compli-
  mentary designation, vir,
  virī, *m.*
manage, administrō, 1.
Manlius, Mānlius, ī, *m.*
many, multī, ae, a ; so many,
  tot, *indecl.*
march (*noun*), iter, itineris, *n.*
(March), of March, Mārtius,
  a, um.
march (*verb*), iter faciō, ere,
  fēcī, factus.
march forth, march out,
  ēgredior, ī, gressus sum.
Marcus, Mārcus, ī, *m.*; *abbreviated* M.
maritime, maritimus, a, um.
Marseilles, Massilia, ae, *f.*
massed together, cōnfertus,
  a, um.
matter, thing, rēs, reī, *f.*
(May), of May, Majus, a, um.
may, licet, ēre, licuit, *with the
  subjunctive or inf.*
meanwhile, intereā.
meet (*trans. or intrans.*), conveniō, īre, vēnī, ventus ;
  meet, encounter, oppetō,
  ere, īvī, ītus.
memory, memoria, ae, *f.*
Menapii, Menapiī, ōrum, *m.*
mention, commemorō, 1.
merely, tantum.
message, nūntius, ī, *m.*
Messalla, Messalla, ae, *m.*
Messana, Messāna, ae, *f.*
messenger, nūntius, ī, *m.*
Metellus, Metellus, ī, *m.*
middle, middle of, medius, a,
  um.

midnight, media nox, mediae
noctis, *f.*
midst, midst of, medius, a, um.
mile, mīlle passūs, *lit.*, thousand paces; *pl.*, mīlia
passuum.
military, mīlitāris, e; military
science *or* matters, rēs
mīlitāris, reī mīlitāris, *f.*
mind, animus, ī, *m.*
mindful, memor, oris.
mine, meus, a, um.
minor, lesser, minor, us.
mistake, make a mistake,
peccō, 1.
Mithridatic, Mithridaticus, a,
um.
Molo, Molō, ōnis, *m.*
money, pecūnia, ae, *f.*
month, mēnsis, is, *m.*
monument, monumentum, ī, *n.*
more, amplius; magis, *adv.*
more, plūs, plūris, *n.*, *substantive.*
Morini, Morinī, ōrum, *m.*
most, plērīque, aeque, aque.
for the most part, maximam
partem.
mother, māter, mātris, *f.*
mountain, mōns, montis, *m.*
move, affect, moveō, ēre, mōvī,
mōtus; move (*make a
motion*), cēnseō, ēre, uī,
cēnsus.
move out, move away, dē-
migrō, 1.
much, multus, a, um; *adverb-
ially*, multum.
multitude, multitūdō, inis, *f.*
murder (*noun*), caedēs, is, *f.*

murder, occīdō, ere, cīdī, cīsus.
murderer, interfector, ōris, *m.*
my, meus, a, um.

N

name (*noun*), nōmen, inis, *n.*
name (*verb*), nōminō, 1.
Nantuates, Nantuātēs, ium, *m.*
Naples, Neāpolis, is, *f.*
Narbo, Narbō, ōnis, *m.*
near, neighboring, fīnitimus,
a, um.
near, *with town names*, ad,
*prep. with acc.; with other
words*, prope, *prep. with
acc.*
nearer, propius, *adv. and prep.
with acc.*
nearest, proximus, a, um.
nearly, prope.
necessary, it is necessary,
necesse est.
need, there is need, opus est.
nefarious, nefārius, a, um.
neglect, neglegō, ere, lēxī, lēctus.
neighbor, vīcīnus, ī, *m.*
neighborhood, in, *or* to, the
neighborhood of, ad, *prep.
with acc.*
neighboring, fīnitimus, a, um.
neither . . . nor, neque . . .
neque; nec . . . nec.
Nervii, Nerviī, ōrum, *m.*
never, numquam.
nevertheless, tamen.
new, novus, a, um.
news, nūntius, ī, *m.*, *or* nūntiī,
ōrum; *as gen. of the whole,*
novī.

next, proximus, a, um.
Niger, Niger, grī, *m.*
night, nox, noctis, *f.*
ninth, nōnus, a, um.
no, nūllus, a, um.
no, *with adjectives used substantively,* nēmō *(defective).*
no one, nēmō *(defective)*; nē quis.
nobility, nōbilitās, ātis, *f.*
noble, nōbilis, e; nobles, nōbilēs, ium, *m.*
Nones, Nōnae, ārum, *f.*
nor, neque *or* nec.
not, nōn, nē.
   if . . . not, nisi.
   (not), is not? does not? *etc.,* nōnne.
not even, nē . . . quidem, *with the emphatic word between.*
not know, nesciō, īre, īvī, *or* iī.
not only . . . but also, nōn sōlum . . . sed etiam.
not that, nōn quō.
not yet, nōndum.
nothing, nihil.
(November), of November, November, bris, e.
Noviodunum, Noviodūnum, ī, *n.*
now, already, jam.
now, at present time, nunc.
now, accordingly, igitur.
nowhere, nūsquam.
number, numerus, ī, *m.*
   numbers, multitūdō, inis, *f.*
   (numbers), in great numbers, frequēns, entis.

O

O, Ō, *interjection.*
oath, jūs jūrandum, jūris, jūrandī, *n.*
obey, pāreō, ēre, uī, itūrus.
observe, servō, 1.
occupy, occupō, 1.
occur, fīō, fierī, factus.
Ocean, Ōceanus, ī, *m.*
Octavian, Octāviānus, ī, *m.*
Octavius, Octāvius, ī, *m.*
(October), of October, Octōber, bris, bre.
Octodurus, Octodūrus, ī, *m.*
of, from, ā, ab, *prep. with abl.*
of, concerning, dē, *prep. with abl.*
of *(partitive)*, ē, ex.
offer, dō, dare, dedī, datus.
   offer battle, proeliō lacessō, ere, lacessīvī, lacessītus; *lit.* harass by battle.
office, honor, ōris, *m.*; magistrātus, ūs, *m.*
often, saepe.
old, vetus, eris.
   old man, senex, senis, *m.*
omit, omittō, ere, mīsī, missus.
on, in, *prep. with abl.*
   on, concerning, dē, *prep. with abl.*
   on all sides, from all sides, undique.
once, once upon a time, quondam; ōlim.
   at once, statim.
one, ūnus, a, um.
   one another, *use the reflexive pronoun.*

one . . . another, alius . . .
alius.
the one . . . the other, alter . . . alter.
only, tantum.
only one, ūnus, a, um ; sōlus,
a, um.
onset, impetus, ūs, *m.*
open, aperiō, īre, uī, ertus.
openly, apertē ; palam.
opinion, deliberate judgment,
sententia, ae, *f.*
opportunity, facultās, ātis, *f.* ;
occāsiō, ōnis, *f.*
oppress, premō, ere, pressī,
pressus.
optimates, optimātēs, ium, *m.*
or, aut ; vel.
or, *in second member of a
double question,* an *or* -ne.
or not, *in questions,* annōn,
necne.
oration, ōrātiō, ōnis, *f.*
orator, ōrātor, ōris, *m.*
order (*noun*), mandātum, ī, *n.*
order, by the order, *or* at
the order, jussū.
in order that, ut, quō ; in
order that not, nē.
order (*verb*), jubeō, ēre, jussī,
jussus.
Orgetorix, Orgetorīx, rīgis, *m.*
other, another, alius, a, ud.
other, the other, alter, a, um.
others, all the others, cēterī,
ae, a.
ought, dēbeō, ēre, uī, itus.
our, our own, noster, tra, trum.
out of, ex, ē, *prep. with abl.*
outrage (*verb*), abūtor, ī, ūsus.

outside, extrā, *prep. with acc.*
overflow, redundō, 1.
overtake, cōnsequor, ī, secū
tus.
overthrow, ēvertō, ere, vertī
versus.
owe, dēbeō, ēre, uī, itus.

P

pace, passus, ūs, *m.*
pacify, pācō, 1.
pain, dolor, ōris, *m.*
pains, care, dīligentia, ae, *f.*
pains-taking, dīligēns, entis.
panic, pavor, ōris, *m.*
pardon, venia, ae, *f.*
part, pars, partis, *f.*
particularly, praecipuē.
partly, partim.
party, partēs, ium, *f.*
pass over, omittō, ere, mīsī,
missus.
pass the winter, hiemō, 1.
patience, patientia, ae, *f.*
pay (*noun*), stīpendium, ī, *n.*
pay (*verb*), pendō, ere, pependī,
pēnsus ; solvō, ere, solvī,
solūtus.
peace, pāx, pācis, *f.*
Pedius, Pedius, ī, *m.*
penalty, poena, ae, *f.*
people, populus, ī, *m.*
perceive, sentiō, īre, sēnsī, sēnsus.
perform, fungor, ī, fūnctus
sum.
peril, perīculum, ī, *n.*
period of life, aetās, ātis, *f.*
perish, die, intereō, īre, fi
itūrus.

permanent, sempiternus, a, um.
permit, permittō, ere, mīsī,
    missus; sinō, ere, sīvī,
    situs; be permitted, it is
    permitted, licet, ēre, uit.
persuade, persuādeō, ēre,
    suāsī, suāsum.
Philippic, Philippica, ae, *f.*
philosopher, sapiēns, entis, *m.*
picked, chosen, dēlēctus, a,
    um.
pilot, gubernātor, ōris, *m.*
pirate, praedō, ōnis, *m.*
Piso, Pīsō, ōnis, *m.*
pitch, pōnō, ere, posuī, itus.
pity, it excites pity, miseret,
    miserēre, miseruit, *imper-*
    sonal; also misereor, ērī,
    itus.
place, locus, ī, *m.*
place, collocō, 1; place, pitch
    (*a camp*), pōnō, ere, posuī,
    positus.
    place around, circumdō, are,
        dedī, datus.
    place before, antepōnō, ere,
        posuī, positus.
    place in charge, place in
        command over, place
        over, praeficiō, ere, fēcī,
        fectus, *with the dat. of in-*
        direct obj.
plan (*noun*), cōnsilium, ī, *n.*
plan (*verb*), cōgitō, 1.
Plancus, Plancus, ī, *m.*
please, placeō, ēre, uī, itūrus.
plot (*noun*), īnsidiae, ārum, *f.*
plot (*verb*), cōgitō, 1.
plunder (*noun*), praeda, ae *f.*
plunder (*verb*), spoliō, 1.

Pompey, Pompejus, eī, *m.*
popularity, grātia, ae, *f.*
possess, possideō, ēre, sēdī, ses-
    sus.
    (possession), gain possession
        of, potior, īrī, ītus sum.
post, place, locus, ī, *m.*; *pl.*
    loca, ōrum, *n.*
power, potestās, ātis, *f.:* po-
    tentia, ae, *f.*
powerful, potēns, entis, *m.*
practice, ūsus, ūs, *m.*
praetor, praetor, ōris, *m.*
praise (*noun*), laus, laudis, *f.*
praise (*verb*), laudō, 1.
precede, antecēdō, ere, cessī,
    cessūrus.
prefer, mālō, mālle, māluī.
prepare, prepare for, parō, 1,
    with acc.
prepared, parātus, a, um.
present, be present, adsum,
    esse, fuī, futūrus.
preserve, cōnservō, 1.
prestige, auctōritās, ātis, *f.*
pretend, simulō, 1.
prevail over, vincō, ere, vīcī,
    victus.
prevent, dēterreō, ēre, uī, itus;
    prohibeō, ēre, uī, itus:
    arceō ēre, uī.
previously, before, anteā, *adv.*
prisoner, captive, captīvus, ī,
    m.
private, prīvātus, a, um.
Procillus, Procillus, ī, *m.*
procure, get ready, parō, 1.
profession, ars, artis, *f.*
promise (*noun*), pollicitātiō,
    ōnis, *f.*

promise (*verb*), polliceor, ērī, itus ; prōmittō, ᵓre, mīsī, missus.

propose, prōpōnō, ere, posuī, positus.

proscribe, prōscrībō, ere, scrīpsī, scrīptus.

prosecutor, āctor, ōris, *m.*

protect, prōtegō, ere, tēxī, tēctus ; tueor, ērī.

protection, praesidium, ī, *n.*

provide, provide for, cūrō, 1.

provided, provided that, dum ; **provided only,** dum modo.

province, prōvincia, ae, *f.*

provincials, sociī, ōrum, *m.*

prudence, prūdentia, ae, *f.*

public, pūblicus, a, um.

publish, ēdō, ere, ēdidī, itus.

Publius, Pūblius, ī, *m.* ; *abbreviated,* P.

punishment, supplicium, ī, *n.*

purpose, cōnsilium, ī, *n.*

pursue, sequor, ī, secūtus ; persequor, ī, secūtus.

pursuit, studium, ī, *n.*

put in charge, praeficiō, ere, fēcī, fectus ; *governs acc. and dat.*

put to death, interficiō, ere, fēcī, fectus,

put to flight, to rout, fugō, 1.

Q

quaestor, quaestor, ōris, *m.*

quickly, celeriter.

Quinctius, Quīnctius, ī, *m.*

Quintus, Quīntus, ī, *m.* ; *abbreviated,* Q.

Quirites, Roman citizens, Quirītēs, ium, *m.*

R

rank, dignitās, ātis, *f.*

rashly, temere.

ratify, cōnfīrmō, 1.

ravage, vexō, 1 ; populor, 1.

read, legō, ere, lēgī, lēctus.

read (*aloud*), recitō, 1.

ready, parātus, a, um.

reap, capiō, ere, cēpī, captus.

reason, causa, ae, *f.*

receive, accipiō, ere, cēpī, ceptus.

recent, recēns, entis.

reckon, numerō, 1 ; habeō.

recognize, cognōscō, ere, gnōvī, gnitus.

recollection, memoria, ae, *f.*

recount, ēnumerō, 1.

recover, recuperō, 1.

reduce, redigō, ere, ēgī, āctus.

refuse, recūsō, 1.

regal power, rēgnum, ī, *n.*

regard, habeō, ēre, uī, itus ; exīstimō, 1.

regret, it causes regret, paenitet, ēre, uit, *impersonal.*

reject, respuō, ere, uī,

rejoice, gaudeō, ēre, gāvīsus.

relieve, free from, līberō, 1.

relying, frētus, a, um.

remain, maneō, ēre, mānsī, mānsūrus.

remaining, remainder of, *in plu.,* reliquus, a, um ; *for sing. use* reliqua pars *with dependent gen.*

remember, bear in mind, meminī, isse ; reminīscor, ī, *supplies the present participle* of meminī.

Remi, Rēmī, ōrum, *m.*

remind, admoneō, ēre, uī, itus.

remove, tollō, ere, sustulī, sublātus.

render (*thanks*), agō, ere, ēgī, āctus.

renew, renovō, 1.

repair, reficiō, ere, fēcī, fectus.

repent, it repents, paenitet, ēre, uit, *impersonal.*

reply, respondeō, ēre, respondī, respōnsus.

report, announce, nūntiō, 1 ; dēferō, ferre, tulī, lātus.

report, fāma, ae, *f.* ; nūntius, ī, *m.*

reproach, incūsō, 1.

republic, rēs pūblica, reī pūblicae, *f.*

repulse, repellō, ere, reppulī, pulsus.

reputation, fāma, ae, *f.*

request, petō, ere, īvī, *or* iī, ītus.

resist, resistō, ere, restitī, *with dat.*

resolution of the Senate, senātūs cōnsultum, ī, *n.*

(resolve), it is resolved, placet, ēre, uit, *lit., it pleases.*

rest, the rest, cēterī, ae, a ; *with the sing.*, reliqua pars.

restore, replace, restituō, ere, uī, ūtus ; restore, return, reddō, ere, reddidī, redditus.

retain, retineō, ēre, uī, tentus.

retreat (*noun*), receptus, ūs, *m.*

retreat (*verb*), recipiō, ere, cēpī, ceptus, *with the reflexive.*

return (*noun*), reditus, ūs, *m.*

return (*verb*), go back, redeō, īre, iī, itum ; revertor, ī.

return (*trans.*), reddō, ere, reddidī, itus.

reveal, indicō, 1 ; patefaciō, ere, fēcī, factus.

review, recognōscō, ere, nōvī, nitus.

revolt, dēficiō, ere, fēcī, fectus.

reward (*noun*), praemium, ī, *n.*

reward (*verb*), remūneror, 1.

Rhine, Rhēnus, ī, *m.*

Rhone, Rhodanus, ī, *m.*

rich, dīves, itis.

right, jūs, jūris, *n.*

rightly, rēctē.

rise up, cōnsurgō, ere, surrēxī, surrēctum.

risk, perīculum, ī, *n.*

river, flūmen, inis, *n.*

road, iter, itineris, *n.* ; via, ae, *f.*

Roman, Rōmānus, a, um ; *as noun*, Rōmānus, ī, *m.*

Rome, Rōma, ae, *f.*

Roscius, Rōscius, ī, *m.*

rouse, sollicitō, 1.

rout, put to rout, fugō, 1.

route, iter, itineris, *n.*

rower, rēmex, igis, *m.*

ruin, ruīna, ae, *f.*

rule (*noun*), imperium, ī, *n.*

rule (*verb*), imperō, 1.
rumor, rūmor, ōris, *m.*
runaway slave, fugitīvus, ī, *m.*

S

Sabinus, Sabīnus, ī, *m.*
sacred, sacer, cra, crum;
sānctus, a, um.
safe, tūtus, a, um salvus, a, um.
safety, salūs, ūtis, *f.*
sail (*verb*), nāvigō, 1.
sake, for the sake, causā (*abl.*)
with gen.; the gen. always
precedes.
sally, ēruptiō, ōnis, *f.*
salute, salūtō, 1.
same, īdem, eadem, idem.
save, servō, 1.
say, dīcō, ere, dīxī, dictus.
scale (*trans.*), trānscendō, ere,
endī,
scarcely, vix.
scattered, rārus, a, um.
Scipio, Scīpiō, ōnis, *m.*
scout, explōrātor, ōris, *m.*
sea, mare, is, *n.*
seal, signum, ī, *n.*
seamanship, rēs nauticae, rērum nauticārum, *f.*
second, secundus, a, um.
second time, iterum.
secure, procure, parō, 1; secure one's request, im-
petrō, 1.
see, videō, ēre, vīdī, vīsus;
see to it, prōvideō; cūrō,
1.
seek, petō, ere, īvī (iī), ītus.
seem, videor, ērī, vīsus.
Seine, Sēquana, ae, *f.*

seize, occupō, 1.
self, oneself, suī, sibi, sē.
self, *i.e.*, *I myself, you yourself, etc.*, ipse *in apposition
with a noun or pronoun.*
sell, vēndō, ere, vēndidī, vēn-
ditus.
Senate, senātus, ūs, *m*; senate-house, cūria, ae, *f.*
senator, senātor, ōris, *m.*
send, mittō, ere, mīsī, missus.
send ahead, praemittō, ere,
mīsī, missus.
send back, remittō, ere,
mīsī, missus.
(September), of September,
September, bris, bre.
Sequani, Sēquanī, ōrum, *m.*
serious, gravis, e.
set, appoint, cōnstituō, ere, uī
ūtus.
set forth (*trans.*), expōnō, ere,
posuī, positus.
set on fire, incendō, ere, cendī,
cēnsus.
set out, proficīscor, ī, fectus.
set up, collocō, 1.
settle, collocō, 1.
seven, septem.
seven hundred, septingentī, ae,
a.
seven hundredth, septingen-
tēsimus, a, um.
seventh, septimus, a, um.
several, complūrēs, a or ia.
severe (*of persons*), sevērus, a,
um; (*of things*), gravis, e.
severity, sevēritās, ātis, *f.*
Sextius, Sextius, ī, *m.*
Sextus, Sextus, ī, *m.*

shield, scūtum, ī, *n.*
ship, nāvis, is, *f.* ; ship of war, nāvis longa.
shore, lītus, oris, *n.*
short, brevis, e.
shout, clāmō, 1.
show, ostendō, erə, endī, entus; show (*oneself*), praestō, āre, praestitī, praestitus.
side, latus, eris, *n.*
Sicilians, Siculī, ōrum, *m.*
Sicily, Sicilia, ae, *f.*
(side), from all sides, on all sides, undique; this side of, citrā, *prep. with acc.*
siege, obsidiō, ōnis, *f.*
sight, cōnspectus, ūs, *m.*
Silanus, Sīlānus, ī, *m.*
silent, be silent, become silent, taceō, ēre, uī, itus.
silently, silentiō.
since (*causal*), cum ; *as prep.*, ex, *with abl.*
six, sex.
six hundred, sexcentī, ae, a.
sixteen, sēdecim.
sixteenth, sextus decimus.
sixth, sextus, a, um.
sixty, sexāgintā.
size, magnitūdō, inis, *f.*
skilled, perītus, a, um
slaughter, caedēs, is, *f.*
slave, servus, ī, *m.*
slavery, servitūs, ūtis, *f.*
slay, occīdō, ere, cīdī, cīsus.
slinger, funditor, ōris, *m.*
small, parvus, a, um.
smoothness, lēnitās, ātis, *f.*
so (*of degree*), tam, adeō.

so, thus (*of manner*), sīc, itə so great, tantus, a, um.
so greatly, tantopere.
so many, tot, *indeclinable.*
so much, tantopere.
soldier, mīles, itis, *m.*
some, something, aliquis, aliqua, aliquid *or* aliquod; nōnnūllus, a, um.
some one, aliquis.
some . . . others, aliī . . . aliī.
some (*persons*), nōnnūllī, ōrum.
somehow or other, nesciō quō pactō.
son, fīlius, ī, *m.*
soon, quickly, mox, cito ; soon after, paulō post.
as soon as, simul atque (ac).
sooner, citius.
Spain, Hispānia, ae, *f.*
Spanish, Hispānus, a, um.
spare, parcō, ere, pepercī, parsūrus, *with dat.*
speak, loquor, ī, locūtus ; dīcō, ere, dīxī, dictus.
spear, tēlum, ī, *n.*
speech, ōrātiō, ōnis, *f.*
speed, celeritās, ātis, *f.*
spend, dēgō, ere, dēgī.
spring, vēr, vēris, *n.*
stand, stō, āre, stetī, statūrus ; stand around (*trans.*), circumstō, āre, stitī.
standard, signum, ī, *n.*
state, cīvitās, ātis, *f.*
station, collocō, 1.
statue, statua, ae, *f.* ; signum, ī, *n.*

stayer, supporter, Stator, ōris,
m.
steadfastness, cōnstantia, ae,
f.
still (temporal), adhūc; still
(= nevertheless), tamen.
stir up, excitō, 1.
stone, lapis, idis, m.
storm, tempestās, ātis, f.
(story), the story goes, trādi-
tur, trādī, trāditum est,
lit. it is handed down.
strange, novus, a um.
stream, flūmen, inis, n.
strength, vīrēs, ium, f.; pl. of
vīs.
strengthen, fortify, mūniō, īre,
īvī, ītus.
strict, sevērus, a, um.
strive, nītor, ī, nīxus or nīsus.
strong, validus, a, um.
sturdy, fortis, e.
subdue, pacify, pācō, 1.
substitute, substituō, ere, uī,
ūtus.
such, tālis, e; such as, quālis,
e.
sudden, repentīnus, a, um;
subitus, a, um.
suddenly, subitō.
suddenness, celeritās, ātis, f.
Suebi, Suēbī, ōrum, m.
Suessiones, Suessiōnēs, um, m.
Sugambri, Sugambrī, ōrum, m.
suffer, patior, ī, passus sum.
suffer from, labōrō, 1.
sufficient, sufficiently, satis.
suitable, idōneus, a, um.
suited, accommodātus, a, um.
summer, aestās, ātis, f.

summit of, summus, a, um,
limiting a substantive.
summon, vocō, 1 ; convocō, 1;
arcessō, ere, īvī, ītus.
supplies, commeātus, ūs, m.
support, aid (noun), subsidium,
ī, n.
support (verb), dēfendō, ere,
fendī, fēnsus.
surpass, praecēdō, ere, cessī,
cessūrus; superō, 1.
surrender (noun), dēditiō, ōnis,
f.
surrender (verb), of persons,
dēdō, ere, dēdidī, dēditus,
with reflexive pron. ; of
things, trādō, ere, trādidī,
trāditus.
surround, circumveniō, īre,
vēnī, ventus; circumeō,
īre, iī, itus; circumdō,
dare, dedī, datus.
suspect, suspicor, 1.
suspicion, suspīciō, ōnis, f.
swamp, palūs, ūdis, f.
swarm, agmen, inis, n.
swiftness, celeritās, ātis, f.
sword, gladius, ī, m.
Syracuse, Syrācūsae, ārum, f.
Syracusans, Syrācūsānī, ōrum,
m.

T

take, capiō, ere, cēpī, captus;
of punishment, sūmō, ere,
sūmpsī, sūmptus.
take away, tollō, ere, sustulī,
sublātus.
take from, adimō, ere, ēmī,
ēmptus.
take by storm, expugnō, 1.

take possession, occupō, 1 ;
possīdeō, ēre, sēdī, sessus.
take (with one), addūcō,
ere, dūxī, ductus.
talent, ingenium, ī, n.
talk, dīcō, ere, dīxī, dictus.
tamper with, solicit, sollic:tō, 1.
tarry, moror, 1.
teach, doceō, ēre, uī, doctus.
taught, ēdoctus.
teacher, praeceptor, ōris, m. ;
praeceptrīx, īcis, f.
tear down, rescindō, ere, scidī,
scissus ; dīruō, ere, ruī,
rŭtus.
tell, say, dīcō, ere, dīxī, dictus.
temper, animus, ī, m.
temple, aedēs, is, f. ; templum,
ī, n. *When used with
precision,* aedēs *refers to
the building only, while*
templum *includes the con-
secrated area as well.*
ten, decem.
tend, pertineō, ēre, uī.
tenor, sentiment, sententia,
ae, f.
tenth, decimus, a, um.
terms, conditions, condiciōnēs,
um, f.
terrify, terreō, ēre, uī, territus ;
greatly terrify, perterreō, ēre,
uī, itus.
territory, fīnēs, ium, m.
Teutons, Teutonī, um, m.
than, quam, *conj.*
thanks, grātiae, ārum, f.
thanksgiving, supplicātiō, ōnis,
f.

that, ille, illa, illud ; is ea, id;
that of yours, iste, ista,
istud.
that (*rel. pron.*), quī, quae,
quod.
that, in order that, ut ; quī,
quae, quod *with the sub-
junctive; with compara*
tives, quō.
that, lest, *with verbs of fearing,* nē.
that not, in order that not,
nē.
that not, *with verbs of fearing,* ut.
that (*of result*), ut ; that
not, ut nōn.
that, the fact that, as to the
fact that, quod, *conj.*
that, on the ground that,
quod.
that, *after verbs of doubt-
ing, etc.,* quīn, *lit. why
not?*
the . . . the (*with compara*-
tives), quō . . . eō.
theft, fūrtum, ī, n.
their, their own, suus, a, um.
then, afterwards, deinde.
then, accordingly, igitur.
then, at that time, tum.
there, ibi.
therefore, itaque ; *or* igitur
*following one or more
words of the sentence;*
proptereā.
thick, crassus, a, um.
thing, rēs, reī, f.
thing, a thing which, id
quod, *or simply* quod.

think, putō, 1; sentiō, īre; sēnsī, sēnsus; arbitror, 1.
think, reflect, cōgitō, 1.
think, regard, exīstimō, 1.
third, tertius, a, um.
third, third part, tertia pars.
thirteenth, tertius decimus.
thirty, trīgintā.
this, hīc, haec, hōc; this side of, citrā, *prep. with acc.*
thither, eō.
those (*as antecedent of relative*), eī, eae, ea.
thou, tū, tuī.
though, quamquam, quamvīs, etsī, cum.
thousand, mīlle, *pl.* mīlia, ium, *n.*
threaten, immineō, ēre; threaten (*to do something*), minor, 1.
threats, minae, ārum, *f.*
three, trēs, tria.
   three days, trīduum, ī, *n.*
   three hundred, trecentī, ae, a.
   three times, ter, *adv.*
   three years, triennium, ī, *n.*
through, through the instrumentality of, per, *prep. with acc.*
throw, jaciō, ere, jēcī, jactus.
throw into confusion, perturbō, 1.
thus, ita; sīc.
thwart, obsistō, ere, obstitī, *with dat.*
Tiberius, Tiberius, ī, *m.*
till, dum, dōnec, quoad, *conj.*
till, up to, ad, *prep. with acc.*

time, tempus, oris, *n.*
tithe, decuma, ae, *f.*
Titurius, Titūrius, ī, *m.*
Titus, Titus, ī, *m.*
to, ad, *prep. with acc.*
   to which, whither, quō, *adv.*
to-day, hodiē.
to-morrow, crās.
too, too much, nimium, *adv.*
(too), and that too, et is, ea, id.
top of, summus, a, um.
Tolosa, Toulouse, Tolōsa, ae, *f.*
towards (*of feeling*), in, ergā, *with acc.; of motion*, ad, *with acc.*
town, oppidum, ī, *n.*
transport, trānsportō, 1.
treachery, īnsidiae, ārum, *f.*; perfidia, ae, *f.*
treaty, foedus, eris, *n.*
trench, fossa, ae, *f.*
Treveri, Trēverī, ōrum, *m.*
trial, jūdicium, ī, *n.*
tribe, gēns, gentis, *f.*
tribunate, tribūnātus, ūs, *m.*
tribune, tribūnus, ī, *m.*; tribune of the people, tribūnūs plēbis.
tribute, stīpendium, ī, *n.*
troops, cōpiae, ārum, *f.*
true, vērus, a, um.
trust, cōnfīdō, ere, fīsus, *semi-dep.*
trusty, fidēlis, e.
try, conor, 1.
turn, convertō, ere, vertī, versus.
Tusculum, Tusculum, ī, *n.*
twelfth, duodecimus, a, um.
twelve, duodecim.

twenty, vīgintī.
two, duo, duae, duo.
two days, bīduum, ī, *n.*
two hundred, ducentī, ae, a.
two years, biennium, ī, *n.*
tyrant, tyrannus, ī, *m.*

U

Ubii, Ubiī, ōrum, *m.*
unbroken, uninjured, integer, gra, grum.
uncertain, incertus, a, um.
uncle, avunculus, ī, *m.*
undergo, subeō, īre, iī, itūrus.
understand, intellegō, ere, lēxī, lēctus.
undertake, suscipiō, ere, cēpī, ceptus.
unharmed, incolumis, e.
unjust, injūstus, a, um.
unless, nisi.
   unless indeed, nisi vērō, nisi forte.
unpopularity, invidia, ae, *f.*
until, dum, dōnec, quoad; *as prep.*, ad *with acc.*
unwilling, invītus, a, um.
   be unwilling, nōlō, nōlle, nōluī.
uprightness, probitās, ātis, *f.*
uprising, tumultus, ūs, *m.*; mōtus, ūs, *m.*
urge, hortor, 1.
us, nōs, nostrum, nostrī, *pl. of* ego.
use (*noun*), ūsus, ūs, *m.*
use (*verb*), ūtor, ī, ūsus.
Usipetes, Usipetēs, um, *m.*
utter, dīcō, ere, dīxī, dictus.
utterance, vōx, vōcis, *f.*

V

valiantly, fortiter.
valley, vallis, is, *f.*
valor, virtūs, ūtis, *f.*
value, aestimō, 1.
vanquish, vincō, ere, vīcī, victus.
Veneti, Venetī, ōrum, *m.*
(vengeance), take vengeance on, ulcīscor, ī, ultus.
venture, audeō, ēre, ausus.
Veragri, Veragrī, ōrum, *m.*
Vercingetorix, Vercingetorīx, rīgis, *m.*
Verres, Verrēs, is, *m.*
versed in, perītus, a, um.
very, *with adjectives, expressed by the superlative degree; elsewhere*, valdē.
   with substantives, ipse, a, um; *with superlatives*, vel.
very many, complūrēs, ia.
Vesontio, Vesontiō, ōnis, *m.*
Vestal Virgin, virgō Vestālis, virginis Vestālis, *f.*
veteran, veterānus, a, um.
vice, improbitās, ātis, *f.*
vicinity, in the vicinity of, for the vicinity of, ad, *with acc.*
victory, victōria, ae, *f.*
village, vīcus, ī, *m.*
violate, violō, 1.
Viromandui, Viromanduī, ōrum, *m.*
virtue, virtūs, ūtis, *f.*
visit, adeō, īre, iī, itus; visit (*with punishment, etc.*), afficiō, ere, fēcī, fectus.

voice, vōx, vōcis, *f.*
Volusenus, Volusēnus, ī, *m.*

W

wage, gerō, ere, gessī, gestus.
wait, exspectō, 1.
wall, mūrus, ī, *m.*; **wall of a
house,** pariēs, etis, *m.*
war, bellum, ī, *n.*
war-chariot, essedum, ī, *n.*
ward off, dēpellō, ere, pulī,
pulsus.
warlike, bellicōsus a, um.
warn, moneō, ēre, uī, itus.
(warning), **give a warning,** admoneō, ēre, uī, itus.
watch, vigilia, ae, *f.*
water, aqua, ae, *f.*
way, **manner,** modus, ī, *m.*
way, **route,** iter, itineris, *n.*
weak, dēbilis, e.
weakness, īnfīrmitās, ātis, *f.*
weakened, cōnfectus, a, um.
wealth, dīvitiae, ārum, *f.*
wealthy, dīves, itis.
weapons, arma, ōrum, *n.*
welcome, grātus, a, um.
well, bene.
what (*interrog.*), quid, *subst.*;
**what kind, nature, of
what nature,** quālis, e.
whatever, quisquis, quicquid.
when? quandō.
when (*relative*), cum, ut,
ubi.
whenever, ut, cum.
where? ubi.
where (*relative*), ubi; **wher-
ever,** ubicunque.

whether, num, -ne.
whether . . . or, utrum . . .
an; **whether . . . not,**
nōnne.
which, quī, quae, quod.
while, dum, dōnec, *conj.*
whither, quō.
who? quis.
who, which (*rel. pron.*), quī,
quae, quod.
who (does) not, who (is) not,
quīn.
whole, tōtus, a, um.
why? cūr, quid, quam ob rem.
why not, *after* nūlla causa
est, *etc.*, quīn.
wicked, scelerātus, a, um.
wickedness, scelus, eris, *n.*
wide, lātus, a, um.
wife, uxor, ōris, *f.*
will, testāmentum, ī, *n.*
willingly, **readily,** libenter.
win, **attain,** adipīscor, ī, adeptus; **win over,** conciliō,
1.
winter, hiems, emis, *f.*
winter quarters, hīberna,
ōrum, *n.*
wisdom, sapientia, ae, *f.*
wise, sapiēns, entis.
wish, volō, velle, voluī.
with, cum, *prep. with abl.*
with (*not involving partici-
pation*), **at the house of,**
apud, *prep. with acc.*
withdraw (*trans.*), subdūcō,
ere, dūxī, ductus; (*in-
trans.*), dēcēdō, ere, cessī,
cessūrus.
within, intrā, *prep. with acc.*

without, sine, *prep. with abl.*
  be without, careō, ēre, uī, itūrus.
withstand, sustineō, ēre, uī, tentus.
witness, testis, is, *m.*
woman, mulier, eris, *f.*
wonder, mīror, 1.
wonderful, mīrābilis, e.
wont, am wont, *perf. of* cōnsuēscō, ere, suēvī, suētus.
woods, silva, ae, *f.*
word, verbum, ī, *n.*
work (*a work*), opus, eris, *n.*
worship, veneror, 1 ; colō, ere, coluī, cultus.
worthy, dignus, a, um.
wound, vulnus, eris, *n.*
wounded, saucius, a, um.
wreck (*of vessels*), frangō, ere, frēgī, frāctus.
wrest, extorqueō, ēre, torsī, tortus, *with dat. of person from whom.*

wretched, miser, a, um.
write, scrībō, ere, scrīpsī, scrīptus.
wrong, injūria, ae, *f.* ; wrongdoing, injūriae, ārum, *f.*

Y

year, annus, ī, *m.*
yet, nevertheless, tamen.
  not yet, nōndum.
yield, cēdō, ere, cessī, cessūrus.
you, tū, tuī; vōs, vestrum *or* vestrī.
young man, juvenis, is. *m.*
your, your own, tuus, a, um ; vester, tra, trum.
youth, period of youth, adulescentia, ae, *f.*

Z

zeal, studium, ī, *n.*

A primer to the composition of Latin verse

Tonight They All Dance: 92 Latin & English Haiku

by *Harundine*, A Belgian group of Latin haiku poets

edited by Dirk Sacré and Marcel Smets

illustrated by Mark McIntyre

translated into English by Herman Servotte

- ✦ Introduction with tips on composing Latin haiku
- ✦ 92 Latin haiku with English translations
- ✦ Four sections: *Caelestia, Terrestria, Animalia,* and *Humana*
- ✦ Brief, helpful notes; full vocabulary
- ✦ Dramatically illustrated throughout

Hac nocte saltant
viri mulieresque,
saltant et umbrae.

Tonight they all dance
the men and the women and
their shadows as well.

Tonight They All Dance can serve as a primer to the composition of Latin verse and, as such, can lend students and scholars alike insight into the intricacies and joys of writing poetry in a non-native language. Haiku, with its short form and engaging content, is the ideal instrument for a first exploration of Latin poetic composition. By modeling the composition of Latin haiku and translating both the substance and the form into English haiku, students will begin to understand the challenges of accurate and beautiful translation. It is only through such intimate experience that a true sense of Latin verse can be gained.

What an unusual and interesting way to teach intermediate and early advanced students both Latin and effective English expression!
— **A. W. Godfrey,** *Newsletter*
The Classical Association of the Empire State

(1999) Paperback, ISBN 0-86516-440-1; Hardbound, ISBN 0-86516-441-X

Bolchazy-Carducci Publishers, Inc.

References for Teachers and Students

NEW LATIN GRAMMAR by Charles E. Bennett

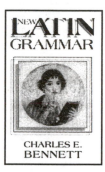

CHARLES E.
BENNETT

Great pleasure attends the reissue of Bennett's New Latin Grammar *by Bolchazy-Carducci...Teachers and students alike can rejoice at its reappearance. Bennett's definitions and explanations of the basic grammatical and syntactical points are a paragon of clearness and succinctness. I strongly recommend it for high-school teachers and for undergraduates at all levels; for graduate students and scholars it is ideal for a quick look since the organization is clear and 'user-friendly'.*

Robert I. Curtis, *Univ. of Georgia*

xvi + 287 pp., (1908, reprint 1995)
Paperback, ISBN: 0-86516-261-1

GRAPHIC LATIN GRAMMAR

Latin grammar constructions (color-coded) on four, coated cardstock pages, ready for insertion in a 3-ring binder. **Great for Students & Teachers alike!**

Four 3-hole-punched reference cards, laminated
(1961, reprint 1995), ISBN 0-86516-460-6

A NEW LATIN SYNTAX by E. C. Woodcock

E. C.
WOODCOCK

This book gives a historical account of the chief Latin constructions in twenty-five chapters arranged in such order as to make it useful as a progressive revision course in syntax for Advanced Level and University students.

xxiv + 2687 pp., (1959, reprint 1987)
Paperback, ISBN: 0-86516-126-7

GILDERSLEEVE'S LATIN GRAMMAR
by B. L. Gildersleeve and G. Lodge

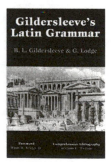

The classic Latin grammar favored by many students and teachers with two new additions

- ❖ Foreword by **Ward W. Briggs, Jr.**
- ❖ Comprehensive bibliography by **William E. Wycislo**

The *45-page bibliography* that accompanies our new reprint is designed primarily but not exclusively for an English-speaking audience, comprising scholarship produced on Latin grammar in English during this century.

613 pp. (1895, third ed., reprint with additions 1997)
Paperback, ISBN 0-86516-353-7
Hardbound, ISBN 0-86516-477-0

http://www.bolchazy.com